CHILDHOOD UNBOUND

Saving Our Kids' Best Selves—Confident Parenting in a World of Change

Ron Taffel

FREE PRESS

New York   London   Toronto   Sydney

Free Press
A Division of Simon & Schuster, Inc.
1230 Avenue of the Americas
New York, NY 10020

Copyright © 2009 by Ron Taffel

First Free Press hardcover edition January 2009

For information about special discounts for bulk purchases,
please contact Simon & Schuster Special Sales at
1-800-456-6798 or business@simonandschuster.com

Manufactured in the United States of America

1   3   5   7   9   10   8   6   4   2

Library of Congress Cataloging-in-Publication Data

Taffel, Ron.
Childhood unbound : saving our kids' best selves—confident parenting
in a world of change / Ron Taffel.
p.   c.m.
Includes bibliographical references and index.
1. Parenting   2. Child rearing.   I. Title
HQ755.8.T33   2009
649'.1—dc22   2008038115

ISBN-13: 978-1-4165-5927-6
ISBN-10:   1-4165-5927-2

I dedicate this book to my greatest generation parents, Leo and Lotte Taffel, forged by the trials and challenges of the twentieth century, who instilled in me a moral compass—their hard-won certitude and determination to make the world a better place.

I dedicate this book to my childhood friends, boomers all, an extended family of deep-down decency I still know today—whose unswerving loyalty and spirit of neighborhood helped me feel an envelope around me and an anchor within.

I dedicate this book to my slightly less rooted circle of post-boomer friends and colleagues and especially my wife, Stacey, who opened my previously sure but shuttered eyes onto a world of greater paradox, creativity, and comfort with change.

And, I dedicate this book to my free-est generation children, Leah and Sam and their many peers, whose sometimes exasperating but always exhilarating sense of hope and improbable ease despite the challenges of a world forever different, will lead us into an enlightened time.

much good to quote and report on about these kids that you will be heartened as well.

To Other Professionals

Thousands of you have attended workshops I've given or read my other books and articles over the years. It will not surprise you to hear me once again state clearly that any suggestion I make needs to be sorted through your own set of values, your own supervision, your own agency and local regulations, which, as you know, vary from state to state. I do not say this as a rote caveat. I firmly believe that each of us needs to work in ways that conform to our own values and professional requirements. In the last analysis, stay within your perspective and framework. Do what is right for you personally and professionally, for your clients and for your students.

To Mothers and Fathers

Finally, to you parents, the tens of thousands with whom I've spoken over the decades, I have always been impressed by your basic good sense, no matter how you (and myself and my wife as parents) are often characterized. Much of what I write here reflects your ideas and experiences about what works in these times, as well as your concerns about what doesn't. Having said this I will repeat what I write in every book and say in every talk: when it comes to my suggestions, you are the final judge of what to listen to, you are the final judge of what to try, and you are the final judge of what to ignore. While I deeply understand your hunger for information and guidance, I also respect that these are your children and you ultimately know them better. No matter how compelling my message, the final arbiter of what ought to be done is you.

In all situations, however, if you are worried about the safety of your child or anyone in your family, immediately skip these pages and seek a local mental health resource or hospital to guard your child's, your own, and your family's safety.

I will end this beginning with a brief story that represents the basic theme of what you have just read. While I was growing up our family had a small shoe store in a small town. It was a family store, so we all helped out. For decades I watched my father go through the following scene: Someone would try on a pair of shoes that they or their kids loved, but to my father's eye they were not a good fit. He'd then say over their strong objections, "These shoes are not right for you. They look good and they feel good now, but they won't fit you later." No matter how much they disagreed, even argued with him, he would refuse to sell them the shoes, saying, "I'm sorry, but this is not a fit for you."

My father's way is how to think about *Childhood Unbound*—if a particular piece of advice I give is not a fit for you or your children, let it go. There is so much in these pages I know you will find other advice that better matches your values, your beliefs and, most important, your children.

Ron Taffel
September, 2008

CHILDHOOD UNBOUND

1

PARENTING IN THE POST-BOOMER ERA

The Thrills and Challenges of Modern Child Rearing

L ET'S STATE THE EVERYDAY REALITY FIRST: parenting today is a wildly challenging, confusing job, far beyond anything most of us expected. For sure, raising children has always been a struggle, but kids' lives in these times, and our relationships with our children, present a host of contradictions that are especially tricky to navigate. Kids at increasingly younger ages are coarse, crude, jarring, and wild. But at the same time, they are filled with exhilarating and tender surprises; they can be more gratifying and exciting to live with than one would ever have imagined. We parents love the casual openness in our relationships with our kids, but at the same time we are often taken aback by their ability to say whatever crosses their minds. We love their sense of "rights," and the way they stand up for their views, yet we cringe at the entitlement that is so often expressed in their demands. We encourage freedom of expression even as we end up depleted by relentless negotiations, beginning as early as the nursery school years.

We worry that kid humor has become too fierce, too ironic and callous, and that a moral relativity we sometimes hear from our children will grow into amorality. Yet we also find ourselves laughing hysterically at their irreverent jokes and, when we're not annoyed, twinkle with pride at their ability to spar with us so adroitly over explanations we've given about why they can't do this or that, challenging us on our own inconsistencies. We worry about pop culture playing such a powerful role, perhaps replacing real passions that would be more meaningful. Yet many of us are avid consumers of pop culture ourselves, which we participate in right alongside our children. We are concerned by the frenzied way they do everything at once at earlier and earlier ages—they're online with five buddies, text messaging, Facebooking almost constantly—all the while supposedly doing homework. Yet we admire their proficiency with things high-tech, and given that we are doing our own version of frenzied multi-tasking, we know too well how important that ability is in this twenty-first century world. We are worried about how our children will cope with the stresses and social influences that assault them. But we are also delighted by and proud of their ability to manage so many demands on their time.

Given these extraordinary crosscurrents, a great deal has been written in recent years about disturbing behavior among today's children and teens, and how parents have failed to rein in that behavior. In light of all of that criticism, parents sometimes feel under siege, not to mention confused. With my wife, Stacey, I am a parent of two children, and we both understand the endless maze of commentary and advice parents find themselves in.

We parents are drowning in a sea of conflicting child-rearing fads, most of which we find inadequate, or even offensive. And even as parents have come under so much criticism, many of us secretly sense that we are doing a better job than our parents' generation did, and their parents before them. For one thing, we know we are closer in many ways to our children, even our teenagers. We do not feel the generation gap that was the source of so much parent-child conflict and alienation in prior generations. We allow for back talk that would have brought down the houses our mothers and fathers grew up in and maybe our own homes too. Yet we will not be argued out of our forbearance, because at all costs we want to make sure the lines of communication with our young and older children alike remain open. Despite critiques that we have been over-indulgent, we are determined to praise our children and give them positive feedback, even if we wonder how kids in earlier eras ever grew up, hearing only a fraction of the praise that children now hear in a single day.

These paradoxes of contemporary parenting, the mind-boggling contradictions about how to raise our kids, are the sub-text of every talk I give to mothers, fathers, and educators, and of every discussion I have with children, from preschool through high school. Intense heat is also generated regarding these issues in almost every meeting with parents and school personnel: opinions vary wildly about what to think about the state of our children's lives and how we should be facing these challenges.

Much like the endless debate over global warming, a debate rages across the country about whether kids, and their behavior, are really so different today, and if so, how parents should respond. Some of us aren't convinced there is any particular cause for worry, thinking, "Kids are still kids. Nothing is fundamentally different." Others are seriously concerned. Many parents, of course, are in the midst of dealing with child-rearing crises; there is no question for them that all is not well in the lives of contemporary children.

The debate about whether anything is truly different, though, has ended for me. From my twenty-five years as a counselor to children, teens, and their parents, as well as from over a thousand talks in schools, churches, synagogues, and community agencies around the country, I am convinced that not only are kids' lives qualitatively different today from those of earlier eras, but that parents today are uniquely different, and therefore the parent-child relationship has fundamentally changed as well.

Because of this I am convinced that a distinctive breed of child-rearing techniques is now required for raising children, and here is the good news—that today's parents are uniquely qualified for providing exactly what our children need.

The underlying reasons for this are not those, however, that have been emphasized in so much of the media coverage. Rather than focusing on criticism of parents and the pathologizing of their kids, we should put our emphasis elsewhere. Instead, our first emphasis should be on the massive social upheaval that has been underway in our society for decades. A great deal of insight into how we might parent more effectively arises from appreciating that these social changes (rather than just our failures) are the true causes of the troubling paradoxes in children's behavior. Understanding how a changing context has shaped our lives and our children's lives so profoundly will then point toward the new style of parenting I will present in this book, one that meets the demands and challenges we face every day.

THE POST-BOOMER ERA

The key new reality to appreciate is that we are living in what I call the "post-boomer" era of parenting.

Why is post-boomer such an important characterization? A couple of years ago I realized that for the first time a vast majority (over two-thirds) of parents who currently have kids in the prime child-rearing years—from preschool through high school—are *post-boomers*, born after the boomer years of 1946–1964. I also realized that even late-boomer parents—born between 1955 and 1964—were far too young to have experienced the sixties as teens or young teens. (Think about it: most late-boomers with under-seventeen-year-old kids today, were quite young during the sixties' major events.) Their lives have been shaped at least as much by profound post-boomer era changes as they have been by Woodstock Nation, now forty + years in the past.

Generational characterizations can be grossly over-drawn and sometimes meaninglessly narrow, as in the designations Gen X, Gen Y, and Gen Z, which have been popularized largely by marketers and have questionable value as tools for understanding child-rearing issues. The divide between the era of the baby-boomers and the era that began during the coming of age of post-boomers is, however, another story. Just as the youngest boomers and the oldest of today's post-boomer parents were growing up—in the late seventies and early eighties—a torrent of familial-social developments got underway that impacts parenting today at every turn.

ARE YOU A POST-BOOMER PARENT?

You Almost Definitely Are and That's Good News for You and Your Kids

Some parents have trouble deciding whether they are boomer or post-boomer parents. I believe that the vast majority of today's parents of kids 18 and younger need to be considered post-boomers. Here's why:

The usual definition of a "boomer" is that you were born from 1946 to 1964, which at this time puts boomers between the ages of 45–63. The usual definition of a "post-boomer" is that you were born after 1964; the majority now between 25–45 years old, prime child-rearing ages.

The math bears this out. According to The Yankelovich report, *Zapping the Gap*, published in 2005, only 33 percent of parents were boomers while 66 percent were already post-boomers back then. Obviously there are even more post-boomer parents today.

(continued)

OK—so according to the math, whether you realize it or not, you are most likely a post-boomer parent.

However, when it comes to such an emotionally rich experience like parenting, math doesn't always do justice. Even "by-the-math" boomer parents, especially those born towards the middle-end of the boomer years are really post-boomers: most of your growing up, especially those crucial pre-teen and adolescent years, happened *after* sixties' world events and the Woodstock Nation revolution. Check it out:

- How old were you when JFK was assassinated in the early sixties?
- How old during the introduction of "the pill" and its sudden impact on sexual mores?
- How old when drugs such as marijuana and LSD first appeared on the scene?
- How old were you during the civil rights marches and "I Have a Dream?"
- How old were you during the mid-sixties' Vietnam build-up, the protests and the marches?
- How old were you during Woodstock in 1969—old enough to have attended?

Probably, then, if you have children from three to eighteen, the focus of *Childhood Unbound*, you were quite young during the sixties. Your first-hand experiences growing up (though informed by that tumultuous decade) actually happened in a post-boomer world, from the seventies on.

Post-boomer experiences are the ones most meaningful to both you and your kids—the growth of suburbia, exurbia, divorce, moms in the workforce, geographic relocation, ATM machines, over-scheduled lives, technology, and globalization. And, these are just some of the reasons that as a post-boomer parent you have a far better capacity to understand the world of kids and teens today. You are more alike than any parent-child combination coming of age after the Second World War—and the chance for authentic engagement between you and your child or teen is greater than ever before.

Massive social changes have exponentially accelerated in the years since, and they have had profound effects on family life and the parent-child relationship. It is the cumulative effect of these forces that now is so dramatically shaping children's lives and behavior, and our relationships with them. Rather than focusing only on negative characterizations of generational groups—for example, the criticism that Gen Y is pathologically "narcissistic" and "entitled" or the tendency to pejoratively pigeon-hole today's parents as "helicopter" moms and dads—we need to begin appreciating the role of this tectonic shift.

The current wild and troubling aspects of kids' lives are largely the result of four decades of post-boomer change.

And this is basically hopeful news. Parents today are the ones who first dealt with the brunt of the shifting post-sixties social landscape. We are the ones whose lives were the first to be formatively shaped by those changes. We therefore have an authentic capacity to understand what our kids are going through.

We appreciate the many ways in which children's ability to adapt to contemporary realities will prepare them for the demands of twenty-first century life. In fact, living together in a post-boomer world (rather than being at war with one's elders—which was so often the case in boomer times) is a main reason that parents today are so close to their children and sympathetic about the hidden good in how youngsters must make their way through a complicated world.

This is why mothers and fathers now are intent not to throw the baby out with the bathwater. We highly value this newfound closeness with our children and teens and would rather contend with rudeness than be dictatorial in ways that might drive them away. We respect kids' agility with technology, and don't want to cut them off entirely from the vital manner in which it's become part of their lives. Do we really wish our own kids to be the only ones not engaged in social networking? We truly are much more team oriented and friendlike to our children than parents have tended to be in the past, in large part because we too identify with many of the peer and academic pressures that kids now face.

In the post-boomer era, parents and their children are far more similar than different, which is a revolutionary way for parents and kids to feel, and a revolutionary way to think about child rearing. All in all, it is a welcome development. This doesn't mean, though, that these same forces of change don't present daunting challenges, and serious dangers; they do.

In the next chapter, I will give a more detailed description of specific social forces, and how attempts to contend with them spawned a confusing, contradictory range of parenting advice—and wild acting-out in kids. But first it is important to give a broad stroke overview of how cultural shifts play out in our daily family lives. This initial description will help us to appreciate why we must turn our attention away from destructive finger pointing toward a new approach to bring out our kids' best selves.

FORCES OF CHANGE

What characterizes the post-boomer era is the sudden cessation and replacement of inter-generational warfare with a constant tension between family fragmentation and the desire for closeness. Post-boomers and their kids today are kindred spirits, fellow travelers in a world increasingly defined by the struggle of disconnection versus engagement.

For example, one of the most pervasive of post-boomer changes has been that society has become ever more "atomized," with many of the older bonds of family life and of community progressively weakened. By the mid-seventies, geographic mobility had become commonplace, as people increasingly moved around the country for job opportunities and changes in lifestyle. Also, divorce rates spiked in the 1970s, when post-boomer and late-boomer parents were coming of age. During their adolescence it became almost as common to be a child of separated mothers and fathers as one whose parents had stayed together. A striking effect of this increase in divorce was the rise of single motherhood, and over time, a much wider range of family arrangements including women (and some men) choosing to have kids entirely on their own.

One result of this atomization is that in the seventies and eighties, post-boomer age groups exhibited diminished community involvement, becoming less neighborhood-oriented and less participative in hierarchical, organized religion. They placed far more emphasis on individualism and on crafting their own tailor-made religious/ spiritual and political beliefs, accompanied by waning participation in and formal allegiance to rigid "party lines." This constituted the "bowling alone" phenomenon, a term sociologist Robert Putnum famously coined to describe the diminishment of American community life.

And yet, a counter-intuitive consequence of this atomization and family fragmentation has been an increasing focus on closeness within the immediate family. Our lives have become far more child-centric—the latch-key phenomenon being mostly a thing of the past. Another measure of desired closeness is that so many post-boomers feel a strong desire for better work-life balance. Evidence of this has been the number of post-boomer mothers opting to leave the workforce during key child-rearing years, rejecting the "supermom" ideal boomers had popularized, and forging a distinctive blend of career dedication and parenting. And, of course, the growth of mega-faith communities is in no small measure due to its emphasis on family building and community connection.

The tension between fragmentation and engagement took hold on the world stage as well. In addition to the many forces of disconnection that defined the seventies, the process of globalization steadily accelerated. As resulting worldwide population shifts picked up speed, our lives became much more connected and diverse. Waves of immigration changed the fabric of our own society, a new openness (as well as fear) toward diversity and diverse lifestyles evolved, and the culture slowly became less dominated by singular viewpoints and strictures. Throughout the post-boomer era, this process of fragmentation and push toward re-engagement has fitfully, but inexorably played out: family configurations that defy rigid notions have proliferated; cross-cultural marriages led to more families with blended cultural heritage; gays began to come out of the closet and then to raise families; and attitudes about sex and sexuality have begun to undergo fundamental re-definition, especially for adolescents, and more recently for younger children.

At the same time, globalization's effects on the economy made working life more demanding and competitive, as well as fueling an ever-growing entrepreneurial spirit. Each day, it seems, has brought previously unimaginable inventions, affecting the very fabric of family life. Years before the dual shock of the credit and energy crises, our work lives had changed in many ways. As massive layoffs became a means of corporations adjusting their balance sheets, we saw far less commitment to the notion of staying at one company, or even staying with one career, and an accompanying rise of "free agent" thinking, even as we begin to focus more on a team approach and responsive work environments, witness the rise of Human Resources, EAPs, and family-friendly policies. We demand these days to know what a company is going to do for us, and we are much more prepared to move from job to job in order simply to survive or pursue life-fulfilling goals. These changes in attitude, from anchored permanence to portability, and an expectation to be "heard" in turn influenced our children, way before *YouTube* hit the scene.

Obviously, one of the most powerful of the shaping forces in the post-boomer period has been warp-speed technology. It has assured that the one constant we can count on is constant movement, which both fragments focused connection while creating endless possibilities for connection. Just as the oldest of the post-boomer parents were emerging into adulthood, clunky computers and then an explosive range of new technologies began to exercise an ever-more powerful influence on our lives. With the evolution, first of e-mail, then of cell phones and hand-held computers, we late-boomers and post-boomers ceaselessly multitask, with ever more expectation—and demand—always to be in touch. And our kids are no different.

A change that is perhaps more subtle, but also quite significant, is that the post-boomer era has been characterized by the absence of an overwhelmingly catastrophic national crisis. The greatest generation was unalterably influenced by the Depression and World War II, and readily defined itself as such. Boomers were profoundly influenced by civil rights and Vietnam, and polarized around their support for or protest against these events and movements. A great deal of intense conflict revolved around how parents and their children defined themselves as members of very different generations.

In the post-boomer era, however, even as we are in the midst of tightening financial stressors, there has, as yet, been no single defining crisis to *divide* the generations. Even research about 9/11 has shown that its impact on those coming-of-age at the time has not been permanently transformative. The lack of a chronic, defining crisis from the 1970s on has eased the way for today's parents and children to avert what might have become the next generation gap or cause of generational friction. Today's post-boomer parents and their children can hardly imagine the intra-familial rage that passed for family life just a few decades ago. This is another reason that despite all the fearsome headlines, and daily disconnection, contemporary parents and children generally understand each other, talk more openly together, and feel closer in values and spirit than generations before.

Of course, the effects of a decades-long upheaval and tension around social-familial fragmentation and desire for connection have not been easy. Parents have every reason to feel confused and somewhat scared bringing children up in a post-boomer world.

CHILDHOOD UNBOUND

What has the culmination of all of these changes led to in the lives of children?

In many ways, children and teens today are, for better and worse, kids who know no bounds. Because of this I have come to think of them as the "Free-est Generation."

They have an all-access pass to the infinite reach of the internet and are exposed at ever-earlier ages to categories of sex and violence that post-boomer and boomer parents learned about much, much later in life. Cell phones, texting, and online networks afford kids endless freedom in socializing, breaking the old bounds of school and of town. They participate day and night in a kind of instantaneous connection that is even more intense than that of their post-boomer parents with their cell phones and Blackberries. The loss of the town center with its eyes and ears—meaning shopkeepers, church, community groups, and school—has left children of all ages more scheduled, but much less policed by the adult world. Even though we are closer as families in many ways, kids today live behind a wall of silence that the most informed parent has little ability to breach.

Children are also freer from the constraints of history: the stories of generations past are missing. Yesterday is a speck on the consciousness of most kids; decades ago is another universe. Children and teens often feel less guilt and connection to the everyday job or career sacrifices of their parents. When pressed, many cannot even describe what their parents do, in an increasingly service-oriented economy. Also, fewer of them are held emotionally hostage by the threat of divorce. Step- or gender-bending family configurations that rocked the late seventies and eighties have become familiar, and kids know that life does go on despite these life-altering upheavals.

Trying to make sense of post-boomer changes as they have played out, and how parents need to cope with them, has led to the proliferation of confusing, contradictory diagnoses about the serious problems in parenting and in kids' behavior that we've seen in the last decades. These problems in turn have spawned confusing, often contradictory advice about how parents should be child-rearing, with too much blame aimed at both kids and parents. Coping with so much change has rightfully been challenging.

THE BEST OF TIMES—THE WORST OF TIMES

This accident of history—that today's kids are freer now than ever before—is a mixed blessing. With freedom comes a great deal of childhood-teen anxiety and acting-out, as well as instense parental fear and frustration.

At one and the same time, the free-est generation stuns and delights parents. We are awed by kids' ability to discuss just about everything—when they choose to. We are inspired by acts of friendship between supposed-to-be oblivious boys, and admire, almost as much as we cringe at, girls who are queen bees, leaders even in early elementary school. Parents marvel at the close friendships between boys and girls that have broken down that gender divide which we ourselves were just beginning to experience when we were growing up. (Sorry, Alanis, these friendships are mostly without benefits.) We are stunned at the ease with which kids travel across the globe, make cyberconnections, and break geographic boundaries once walled off for grown-ups only. We are stupefied by how our children deal every day with bullies online and in the schoolyard, and envious of their seamless communication possibilities—allowing kids to stay in touch with each other 24/7. We watch our teens willingly participate in community service (not always just for the points) and admire that children give of themselves more generously and at earlier ages than we ever thought to give of ourselves.

But freedom brings anxiety, and trouble is its companion, driving both kids and parents a little crazy.

The free-est generation is living with a great deal of anxiety: the anxiety of daily life filled with such endless choice, hours so crowded with online and schoolyard dangers, so rife with flagrant sexuality, financial, academic, and social competition that we parents sometimes worry our children are coming apart at the seams. And for too many kids, that's true. Children of all ages today binge-drink in excess; self-cutting is on the rise; and coarseness is normal, both around the house toward parents and, in school, toward teachers and each other. Depression is at epidemic proportions, along with eating disorders. Social cruelty begins in ever-lower grades. Even kindergarteners strive to be cool. Exclusion and cliques, scape-goating, and physical violence are what we personally deal with or read about every day.

Yet despite all this, post-boomer parents know our kids are capable of showing a better self, a more empathic, considerate, and sophisticated self than we ever could have possibly imagined for ourselves.

WHAT KIDS NEED—AUTHENTIC ENGAGEMENT

Because we live in times that are balanced between fragmentation and connection, of unanchored families and exponentially ramped-up change, a new style of parenting is needed. I do not believe that a return to the parenting methods of prior generations is the answer. Everything about the world is almost unrecognizable—except to post-boomer parents and their kids, who have grown up more alike than different, more capable of connection than we usually realize.

It is our job, then, as parents and grown-ups, to recognize the changed state of affairs—the positive side as well—and begin to guide our children and teens in a powerful new way. To paraphrase from that old expression about what matters in real estate, kids of all ages need three things: *engagement, engagement, and engagement.* Parents must (and can) learn that what I call "authentic engagement" is the essential component to successfully raising twenty-first century kids. For every aspect of what is different, what it is that post-boomers "get"—meaning the endless choices; the parallel lives of kids and parents; the loss of historical anchoring, of close kinship, neighborhood, and town; and the anxiety of life that every day threatens to run helter-skelter off the tracks—for all this the answer is *authentic engagement.*

This engagement does not conform to the old rules of engagement that swung wildly between the greatest generation's authoritarian "children should be seen ..." and the boomers' laissez-faire child-centeredness. As I will show, post-boomer loving is different. Limiting is different. Listening is different. Community is different. In this book, I will describe an approach to engagement with our children that is often counter-intuitive; it may sometimes feel overly tough, sometimes overly tender. But it is a style of parenting that fits today's parents as much as the kids who depend on us—one that reaches beneath the sophisticated, cool façade that twenty-first century children and teens have learned to put up, revealing the heart, passion, and unlimited potential that lie within them. Authentic engagement is a way to bring out the best selves in our kids.

TOWARD A NEW AGE OF CHILD REARING

From my many years of counseling and presentations across the country, I firmly believe that with attuned guidance, our kids have great potential to reconcile the contradictions in their lives. There are so many reasons to believe they will become more well-rounded, fulfilled, and balanced adults than we have been; more genuinely open to the diversity of cultural perspectives around the world; more aware, comfortable, and healthy in their sexual lives; more able to understand and empathize with generations other than their own.

While we watch with a mixture of awe and fear, kids are continuing the quest for improvement in our lives that post-boomer parents began. Just like you, their parents, today's kids are in the process of re-defining focus for the better, even as it looks like their concentration is scattered beyond belief. Just like you, they are re-defining sexual mores (in often unnerving ways), at the same time that they are moving toward a new sexual restraint. And just like you, they are re-defining relationships with greater openness toward each other *and* toward adults. Kids' sense of entitlement today, which drives us all crazy, is matched by a new sense of giving, built upon your values and absolutely unprecedented in its scope. The casual coarseness, rough-talk and mean talk—which you are no stranger to—is matched by a far greater capacity for empathy, including empathy toward mothers and fathers. And most significant for the future, kids are in the process of re-defining a new tolerance and love of teamwork that started gaining momentum when you were coming up, and that may forever change, if not save our world.

This is, indeed, a special moment in time—one that like a great painting may take just a few days to paint, but has taken decades of trial-and-error learning and many wrong turns to conceive. We are ready for this change now. We have been loosened from the grip of the twentieth century and its strictures regarding the ways that parents and kids should relate; and we are fully prepared to engage in a twenty-first century manner of parenting.

I believe that we are at the dawn of an enlightened period of child rearing—even as we wring our hands in concern.

Besides the fact that parents are ready for change and that their kids are showing signs of constructive transformation beneath the scary headlines, the field of child development is maturing in ways that will support parents as never before. Throughout these pages I introduce surprising trends, scientific and research findings, observations from my counseling and workshops with families, and concrete techniques (many of them counterintuitive) that will reveal why there is much reason for hope—if we learn to practice authentically engaged parenting.

I will start by taking you on a journey of discovery I went through over the past decades as I wrestled with startling and deeply troubling developments in children's behavior: something changed in the way they related to their parents and each other during the 1990s, leading up to the challenges and hopes of today. As I've said, we have heard a great deal about the many shocking behaviors kids began to exhibit during those years. But I believe that we have largely failed to understand the true, underlying causes, and this has contributed to the confusion about how to adjust our parenting methods *now*.

As I reflected on the current situation between parents and kids, I realized that it was impossible to learn how to forge a distinctive style of engaged parenting if we didn't have a more cohesive, penetrating understanding of how the social changes I've mentioned have so deeply affected parents and kids, and affected our relationships with one another. I've described the broad social changes, but we must now look into the specific ways they have led to the challenges parents now contend with. Then we must concretely describe new approaches to cope with those challenges.

So come with me as I lead you through the series of realizations about what shifted in parents' and kids' lives, which crystallized for me over decades, and launched me into writing this book.

It is a graphic, rough ride. But we are no strangers to it. We all have grown up, post-boomer parents and our free-est generation kids, in a world forever changed.

2

"OH, THE THINGS I HAVE SEEN"

Why Kids Are the Way They Are— The Great Unraveling

As I'VE SUGGESTED, a major positive characteristic of the relationship between parents and kids in our post-boomer era is the lack of a glaring generation gap: there is much less of the fierce defiance and rigid conformity that characterized the greatest generation and boomer eras in family life. Mothers and fathers feel more involved with their kids. But there is a poignant irony about the very closeness that characterizes post-boomer families.

As the story I tell here reveals, in recent years parents have become subtly distanced from their children's lives in ways that are almost invisible, but have profound effects.

This surprising fact first became apparent to me in the early to mid-nineties. This was when children of the youngest baby-boomers (born in the mid-1950s to the mid-1960s) and the oldest boomers (born from the mid-1940s to the mid-1950s) were beginning to come of age. Around then I started to sense, in my workshops, in my clinical practice, and among the families in our own community, that something fundamental was changing. I began to chronicle these observations in a series of articles. The first, written in 1995, was entitled "The Second Family," and it struck a powerful nerve with child professionals (teachers, counselors, clergy) nationwide, as well as with the increasingly larger parent groups I was presenting to. Here's how the article started, with the story of an in-trouble, but pretty typical kid I called "Jimmy":

Jimmy was a thirteen-and-a-half year old boy on the verge of being expelled from eighth grade because of his obvious, but heatedly denied, pot-smoking habit. Almost as bad, according to his horrified parents, was his intention to make the ultimate fashion statement by having his ear, eyebrow, and lip pierced, and various items of punk jewelry inserted. The boy's problems, previous therapists had said, could be traced to the fact that his father was classically distant and his mother tended to be over-indulgent and intrusive. Together they had not set enough rules and limits for the boy's behavior.

Jimmy's father acknowledged that because of long work hours he had not had as much of a relationship with his son as he would have liked. Meanwhile, Jimmy's mother said that she had "emotionally spoiled" him. Because she had gone back to work when he was a toddler, she was always feeling guilty and became overly indulgent, trying to make up for lost time with him.

At first these issues seemed pretty standard stuff. I had heard many such family stories. But then I made note of a significant feature of Jimmy's behavior that I began to understand was indicative of a change I hadn't appreciated, and which had been underway in family life everywhere:

His mother reported that since the age of eight or nine, Jimmy had gradually been moving "out of her orbit." She then went on to describe how deep into his own world her son had disappeared. During the last couple of years, I wrote, she didn't think he'd said five words to her that weren't requests to buy him something, give him money, or grant a new privilege.

This subtle distance, without a great deal of fighting, was in progress long before adolescence officially began—a phenomenon I had been observing in other families for a number of years.

When Jimmy and I subsequently met, I realized that the degree to which he had become disengaged from his parents was profound. I asked who had been the significant adults in his life, and he responded with nothing more than a blank stare. He was busy with plenty of adult-run activities, but as I looked beneath the surface of his tightly scheduled life, it quickly became obvious that this boy hadn't experienced any ongoing, deep connection with a grown-up—including, to a troubling degree, his parents—since middle childhood, not adolescence as one would expect.

Beginning in about mid-elementary school, Jimmy had almost completely drifted into the closed society of kid pop culture—communing mostly with his TV, Nintendo, Sega Genesis (remember that one?), CDs, and action comic books. Friends came to hang out but were near invisible, except for brief sightings as they slunk from the front door to Jimmy's inner sanctum and out again. Insidiously, without his parents noticing, Jimmy had become almost completely engulfed by a voracious, commercially-driven kid-universe, what I went on to call "*the second family*" of his peers and pop culture. This second family in many ways, had become his primary family.

I realized that what was true for Jimmy's family was true for millions of others. Trends begun in the seventies, I continued in my article, having lessened the gravitational force of the first family. As we know, divorce (50 percent of marriages), mobility (up to 20 percent of the population moves every year), and economic pressures that generally require both spouses to work ever-longer hours have undermined the old stability of the family. The "traditional" configuration of male breadwinner and wife at home fits only 11 percent of today's households. Furthermore, the informal support systems—the extended kin networks, church and community organizations, PTA and neighborhood ties—that buttressed family life have gradually disintegrated.

For example, PTA membership since 1964 has fallen from 12 million to 7 million. And while Main Street, with its network of well-known shopkeepers and familiar customers greeting one another every day is too often deserted and half boarded-up, huge, impersonal malls on the fringes of town are the real center of urban and suburban life in America.

Into the void left in the old family and neighborhood order had rushed the influence of the peer group and popular culture. Because of this, I concluded, "Today's child has more than likely already been pried out of the family long before adolescence."

I cannot describe the reaction these ideas triggered over a dozen years ago. For some parents, the notion of a powerful new kid-universe competing with adult authority, even before adolescence, was puzzling, especially because they were increasingly involved with their kids' lives. They felt so much more involved with the day-to-day details of their children's schedules, and felt that they understood their children far better than their parents had understood them.

Despite this counter-intuitive description of family life, thousands of mothers and fathers I talked to at lectures told me what a relief it was to finally hear someone validating their experience: the power of the first family at home had somehow been overshadowed by the force of the second family—the peer-group and the pop culture "out there." And this didn't feel good to parents, who knew they were supposed to be more in charge and feel more connected to the kids they so loved.

THE NEW ANGER

Once I understood the emergence of this powerful second family, a number of other discoveries followed. For one thing, children were far more angry than we had realized. Kids saw that their mothers and (some) fathers were deeply involved in the scheduling details of their lives, but were multitasking to the point of often ignoring potential moments of focused attention. Children often see what we adults miss. Management of their time was one thing, but it couldn't replace Mom or Dad's full attention. Children were angry about this lack of genuine connection with their parents, much angrier than I and most other professionals had realized at that point.

In the mid-nineties I did a segment for the TV series *Dateline*. The theme of the show was the difficulty families had with creating rules for their kids. For God knows what reason, a family let *Dateline* set up cameras around their house, an early version of reality TV. While watching hundreds of hours of tape, I was struck when suddenly one of the younger kids in the family, her face magnified by a tight close-up, began to sob because her mother was leaving for work. A huge tear descended with hypnotic power, ever so slowly down her face. She then became furious with her mother, who could do nothing but leave. Mom attempted to repair the hurt with a "guilt gift" when she returned home later—only to trigger another angry outburst from her daughter.

I realized that in dealing with the disconnection children were feeling, at first they were sad, then they became angry, and then, at some point in elementary school, they got used to it and began drifting out into the increasingly welcome arms of the second family's peer group, and the enticing world of consumerism and pop culture.

I was so moved by this realization that I decided to ask kids to help me better understand their experience in a changing world. I began interviewing hundreds of children from diverse backgrounds and varied socioeconomic groups, between the ages of four and sixteen. Over time, I asked almost 250 children and adolescents the simple questions: *"What do your parents do that matters?" "What do you like?" "What don't you like?" and "What do you need from them?"*

I was stunned at what I discovered—just how angry many kids were, especially before they were absorbed into the distractions of the second family. This anger was expressing itself in ever more aggressive interactions at home, as well as in school, both among kids and between them and their teachers. By 1998 I saw with shocking clarity that parents and teachers were losing their authoritative grip and kids of all ages were lashing out in ways unimaginable to those who had grown up in previous decades.

"The new anger," as I referred to it, was raw, sudden, and casual; so casual it was becoming the norm in ordinary families around the country. Parents and their children were rewriting what was considered acceptable communication between the generations. One example I wrote about back then has just as much power to shock today.

"Jessica has just been told by her mother to stop watching TV and clean up the table. 'Not now,' Jessica says, without bothering to look up. 'No, Jessica, I mean this minute,' her mother says sharply. 'Later,' Jessica responds, almost absentmindedly. Mom stiffens and threatens: 'Stop it now, or there won't be TV tonight.' Finally, she's got her daughter's attention. Jessica looks her mother squarely in the face and says, 'Fuck you, Mommy!' Jessica is eight years old."

The startling horror of that phrase! Keep in mind that Jessica was not a neglected or abused child in thrall to gang culture. Her parents were middle-class professionals living in a comfortable suburb. Nor was Jessica maladjusted psychologically; she knew her parents loved her, she earned good marks in school and basically got along well with other children. What was really shocking to me was that such exchanges were becoming so much a part of everyday family discourse.

And I heard of plenty more.

A father informed me that his elementary-school son, when asked for the fourth time to turn off the computer game and straighten his room, snarled, "Leave me alone, butthead!" A ten-year-old girl, told by her mother to finish her homework, barely glanced up, uttered under her breath, "What an asshole," and continued to play. I began hearing the "flailing tantrum" story over and over: a parent directed a child not to chew gum or to stop playing and get ready for bed, and the child responded by hurling him- or herself at the parent, flailing away with small fists in a frenzy of anger. "A few times a week, I get so mad, I go into my room and just rip it apart," I was told over and over by angel-faced innocents. "I beat up on my brother and sister whenever I get mad," reported numerous apparently lovely youngsters. "When I get really, *really* angry," one seven-year-old girl said, in keeping with stories dozens of other children had told me, "I go into the bathroom, shut the door, and scream as loud as I can."

Of course, as has by now become all too well known, such outbursts were not confined to the home. Around 1997, I attended my son's weekly softball game led by an experienced coach, and watched it turn into a free-for-all. One seven-year-old was enraged after he struck out, and grabbed home plate, running off in a howling tantrum. Another child, tagged "out," physically attacked the boy who had tagged him. A kindergartner, when she was called out by the umpire, ran up to him, screamed, "I hate you!" and actually kicked him hard three times in the shins—all this in a friendly neighborhood game for kids and their families.

In interviews with non-parental adults in kids' lives—teachers, coaches, principals, community leaders, clergy, camp owners—I heard again and again about disturbing aggression toward adults, manifested by even the tiniest of tykes. One eminent children's theater director described defiance from the most motivated of elementary-schoolers, telling me that in twenty-five years of producing plays, he had seen an increasingly aggressive disrespect for him by his young charges: "I can't describe the enormity of change in the way children behave. I can no longer count on having their respect and attention merely because I am the adult and a teacher—now half the struggle is just to get them to begin to listen to my directions."

DAZED AND CONFUSED PARENTING

What exactly was going on between parents and children? After listening to thousands of mothers and fathers and teachers in my workshops, I concluded that we adults were a large part of the problem.

In the 1999 *Networker* article, I wrote, *"Like deer frozen in the headlights of an oncoming car, parents at all ends of the political and economic spectrum are increasingly at a loss about how to provide leadership in their own families."*

Many parents, suffering guilt about the demands of their responsibilities outside the home, and feeling the power of the second family to hijack their authority, were simply baffled about how to respond. They were of a different time than their greatest generation parents and grandparents. For better or worse, the certitude of that era was gone. Gone too was the pretty unified voice of the adult network that once supported parents. Gone was the phrase "Because I'm the parent and I said so!" Looking back, this should not have been a surprise to me: Many late-boomers and post-boomers didn't want to use the older, more authoritarian approach to parenting of the greatest generation. Decades of decline in rigid moral formulas, tightly-knit neighborhoods, and kinship systems, along with an increase in the importance of personal "self-actualization" had profoundly impacted child-rearing mores. Relativism had replaced the tougher disciplinarian approach that so many of their own parents had used, and which they had come to deeply resent. I cannot overstate how many parents told me in those years: "My parenting approach is the exact opposite of how I was raised. I will *not* squelch my kids the way I was squelched as a child!" And they meant it.

Parents were not just confused, they were beginning to lose their own moral direction. What, for example, happened to Chrissie, who screamed at the umpire and kicked him in the shins at the Little League game? Incredibly, her mother, who was watching, did not reprimand her. The umpire did not kick her out of the game, and a few minutes later, Chrissie received the weekly achievement certificate she'd "earned"—a red ribbon for her participation. Frankly, sitting on the sidelines taking this all in, I was embarrassed to be a parent.

What did many fathers and mothers do when their children cursed at them, flew into a tantrum, or beat up a younger sibling? Not very much, it turned out. Speaking for many, one mother I counseled described her reaction when her six-year-old son, Eric, hit her and screamed at her in the supermarket: "I didn't know whether it was better to smack him on the spot or let him get his feelings off of his chest so they wouldn't fester." Even worse, some parents responded with intense rage and overblown, unenforceable punishments. In the face of her daughter's "fuck you," for example, Jessica's mom immediately spanked her and threatened, unconvincingly, to take all TV away for a whole year. Several weeks later, while watching television together, another version of the same incident occurred.

In addition to the anger, children were increasingly challenging parents with a shockingly early onset of behaviors once reserved for adolescence. For example, ten-year-old Mindy had been invited to a party, where, she said, the kids would be playing make-out games. "What should I do?" Mindy asked her mother, Ann, "when they start kissing?" But Ann was as unsure as her little girl. Finally, after what seemed like an endless hesitation, she recalled to me that she said, "In the end, it's whatever makes *you* feel comfortable with who you are," a well-intentioned but unsatisfying answer that satisfied neither Ann nor her daughter. Mindy was outright annoyed at the lack of guidance. Ann confided to me that she hadn't known what would be better—letting her child "harmlessly" explore her emerging sexuality, or setting strict limits that she might rebel against. Mom worried that doing so would lead Mindy to choose not to confide in her next time.

Bill, the father of depressed, thirteen year-old Jason, was in an equally serious quandary. After a couple of lonely years without friends, Jason had finally seemed to find a buddy—a classmate he brought home during lunch period. The tentative friendship was a real breakthrough, except for one tiny detail: the two boys spent the lunch hour in Jason's room smoking dope. Should Bill ignore the massive infraction of school discipline, not to mention state and federal drug laws, in relief that his son had found a new chum? Or should he crack down on the illegal and dangerous behavior? Which was worse for the boy—being friendless at school or being a budding pot-head with a pal?

MORAL RELATIVITY AND THE NEW ANGER

Moral relativism, especially the view that no one view should dismiss another's equally valid perspective, had become apparent in kids' attitudes, as well. Although younger children I interviewed in the mid-to-late nineties—I'm talking about five-, six-, and seven-year-olds—still strongly believed in right and wrong and were angry when their parents failed to set rules, by fourth or fifth grade they had begun talking in ominously relativistic terms about moral issues. For example, in response to the Columbine murders, many children made remarks like, "I don't think what they did was right, but I don't completely blame them, either. Those kids had their reasons. They were treated badly, and anybody can crack under certain conditions."

One shocking article from 1996 appeared in the *Rockford Register Star*, an Illinois newspaper. In a poll of hundreds of teens in heartland America, the paper asked what moral guidelines they followed. "There aren't any," these kids answered almost unanimously. "You only need to treat others the same way they treat you." Almost none of the teenagers, boys or girls, were prepared to label behavior, no matter how noxious, simply right or wrong.

More disquieting, and perhaps more instructive, was my realization that many of these kids had little faith in their parents' ability to give them good guidance. They truly had begun to live in their own universe. With the explosion of kid-to-kid culture (the number of teen and child magazines, for example, sky-rocketed around this time, from a handful to dozens), TV networks and video games *just* for children seemed to suddenly take over the air waves. In addition, the growing sophistication of peer politics became a major factor far removed from the eyes of most adults. In around the early to mid-nineties, I started to be called into elementary schools, not middle or high schools, to deal with ostracism and social cruelty. Many parents, despite their own post-boomer sophistication, failed to understand the complexities of kids' second-family lives.

Central to the ways kids were behaving, I realized, was the fact that so many perceived their parents had become unsure of their ability to guide them. Kids were more "free," but freedom had started to take quite a toll in terms of everyday family chaos and angry, dismissive children.

PARENTING ADVICE GONE WILD

The more families I counseled and listened to in workshops about these issues, the more I realized the problem of parental confidence in the face of second-family influence had been compounded by the contradictory hodge-podge of child-rearing advice that had been popularized over the last thirty years. Many parents tried out various one-size-fits-all theories, some from decades earlier, some more current. Advice to parents had swung crazily back and forth for years between poles of permissiveness and toughness. Often these off-the-rack approaches were inappropriate for a particular child.

When eight-year-old Peter, for example, got into another bruising battle with his little brother, his mother, Hillary, tried an approach based on Thomas Gordon's Parent Effectiveness Training (P.E.T.) model. This method was first introduced in 1970, in a reaction to the generally stricter greatest generation child-training methods that emphasized that "children should be seen, not heard," "guilt is good," and "you need to do this, just because I said so." P.E.T. stressed the importance of allowing children to express themselves freely and warned of psychological stultification if parents suppress the child's inner spirit. It became a national movement.

While extremely useful for many boomers and post-boomers, as Hillary discovered, this enlightened approach—seriously listening, reflecting back feelings, naming emotions for children—had its limitations. After a while, kids at surprisingly young ages, especially as they became second-family "hip," would tune it out. Using the "active listening" techniques recommended by P.E.T., Hillary asked open-ended questions in an attempt to help Peter express and neutralize his feelings of jealousy. The more she used this kind of therapy-speak, though, the more tight-lipped he eventually became. "Oh, forget it," Peter finally said one day in disgust and walked away. Our own daughter, Leah, did the same to me once. When she was about four she looked at me with irritation after I'd "reflected" her feelings one too many times, saying "Leah, that must have made you very angry"; she retorted: "That again, Daddy!" turning her back to resume playing.

Another, very different approach to parenting that was popularized, following hard on P.E.T., was *tough love,* with its emphasis on limits, structure, and consequences. The advocates of this approach criticized P.E.T.'s encouragement of expressiveness in kids. It too became a national movement, helping many parents develop the nerve to deal more effectively with out-of-control situations. But this one-size-fits-all model also had its limitations, as twelve-year-old Jenny's parents discovered. Jenny had been drinking, hooking up with lots of boys, staying out way past her curfew, and doing poorly in school. Her father, Bob, already overly rigid, treated Jenny to an ironclad discourse on bottom-line consequences. Two days after his hell-and-brimstone sermon, Jenny didn't come home at all. She had found a place to crash with some loosely supervised kids in the neighborhood.

Following *tough love*, yet another wholesale, almost diametrically-opposite approach caught fire: the self-esteem movement. Prompted in large part by the revelations of widespread family abuse and incest that surfaced during the late seventies and early eighties, this movement was originally promulgated by such books as Alice Miller's hugely influential *Prisoners of Childhood,* Marlo Thomas' *Free to be You and Me*, and Haim Ginott's groundbreaking guide *Between Parent and Child,* among so many others. Word spread rapidly throughout the world of post-boomer child-rearing, as well as progressive education; the self-esteem movement attracted millions of followers, just as P.E.T. and *tough love* had. Parents were admonished that children be "empowered" so that their spirits and souls might no longer be cavalierly crushed in abusive family contexts.

Self-esteem-based parenting recommended attention to accomplishments, praise instead of "constructive criticism," and a belief that each child's unique sense of self should be nurtured, rather than ignored. This surge of empathic awareness of kids' emotional needs added immeasurably to a greater understanding of children as sensitive individuals, who would carry a legacy of abuse or neglect well into adulthood. The approach spoke to huge numbers of parents, by then in "sharing-caring groups" or twelve-step programs, who were trying to heal from their own experiences of abuse growing up.

Over time, the self-esteem movement was roundly accused by critics of encouraging the wild behavior so many post-boomer parents are now dealing with. New mothers and fathers I met around the country nonetheless continued to subscribe to the approach, even as others began to rail against what they perceived as its permissiveness.

In response to the self-esteem movement, parenting advice took yet another 180-degree turn, with the advent of the *family values* movement in the late eighties.

Parents were exhorted that if they taught their kids morality, their behavior would take care of itself. Linda and Richard Eyre's *Teaching Your Children Values* became the first parenting book in years to be number one on *The New York Times* best-seller list. The Eyres clearly touched a nerve among parents who believed that child-rearing permissiveness had gone way too far. Either in humorous guides, like Fred Gosman's *Spoiled Rotten,* or in harder-line approaches such as highly structured wilderness programs for out-of-control kids, the message was clear: "spare the discipline and moral clarity, and you risk spoiling the child." Yet even as the values movement gained momentum, with its emphasis on teaching children the importance of honor, truth, respect, obedience, courage, and loyalty, its perspective was soon challenged. The popularization of biological explanations for kids' unruly behavior suddenly emerged on to the national scene.

Scientific discoveries about the effect of "hard-wiring" on behavior swung the pendulum once again, now in the direction of nature, rather than nurture. Forget working to instill self-esteem, forget teaching values; in fact, forget relying on any one "right" parenting approach. Far more important was the understanding of children's immutable biological "programming." Stanley Turecki's *The Difficult Child* strongly suggested that behavior blamed on "bad parenting" lay at the feet of genetic predisposition, chemical imbalances, and inborn temperament. Millions of parents (especially mothers) understandably heaved a sigh of relief, having been previously blamed for their children's bad behavior and for every childhood disorder under the sun, from autism to schizophrenia.

This new biological frontier led to an array of additional childhood diagnoses, such as the pervasive developmental disorders, attention deficit disorder, obsessive-compulsive disorder, affective and bipolar disorders. The role of parents and professionals became helping children take medication to compensate for problems that were seen as largely beyond conscious control. While these diagnoses added immeasurably to understanding psychological and medical conditions in kids' lives, and saving what once had been considered absolutely hopeless situations, they also created a backlash from the next trend in the pop-parenting pipeline.

Criticism mounted around the late-nineties and turn of the century about the over-medication of childhood. In reaction to this biological wave, regarded in some circles as a way to create alibis for the bad behavior of spoiled and undisciplined kids, yet another breed of authoritarianism arose on the scene. "Children should be punished for every act of disobedience, no matter how small," intoned John Rosemond, a popular syndicated columnist and main spokesman for the new movement. Conservative psychologist James Dobson, head of Focus on the Family, advocated bringing spanking back. And, in the shadow of school shootings, a legislative movement gained steam in support of posting the Ten Commandments in every schoolroom in America. Child rearing and the values surrounding it had become a "wedge" issue in political dialogue.

No wonder parents were confused after this series of whiplash changes in advice. Parents often floundered, trying first one and then another of these approaches; and their children became increasingly frustrated with the lack of adult certitude and attention to their main concern: that parents really engage with them.

"HELLO, I MUST BE GOING."

Kids' simple answers to my questions about what worked and what didn't pointed to a consistent theme, a powerful feature of postboomer family life regardless of where one lived or what one believed politically: the pace of life seemed to be lurching out of control, leading to the question of whether, with all of our frenetic activities, we were really getting to know our own children.

"Sometimes," said one of the fifth graders in my study, "I get the feeling my parents don't know me." "Mine, too," yelled an irate classmate from across the room. "We don't spend time together— we're always so busy in my house." Just about every child nodded enthusiastically, some with obvious annoyance.

The more I delved into what was going on with this new breed of kids, the more I became convinced the social changes that had been set in motion in the late seventies and eighties were now playing themselves out in the lives of families. We were becoming, as a famous *New York Times* article put it in 1997, "Addicted to Speed." Take just one look at what ordinary family schedules had morphed into by this time, and it's clear why kids were feeling subtly unknown, despite being so catered to:

9 A.M: Feed Baby Guppies, 10–12- P.M.: Non-Verbal Social-ization Group, 12–3 P.M.: Pre-Nursery Day Care, 3–5 P.M.: All-sport Little Leagues, 5–6 P.M.: Theater for Tweens, 7–11 P.M.: The UPN-WB Teen Network, 11 P.M.–Dawn: My Space, YouTube, Facebook, and Online Poker.

While this frenzied pace of family life may seem normal to parents *now,* it is sobering to recall that for decades before and after the Second World War, such a non-stop conveyor belt life would have been considered, well—insane! The great irony at the heart of family life by the late 1990s, I realized, was that despite all of the greater parent involvement, few parents really knew what their kids were up to a great deal of the time.

This is not easy to say but—for better and worse—over the past twenty years, we parents have been subtly extruded from our kids' lives.

By the turn of the century, we had become managers of our kids. "After decades of social change we are no longer engaged primarily as nurturers or teachers of values. Regardless of headlines labeling us "helicopter" dads and "soccer" moms, in many ways, parents seem almost invisibly removed. Twenty-first century parent-managers, negotiating every single logistical challenge of their kids' crammed schedules became too frenetically busy to be a magnetic presence in the internal landscape of a child's world. On the surface kids are used to it; they adore their newfound freedom and deeply love their parents, but underneath they are troubled by the missing connection.

Free on the surface—inside kids are hungry for non-managerial parental engagement underneath.

Even while being thrown together in car pools, our children understand that most of the time we spend as family could best be described by the old movie line, *"Hello, I must be going!"* They get that life with mom or dad is a series of tightly choreographed transitions, of conversations interrupted, and of moments hurried along so that the next moment can almost happen. They correctly sense that even though we're spending time with them, we are often not as engaged as either they or we would like, forever consumed as we are by the endless list of logistical maneuvers that overpower the most loving families.

Kids' hunger for more connection might seem surprising at first, because data starting back in the nineties indicated that parents were spending the same, if not more time with their kids than June and Ward Cleaver ever did. But when researchers examined what kind of time family members were spending with one another, we got a troubling picture of that so-called family togetherness.

Kids and parents might be spending time near each other, but they are engaged in separate activities, not remotely doing things together. Indeed, a long-distance phone conversation can provide a much closer and more intimate experience of connection than a typical evening in the bosom of the American family in the post-boomer era. In 1999, The Kaiser Family Foundation conducted one of the first extensive studies on TV viewing habits and how families actually spent time at home. They asked the reader to imagine removing the roof of a typical house and look down from above. This is what the Kaiser study found: mother may be supervising her five-year-old in the bath, while calling someone from work to arrange a meeting and an after-school activity for the next day. Sister is e-mailing several buddies and talking with yet another friend on the phone. Dad (whether he lives at home or if it's his weekend with the kids in a divorced family) is busy finishing up a report, looking up every ten minutes or so to announce that it's nearly bedtime, to whatever child might actually be listening.

I realized the question we had to ask ourselves as parents: were we really getting to know our children? In my conversations with students from pre-kindergarten to sixth grade, kids overwhelmingly indicated that what they wanted most from their parents was *undivided* attention—not me instead of my brother, but mom or dad entirely focused on me, rather than multitasking. I would hear, "I want my mom to stop being so busy and just play with me." "I love when my dad sits next to me and we watch movies together." "I want my mommy to lie down with me every night."

I didn't believe then and don't believe now that this is simply whining by a generation of spoiled kids. These were the heartfelt responses of children desperate to be truly known, rather than scheduled and hurriedly attended to on the way to the next activity.

"It is logical that many parents buy great quantities of off-the-rack advice," I concluded in 1998 after listening to the kids, "because, stretched to the limits as we have become, we do not really know the children we have. We cannot always tell the ways in which our kids are uniquely different because we just do not spend enough direct, one-on-one time with them. The hard truth is that parents love their children, but they do not create the time to pay attention to them. They do not really hear them. They do not really see them."

I knew these words sounded harsh, and this point was a bitter pill for overworked parents to swallow, particularly those who felt their lives were already so child-centered. But the issue had to be raised. "What happens," I asked in this *Networker* piece, "to children when they do not get the kind of direct, undivided, personal attention they need from their own parents? When they lack confidence in the capacity of their parents to guide them? Where do they look to find something that promises to assuage their yearnings for attention?"

CELEBRITY NATION IS BORN

"Nature abhors a vacuum," I continued in the article, "and for American children the great, roaring tornado of the mass media culture—particularly the culture of celebrity—rushes in to fill the psychic void that family used to fill."

Twenty years ago, I rarely heard about celebrity fantasies in my work with kids. By the late nineties, I rarely *didn't*. Increasingly, children answered my questions about what they would like most by stating that their greatest wish was to be near a celebrity.

This was sad enough, but it was less ominous than the growing hunger many kids felt to achieve celebrity status themselves, as if this were the one best bet for achieving the attention they craved. Of course, in a celebrity-drenched culture, most of us occasionally think we'd like to be famous. But for children who are angry because they can't get the personal attention of the people they love and need the most, the desire to be seen can become an all-encompassing and toxic need. In a society of increasingly fragmented families, whose members live parallel lives within the home, in which children often feel more catered to than truly known, and where off-the-rack child-rearing techniques too often miss the point, the culture of celebrity is a potentially inflammable ingredient.

"Kids who commit publicly violent acts," I concluded, "have found a metaphor that describes the pain of, as well as the solution for, their invisibility. They engage in such behavior precisely because it makes an unknown child instantly and uniquely recognizable. In a child's mind, public violence appears to be the perfect antidote to the anonymity of his or her life."

In a keynote address to several thousand child-professionals in 1999, I said that given the amount of free-flowing anger I'd heard from kids and the growing influence of the pop culture, I was surprised there wasn't more schoolyard aggression than we had yet seen.

A couple of weeks later Columbine exploded, and it's never been the same since.

It's time to pause on this journey for a moment as we close in on the turn of the century. I had begun to articulate the beginning of major changes that were in progress and, in fact, gaining steam: The first was a slow, but steady disintegration of the greatest generation's family and neighborhood container, and the emergence of a technologically-driven peer group and pop culture—exerting a tremendous pull on the hearts and minds of even our youngest children. The second was the reduction of monolithic authority and power in homes, with an accompanying increase of explosive aggression and casual disrespect from kids toward boomer and post-boomer adults, who were much more confused than their own greatest generation parents. The third was the notion that violence of kids toward each other was an expression of anger at subtle but widespread adult absence (despite their good intentions) and the pressure to be seen in a world obsessed by celebrity.

By the mid-to-late nineties, then, our children were beginning to live in an increasingly powerful, but parallel universe. The second family had taken hold. And not being particularly concerned with adult authority, kid-life inside the second family was becoming wild, very wild indeed.

THE WALL OF SILENCE AND KIDS' NEW FREEDOM

As I continued to deal with families grappling with these issues, I realized that children and teens had increasingly been living behind a "wall of silence," as I called it in my 2001 *Networker* article, unreachable by most parents, and were using that freedom to engage in an entire world of new behavior just beyond the view of adults.

To get behind that wall, I changed some of the ways I worked with kids. I began spending hundreds of hours with young clients studying the "artifacts" of their lives. I listened to their favorite CDs, read their e-mail correspondence—together with them—and leafed through teen magazines, Goth comic books, video game manuals (especially violent ones) and student-run newspapers. This was an eye-opening period during which my hair, not coincidentally, changed from dark brown to a shock of grayish-white. Some of this was, of course, my own father's genetic timetable for middle-year graying, and part was having two youngsters of our own to worry about. But much of it was the sheer magnitude of what I was discovering.

I had been the director of treatment in Child and Adolescent Psychiatry at Brooklyn's Downstate Medical Center during the late seventies, and I had been involved with creating programs for parents and kids in many schools for decades, but nothing I had seen previously prepared me for what became re-defined as ordinary life behind the "wall of silence." The range of activities our kids had begun to engage in is still shocking for most of us parents, especially in relationship to our own children.

Consider "raves" and loft-parties, which were becoming popular events during those years. Although common knowledge now, few parents believed me when I first started talking about them in the nineties. With no adults permitted, raves often began at midnight and continued into the wee hours of the morning, alcohol and drugs freely available to hundreds of mostly unacquainted young teens. When the panic-stricken parents of a thirteen-year-old came to me about how to handle an upcoming loft party, I was stunned to discover that not one other set of parents knew about it. Just about every kid in school had been furiously plotting about how to go—but only this one girl had broken the wall of silence.

Experienced counselors and teachers felt paralyzed, unprepared by their training for dealing with what was looking like a completely new brand of kid. Like me, they met children who vandalized buildings without experiencing any guilt; talked with young teens who had sex in school bathrooms, not caring who walked in on them; and heard about adolescents who broke into abandoned warehouses to hold "x-treme" wrestling matches that continued until one of the participants was left unconscious. (How prescient these kids were: think about the appearance of "x-treme" fighting on TV now.)

Despite the shocking nature of this behavior, one response I heard from many adults was, so what else is new? Since when, during the last forty years, have American teenagers *not* evaded the gaze of adults, incensed their elders, and inspired media jeremiads about juvenile outrages? "Isn't bad behavior now the birthright of the American adolescent?" they'd insist.

KIDS AND PARENTS: A NEW WORLD

Perhaps, but as I reported in the 2001 *Networker* article, I believed that something new *was* happening here. In keeping with national trends, I was seeing an increasing number of clients doing wilder things at younger ages than I had known in almost three decades of treating children and adolescents—and without their supposedly sophisticated parents having any idea of what was going on. I firmly believed back then that we were beginning to see a new kind of kid privately embedded in a far rawer, intense, and pervasive youth culture than ever before, complete with new rules for the pre-teens and adolescence.

But, it was not the actual behavior that was new. After all, many boomers had been outrageously wild. What was new under the sun was the casual unself-consciousness of the kids, the ordinariness of it, often without a trace of kid-teen rebellion against an adult establishment.

Take the case I described back then of a mother and daughter pair I'll call Margaret and Lauren. Margaret thought that she was very close to her daughter. Lauren gossiped to Margaret about her friends, described boys she thought were "hot," and brought kids home to eat and watch TV. In turn, Margaret told Lauren about her own adolescence and how she had yearned for freedom from rigidly moralistic parents who were suspicious of her every move. Margaret was proud of being the kind of with-it mother a girl could really talk to. And then one day she came home to find her daughter having sex with *two* boys in the bathtub. Shrieking, she got the boys dressed and out of the house, and then confronted her daughter.

"You must have been imagining we were having sex because *your* parents were so strict and you were wild as a kid," Lauren said. "Besides, there were bubbles in the tub—how could you know what was really going on?"

For a brief moment, Margaret nearly fell for it—was it possible she had gotten it wrong? Then, furious anew, she asked, "What do you think I am—a damn fool?"

"Yes," Lauren said flatly.

Shocked and frightened, Margaret called the same day to schedule her daughter for a therapy appointment.

During the first few sessions, I learned several things about Lauren's life that her mother did not know. She told me, for example, that she and her friends often smoked pot together, some of her buddies were heavy drinkers, and all engaged in sex—mostly oral or anal, which kept them, technically, "abstinent." Re-definitions of sexuality have now become so ordinary and were already beginning back then. Just recently, in 2008 a distressed mother wrote to me from halfway across the country about her fifteen-year-old daughter, insisting that a friend's "taking it up the ass" meant she was not engaging in sex and was still, in fact, a virgin. Besides the content of what this girl was describing, can you believe she was actually discussing it with her mother? Even the most rebellious boomers would have found this casual exchange with their greatest generation parents impossible.

Not only did Lauren live much of her life in a world entirely beyond her mother's ken; what really stood out was how she lied about her activities with such virtuosity and shamelessness.

This non-conflicted lying was also a new development in my years counseling kids. Parents weren't the only ones confused; we experienced counselors, as well as teachers, felt stunned, unprepared by our training for dealing with what was looking like a completely new brand of kid behind this wall of silence. "I feel shell-shocked," said Alice, who had spent twenty years as a school counselor in Ohio. "Just about every Monday, kids come in showing off their tattoos. They tell me about gang-bangs, binge drinking, raves, and group sex in every possible permutation. These aren't high school seniors, either. I'm talking about thirteen-, fourteen-, and fifteen-year-olds—and the most frightening part is that their parents haven't got a clue."

Yes, there had always been kids who would sneak into their parents' liquor cabinets, but regular, all-night drinking and pot-smoking binges for well-brought-up, barely pubescent boys and girls had been unknown. And, sure, for decades adolescents had worn outlandish clothes, but did fourteen-year-olds routinely have themselves tattooed and their nipples, tongues, and navels pierced? Of course, kid pop music was always about sex, but several decades ago, the most graphic lyrics were *purposely* calculated to upset greatest generation parents. By the nineties, casual obscenity and violence had become an unremarkable feature of the most wildly successful pop lyricists.

Given the distance between themselves and adults, children could afford to lie without qualms because kids of all ages had begun to realize they were unlikely to get caught. Largely unsupervised by overworked and overstressed parents, living in communities where neighbors were strangers to one another, attending large suburban and urban schools where teachers did not always know their names, they knew that adults were increasingly unaware of what they were actually doing.

"*Who,*" as one kid challenged me, "*is going to rat us out—the cashier at K-Mart?*"

By the mid-to-late nineties, the incredible power of the internet to digitize this wall of silence was announced, with the advent of chat rooms and instant messaging. Never before had so many kids spent so much time in direct touch, entirely uncontrolled by their parents. Online they were beginning to assume different personalities, genders, and ages—becoming anyone they wanted to be and interacting with hundreds of chameleons doing the same shape-shifting—and all without their parents being any the wiser.

One mother, Madeline, compared her fourteen-year-old daughter to her nineteen-year-old daughter in a way I will never forget: "My younger one is online every day with friends whom I've never met and never will meet. Five years ago, I might have talked to some of them on the phone when they called, and at least heard their voices, but now, I don't even know who they are or who she is."

Madeline's fourteen-year-old then put the icing on the cake: "Mom, I could have a boyfriend or even two. And if I wanted to keep you in the dark, you wouldn't have any idea at all—you're lucky I'm not like that and that I actually talk to you."

Kids truly were "freer" than kids had ever been before, and I was increasingly aware that freedom came with costs. In this parallel universe, a world behind the wall of silence, post-boomer parents and their free-est generation children were beginning to feel, what in 2003, I first called "the new anxiety."

THE NEW ANXIETY

The flip side of the new freedom was a new anxiety. It was infused by endless access, early decisions about high-risk behavior, the ability to do "whatever" without concerns about being seen, and by the overwhelming reach of technology and the warp-speed of life itself. The free-est generation began to shimmer with neon-bright anxiety. This was different than internal *neurotic* anxiety, by which I mean symptomatic, psychological conflict, thought to be the result of guilt between "right" and "wrong," the struggle between "id" and "superego," and the fear that "bad" thoughts meant being a bad person. In children this anxiety can lead to a raging battle between pleasing parents and pleasing oneself, and even to feeling personal responsibility for the very lives, health, and well-being of one's parents. This type of internal conflict had been the bread and butter of psychoanalysis during the time of the greatest generation and its boomer children.

No, by the second millenium, the kids of older boomers and post-boomers were suffering from a different breed of anxiety, generated by *real-life* forces: intense social, academic, and techno-driven pressures.

Between 1998 and 2003 I felt this anxiety swelling up around the country. At many parent and school conferences, to illustrate what was going on in kids' minds, I would open my presentations by reading a "stream of consciousness" narrative representing the composite thoughts and external pop culture intrusions that were beginning to practically swallow up post-boomer children and their families. My goal then and now, is to help adults feel a tiny bit of the new anxiety I'd been learning about. Here's what could be swirling through your twenty-first century child's consciousness at any given moment:

"Johnny says I'm a faggot. I'll rip his arms out—then we'll see who's gay!" "Bitch! "How did Jenny get that tattoo? I'm going to throw up." "Just do it!" "A lot of kids are going to crash that party." "Parents, the anti-drug." "Mommy will kill me—wait, I'm at Daddy's this week." "Get the stuff!" "I want Game Boy and Play Station 2 . . ." "You've got mail!" "Wazzup!" "You're never too thin!" "Hey, everybody does not think I'm bipolar!" "New standardized tests." ". . . Shit, I don't understand this math, but first, I have to check my e-mails, then burn that CD and . . ." "Twelve more killed in" . . . "I'm so tired, but what's that noise outside?" . . . "Order in the next thirty minutes and" . . . "Mom, I'm in fourth grade—I am not too young for a thong." . . . "New unemployment figures . . ." "Valerie's father died and Betsy's parents just split up and Bobby's family is moving away." . . . "Deal with it!" . . . "I just can't take it anymore."

Around the turn of this century, as I got behind the wall of silence and listened to enough kids express these everyday worries, it often seemed like they were coming apart at the seams. Millenium children of all ages pulsated with this anxiety; they were living in a pressure-cooker youth culture, feeling ever on-edge. Not that I knew it when I first met them back then. For the most part, they didn't and still don't act particularly scared.

In my encounters with kids, though, as I got to know them well, I learned to see the signs. The new anxiety was chaotic, characterized by scattered thoughts as kids restlessly moved from one topic to another in conversation. It was also chronic: every day would bring a different social or academic pressure to be dealt with, as for example keeping up with what item of "gear" must be had; and "cool," super-casual presentations of often high-risk situations that had somehow become ordinary.

Anxiety was all around, more invisible than the air we breathe. By 2003 it had become apparent to me that there was no longer a town in this country that didn't exhibit the signs of epidemic anxiety among our youngsters.

What therapists used to refer to as the "presenting" problem (for example, a child unwilling to go to school) that presumably masked the "real" issue (a depressed parent at home whom the child felt responsible for and didn't want to abandon) was being trumped. The new issue was simply the struggle to keep up with the ever-increasing stressors of normal twenty-first century life, and with a steady diet of aggressive, sexualized pseudo-adolescence that seemed to begin in the early-to-middle years of elementary school. No wonder kids were increasingly anxious and parents equally unnerved.

In my workshops nationwide, during counseling sessions, and from friends, I heard constant reports by distressed parents about the nature of their children's lives. A typical day might bring the following accounts:

Ben stuns his "Not-*my*-child!" mother, Janice, with a straight-from-TV comment I'd warned her was not far away. "Hey, you're some hot, sexy babe, Mom!" says *six year-old* Ben in the middle of their usual bedtime routine. A few minutes later, he's moved off this alpha-male posturing and is worried about a noise outside the window, connecting it to a news story he'd seen that night on what he calls the "terror channel," CNN.

Eight-year-old Tanya is upset because she has been excluded from the recess group in school. She is a fabulous reader and writer of poetry, but is already beginning to hide her abilities, so she won't be seen as one of the class "geeks." Her parents are stunned by this self-negation, something they'd expected would appear in her adolescent years, *not second grade*.

Fifteen-year-old John has been drinking too much and ends up in my office. Yes, his drinking is a troubling concern, but not compared to the viselike grip of anxiety John feels about thirty hours of homework a week, four hours of basketball practice every night, three hours per week of community service, and, of course, two parties a weekend.

What about Julia, who's in therapy because of her almost failing grades? Sure she's worried about school, though what really preoccupies her is the phenomenon the *New York Times* called the *"Whore Wars."* Julia's caught in a bind. She feels she must show as much skin as possible, but how can she do this when she's obsessed with so many different parts of her body being what she calls "absolutely grotesque." Of course, girls have lived with impossible standards of physical perfection for decades, but now it's happening at younger and younger ages—Julia is eleven.

Her friend, Ethan, also a preteen, is one of the growing numbers of *elementary school boys* I know who are obsessed about their bodies—not buff enough, too skinny, and too small. "I might as well be dead," he says to me.

Thirteen-year-old Peter showed up in my office because he was isolated; he turned people off. What is really going on beneath his haughty presentation, though, is that he's been typed as gay. Why? He once put his arm around another boy in a moment of friendship, and since then he's been accused, as if he were a character on *South Park*, of being "ass hungry."

Mona had it all—the perfect look, the perfect body, and super smarts. So, what made Mona so fearful? Precisely because of her magnetism, she'd became the object of anonymous Internet insults, come-ons, and actual threats to her life.

What kept Michael up at night was different—he couldn't possibly turn himself off after an ordinary evening. Ordinary for many kids by the turn of the century was: being online with six people at once, while talking on the phone with two friends on call-waiting, while burning a CD for a pal, while doing homework with a friend, with TV on in the background just "to keep him company."

Don't reflexively blame their mothers or fathers. Most of these children have reasonably responsive, competent parents. They felt as helpless as their kids about how to lessen the grip of this half-crazed pressure. After all, they lived their own version of the same bind, stretched to the breaking point by their own impossible work schedules, endless social obligations, and gut-wrenching economic worries.

A few years into the twenty-first century, my experience told me that parents felt hard-pressed to protect and soothe themselves, much less their kids, from external pressures that essentially colonized the family.

By then, I had begun to realize that kids knew their post-boomer parents felt helpless. Now several steps removed from the anchoring certitude of the greatest generation, many had lost faith in the ability of the adult "container" to protect children from a culture running off the tracks. Studies repeatedly show that when the unthinkable happens, such as schoolyard killings, death-defying parties, or sadistic bullying, kids know something is brewing, but do not approach parents or other adults for guidance. In a vicious circle, the less comfort and trust kids felt in their post-boomer homes, the more they gravitated to the second family of the peer group and pop culture to meet their needs for self-worth and connection. But the second family, by then an all-too-powerful reality, carried its own freight, its own pressures, and its own anxiety.

Like the culture from which it was shaped, the second family had become a world flying off its hinges, making kids freer than ever before and more vulnerable at the same time.

THE DIVIDED SELF

It was around this period, in the early 2000s, that my view of what was happening in kid-world hit rock bottom. I was certainly not alone in my concern. Almost every best-selling child-rearing book published around this time addressed some aspect of the dangers I've described here, and they kept coming: *Reviving Ophelia, The Pressured Child, Raising Cain, Queen Bees and Wannabes, Lost Boys, Odd Girl Out, Kids Who Kill,* and *Another Tribe,* to name just a few. I began to realize that under all of the pressure, a scary adaptation was under way.

The normal "whole" self of children was fragmenting, much like the lives of their parents.

Since WWII, adults, especially post-boomer parents born after 1964, had been learning to operate, with varying degrees of success and stress, on many competing planes at once, running in several different directions just to keep up. They were increasingly juggling child-care expectations at home and demands for greater productivity at work, as well as the logistics of over-scheduling, deepening financial debt—despite both parents working—often with staggeringly longer commutes. And, hopefully, they were scheduling in some relaxation somewhere, sometime.

The emphasis for post-boomer adults was on action, pushing ahead, and handling it all, *fast!* (Why else had there been a veritable explosion of books on "mindfulness?") Picture moms and dads in the morning rush at home trying to ignore and push past their whining, complaining, balking, dawdling, sadness, and angry normal kids, desperately trying to avoid any emotional outburst or behavior that might derail the holy grail of the schedule.

As we moved from the first to the second millennium, kids were expected to speed up too, pushing aside feelings if they got in the way of moving ahead.

DON'T THINK—JUST "DO IT!"

Decades ago, the eminent psychiatrist R. D. Laing observed a fragmented, "divided-self" in adults during the massive social upheaval of the sixties, which he wrote about in his influential book, *The Divided Self*. By divided-self, Laing meant the struggle between a unique true-self, filled with idiosyncratic and genuine emotions, but too insecure to emerge, and the false-self of an external façade, conforming to the relentless circumstances of life. What I'd been seeing in the children of post-boomers was a similar kind of battle between the genuine internal self and the pressured world out there. The divide is different, though, from what Laing described in the sixties.

Today, in order to keep up with the speed of life and a high definition emphasis on the look of things, kids need to push down true-self feelings and keep moving ahead fast! They are not particularly afraid to be unique, as Laing's greatest generation and some boomer children were. No, these free-est generation kids are much more terrorized at falling behind or being weighed down by anything too emotional. The pejorative term now used to describe kids who spend too much time feeling is "Emo!"

Obviously, this is not a healthy division. Children of all ages had to become cool on the surface to skate through things quickly, without being bogged down by the rigors of passion or troublesome conscience. Even very young kids were being conditioned to move too fast to stick with a private world of internal emotions.

The most closely guarded secrets I was learning from kids in therapy were no longer about internal thoughts, dreams, and emotions; in fact, these were often publicly "blogged" and announced in cyberspace for thousands of their closest "friends" to see. What I hear about in embarrassing whispers now are kids' hidden, nonpop-culture passions that have been split-off into dark places: journals, drawings and art that no one has seen or a stash of fantasy stories stored down in a basement.

I began to register that for the past decade, teachers of our youngest children had been telling me about this diminishing world of inner emotion. Decades ago, psychologist Selma Fraiberg in her seminal work *The Magic Years,* wrote about the vital importance of an almost otherworldly childhood era—between toddlerhood and early elementary school—filled with rich fantasy and imagination, unrestrained by time pressures or the constraints of everyday reality. I realized that magic was being assaulted in children of all ages, seeking to keep up with a world based on instant interaction. (I am convinced that one of the little discussed reasons for the *Harry Potter* phenomenon is that J.K. Rowling tapped into this yearning in children, who had been made to leave behind their magic much too early in life). With little room for cumbersome emotion or playful fantasy or idiosyncratic passion they had better learn to move fast and to "Live Free or Die Tryin'," as the older kids might put it.

Why is the inner world of magic, play, and emotion so important? An internal world hits the "pause" button. It stops action and slows down time just long enough to nurture reflection and protect genuine passion. Connecting to one's inner self helps a child learn to handle the ups and downs of everyday life (a lot of conflict can happen during recess) through creative play, rather than instant acting-out. It helps a child learn empathy through the use of role-play and imaginative games (remember dolls and puppets?), rather than the lightning-sharp repartee of social cruelty. It helps a child regulate anxiety, anger, and frustration through a focus on passionate pursuits. Mastery of some interest, whether it's comic books, guitar, or dance, requires kids to put off immediate gratification, and helps them deal with envy and a fear of failing. Without these skills, children tend toward explosions of raw, unprocessed emotion. An inner life also provides ballast, a strong sense of self that helps navigate the unfettered rush of the here and now.

In workshop after workshop, I heard the same concern from parents and educators. Besides the high-risk behaviors they see all around, they have been most worried about the loss of magical passion and unself-conscious enthusiasm that they'd once associated with childhood. "How come my children can't amuse themselves for long—how come they always need to move from thing to thing?" a father in Chicago asked me. "It all has to be connected to the pop culture for my daughter to get involved," a Florida mom complained. "My son's attention span is too short to stick with any passion that isn't on a screen," I heard in a Southern California gymnasium packed with parents. "My kid is able to move on and forget something troublesome that would have preoccupied me for weeks," said a parent in a filled-to-capacity mid-Atlantic school auditorium. And all of these concerns were from a nonclinical population, about mostly "normal" kids with no discernible diagnosis of attention-deficit disorder (ADD).

Children today have not only become "freer" of their parents, but also of their own genuine, inner emotions, and at strikingly early ages.

This twenty-first century divided-self experience poses a serious threat of personal fragmentation, often leading to devastating behavior. Kids' unique, internal, and best-selves (filled with love, empathy, tolerance, imagination, and kindness) can't always compete with the rapid-fire list of external pressure that they face every day.

With a constant eye on pop culture, children of all ages have been "scared straight" into cultivating a fast-moving veneer in order to fit in—to dress right, get the right stuff, and become voracious consumers before the end of nursery school and certainly by kindergarten. They're seduced into worshipping ever-changing definitions of physical perfection from mid-elementary school on, to create, at all costs, a body that looks flawless from the outside—a body "to die for." They're intimidated out of talking about internal experience, which would be soothing, and instead engage in the blinding speed of cruel wit and irony. They're increasingly oppressed by national legislation to keep up to par on standardized tests, from preschool through high school, often without genuinely understanding the material and without acquiring a true love of learning.

"Something's got to give"—and as the headlines too often remind us, something does.

What does this fast-paced, outer-directed divided-self do to relationships between parents and kids? If children are unable to take the time to self-soothe, the demand is for endless emotional supplies from mothers and fathers, expressing a sense of entitlement so unmodulated it can be breathtaking.

A divided-self disses and humiliates, without much empathic care for its impact on the other. As one child put it for millions of others, "I can say anything I want online because I don't have to see the face of the kid I'm saying it to."

A divided-self breaks through to internal numbness with the heat of speed-binge drinking. Ten drinks ("pre-gaming" as it's called) are not unusual before the evening fun begins.

A divided-self pushes an estranged body-as-commodity to excess: starving, purging, and criticizing itself relentlessly.

A divided-self cuts in order to feel for real, carving up an arm or leg expressing an anger so submerged, it isn't even experienced.

A divided-self makes long-lasting commentary through tattoos: imagination and internal imagery writ large for the world to forever see.

A divided-self pierces, a searing penetration toward the core inside, while making a hard-edged statement to the ever-watchful eye of the peer group and the pop culture.

These are not easy realities to absorb. But if we adults do not begin to understand the inherent disconnection, the yearning of these kids for their true, best-selves to be seen and responded to with the kind of authentic engagement twenty-first century children need, our kids are in serious danger.

These realizations about how decades of massive change in our post-boomer society have led us to a new kind of "divided-self" in childhood could well be devastating—if that were where the story ends. But it doesn't, far from it. There is much we can do to help our children become whole again, and there are many reasons for hope.

In recent years, children have demonstrated promising signs that positives are also evolving in their lives, and in our relations with them: boys as emotional caretakers, girls as leaders, boys and girls as fast friends, kids of all ages giving selflessly as never before, and opening up to their parents in ways that greatest generation and boomer parents never could have imagined possible.

Early childhood specialists and the popular press have understandably screamed the negatives, but in the following chapter I will focus on these positive, hopeful trends, despite the challenges. They point the way to understanding how to foster the kind of authentic engagement our children need. Through vivid stories, examples, and practical guidance throughout the rest of the book, I will describe love, limits, listening, and community that fit a post-boomer world and the enlightened age of child rearing we are about to enter.

The free-est generation already senses that we have been moving toward the edge of something new; now we adults need to see what that something is in order to lead them to their best-selves.

3

THE SUN ALWAYS RISES

Hope in a New Age of Child Rearing

DESPITE THE INVISIBLE and frightening acting-out behind that wall of silence, when I wasn't stunned I was also heartened. I was slowly beginning to see that "kid-world" was not only about the negative. The children of boomers and post-boomers were developing new and in some ways more cautious and care-taking selves as well. Even as I was becoming extremely concerned about kids' lives during the nineties and early 2000s, I started to see signs of positive developments. Yes, kids had been engaging in a good deal of frightening behavior. But they also began to exhibit a promising new set of qualities. For one thing, they were acting more as family toward one another.

My perspective started to widen because from the mid-nineties on, I realized that if I truly wanted to understand twenty-first century children, I needed to respect the power of the second family to heal as well as to hurt. In one of those "aha" moments that life brings us when we are ready, I suddenly grasped that the second family of peers was as important to get to know as the first family at home. So, I decided to make a radical change in my therapy practice. In the early nineties, as I reported to professionals in my article "The Second Family," I began meeting with kids' friends in addition to just seeing kids and their parents.

Fifteen-year-old Peter opened my eyes to the need for this change, which was highly controversial at the time. I had noticed that when Peter came for his sessions, he didn't come by himself; he always brought along his buddy Kevin, who sat patiently in my waiting room during each session. Several weeks later, it suddenly dawned on me (amazing it took so long) that Peter was behaving much like the parent of any troubled child seeing a therapist. Might this be Peter's way of introducing me to another kind of family member, his friend Kevin, who also needed help?

One day, I asked Kevin if he also would like to come in (*for any therapists reading, one must still check with agency, insurance, and state regulations about whether this is permissible*). "Okay," Kevin said, and without hesitating even slightly, he walked in, sat down, and began talking about his own truly terrible problems. Kevin lived with a single, alcoholic mother who brought different men home. Peter seemed relieved that someone else besides him knew about Kevin's bad situation. After seeing this small "family" of two for several weeks, I encouraged Kevin, a chronic substance abuser himself, to come clean with his parents and join a drug program.

Now more alert to this caretaking aspect of second-family dynamics, not long afterwards I began seeing Julia, a fourteen-year-old girl with bulimia. I asked her if she would like to invite her best friend, Laurie, to visit for a couple of sessions. She was glad to. While Julia was withdrawn, secretive, and shy, Laurie was gregarious and talkative, a natural leader. Actually, though, Laurie was in more serious trouble than her friend. She had multiple sexual partners and was dealing with the emotional chaos of a savage custody battle between her separating parents. I saw clearly that Julia was taking care of Laurie, acting as a confidante while Laurie spilled her guts.

Two weeks later, when Laurie's mask of bravado cracked, she asked if I could help her. Several phone calls to her parents later, emphasizing the truly perilous state of their daughter's situation, I persuaded them to enter divorce mediation, rather than battling it out via lawyers. Once Laurie's parents had moderated their hostilities, she felt less frantic and could begin to put some emotional energy into improving her own life. Also, because I had taken Laurie's problems seriously and freed Julia from the burden of saving her friend, Julia began to trust me and started talking more freely about her own difficulties.

TENDERNESS BEHIND THE WALL OF SILENCE

These were transformative experiences. I could no longer ignore that behind their wall of silence kids were more openly human toward each other, much more so than most of the greatest generation and boomers had been as children and teens. These free-est generation kids were in many ways harsher, living in a harder-edge world than we did, but they were also capable of being better than we ever were.

Seeing a group of young, teenage girls walking with their arms entwined or baggy-pants boys skateboarding, most adults understandably failed to understand that children, within the confines of the second family, were beginning to hold each other to surprisingly tough expectations and rules of humanistic behavior. Sophisticated subjects regarding morals and ethics, entirely unexplored by kids in earlier times, were being avidly discussed by the late nineties, when teen and pre-teen TV dramas such as *Dawson's Creek* and *7th Heaven* became popular.

I was heartened by the breadth and depth of issues that had now become part of the kid-universe, even at the mid-elementary school age. Among many such topics were: the difficulties of friendship triangles, the initiation and ending of romances, what friends owe one another, the do's and don'ts of cliques, fairness about whom to invite to birthday parties, the importance of sharing, attitudes toward infidelity in love relationships, and when and whether to share confidences. It was like kids were running their own continuing-ed courses every day.

Back in the nineties I was increasingly impressed by this talk, especially compared with my own limited thinking and almost nonexistent emotional vocabulary as a boomer child. I often say, with more than a trace of self-deprecation, given my work as a psychologist: "I don't believe I had a conscious thought until I was in graduate school—it was all reflex: sports, school, and girls."

Some of today's post-boomer parents, especially women, began down this path growing up in the seventies, but today boys and girls, online and in person, are taking it much farther, much earlier. These emotionally-intelligent and socially-versed kids are grappling every single day and night with what were once college-age issues.

This is not meant to suddenly discount all that was described above and say that behind the wall of silence, life in the second family was and is a place of enlightened fairness. Even as we begin to appreciate the softer sides of kids today, I have no intention of painting a halo around the free-est generation. Their more articulate discussion of the ins and outs of social life can turn vicious fast, as in the case of one early elementary school child who reported being approached by a classmate during recess and told to "reconsider her position" about not siding with the popular group against a vulnerable scapegoat—words from a first-grader, not an experienced trial-lawyer!

A fifteen-year-old boy, whose mother had committed suicide, showed me an e-mail from a "friend" saying, in effect, "No wonder your mother 'off-ed' herself. You drove her to it!" A fourteen-year-old girl received a text message that read: "You are such a poseur, trying to act sophisticated—but everybody sees how insecure you really are since your mother walked out on your father and you." Graphic physical threats, including life threats, are common online for both boys and girls: "I'll smear your face into the ground if you show up," was a snarl that one young boy e-mailed to another. "I'll shank your fuckin' balls off if you don't answer," was another message I cringed at, as one preteen girl showed me a screen filled with IMs sent to a friend of hers.

But just as often, the kids I'd begun talking to in my groups and alone, were beginning to exhibit a real capacity for compassion, tolerance of one another's personal foibles, and even common sense. Indeed, in some respects, by the turn of the century they were already becoming far more advanced in the art of friendship than we had been at their age. Back in 1996, I remember our own daughter, Leah, struggling for weeks in *grade school* and then finally confiding to us that she was deeply worried about a friend of hers who the girls thought might be suffering from an eating disorder.

Registering the wear and tear of post-boomer life, turn of the century kids of all ages seemed to be becoming especially aware of each other's vulnerabilities and the need to take some protective action behind the wall of silence.

Sixteen-year-old Brett, for example, whose mother thought of her (and not without reason) as a "selfish, sarcastic bitch," had a reputation for being a guardian angel to her friends. She encouraged one friend, whose father was hitting her, to call an abuse hotline and sat encouragingly with the girl while she made the call. She also offered the guest room in her house to a boy whose mother was often drunk when he arrived home. On behalf of a friend who showed signs of bulimia, she organized several other girls to visit a school guidance counselor. Without divulging the girl's identity, they asked what they might do to help "someone who might have an eating disorder."

Brett was not unusual in her demonstration of openness, warmth, and good sense in her handling of complicated relationship issues. Because they were growing up in a culture suffused with the concepts and language of therapy, kids had begun to talk to one another with more candor, intimacy, and sophistication about everything, even things once considered taboo. In a family I knew, Tony realized that he was gay long before adolescence. Somewhere in the late nineties, he was increasingly enclosed in a cocoon of supportive friends. And while Tony endlessly discussed the complexities of gay and straight love relationships with buddies, he also helped an online buddy with her homework. In the meantime, he became known among his peers as a good mediator and helped settle fights between Marcia and her boyfriend, John, who was caught cheating on her.

Not only were kids becoming more knowledgeable about relationships than we ever had been, but behind their wall of silence I was discovering that they were much more inclined to break down traditional boundaries between males and females. In spite of the viciously sexist lyrics of some pop songs, real friendships between boys and girls of the second family were becoming far more common. Given their close connections established in day care and preschool, the impact of Title IX, and the breakdown of gender divisions in many sports leagues, as well as the fact that both sexes absorbed the same social-emotionally sensitized language, this makes sense. My experience shows that girls are still more expressive than boys, but, as many parents have told me in workshops, the gap is closing. Hanging and chilling in groups, nineties kids developed best friends almost as often from the opposite gender as from their own; and talking about things came along with the shared turf.

Consider thirteen-year-old Tamika, for example. After her parents divorced and her older sister got married, she became increasingly despondent, something she hid from her mother, along with her nightly habit of raiding the liquor cabinet. When Mom brought her in to see me, I asked her whom she would most trust if she needed help. To my surprise, she answered "Tommy and Kirk. They're my closest friends." In fact, it was Tommy and Kirk who broke the wall of silence, alerting her mother about the seriousness of her situation. "Mrs. Washington," they said to her, "we're scared that Tamika might do something bad to herself."

Brett, Tommy, and Kirk: tough-talking, cool "dudes" and powerful "queen bees" needed help, and they knew it. By the 2000s, I realized that these stories were not unusual. Kids may be heedless and driven by their own passions, but they are not stupid. Despite the swagger, the entitlement, and the sophistication about all issues at every age, they know they don't know everything about life or how to grow up.

We adults need to see beyond the "cool" façade kids put on and recognize their internal hunger for engagement with parents. It's not an easy challenge to realize that twenty-first century trash-talk, tough-talk, "Everything's fine, I can do it all" bravado can be just that. But once we get past the divided-self façade, we are able to see emerging, hopeful signs that are an invitation for us to become different along with our children.

Despite the ordinary disconnection of everyday life, my experience with the free-est generation over the past decade has convinced me there has been a quiet, post-boomer sea change that represents a compelling opportunity for parents and kids to connect in a new, powerful way.

For every aspect of what we correctly worry about in our kids' lives, look just beneath the surface, and you will find hopeful developments. Following are eight reasons for hope every parent needs to know.

REBELLING AND THE GENERATION GAP— NOT SO MUCH ANYMORE

In 2005 the Yankelovich Youth Monitor, one of the most respected public opinion research organizations in the country, came to a rather startling conclusion. Their latest survey uncovered a narrowing of "the generation gap." The study concluded that "while this can lead to the delegation of authority to children in some families" (a scary side aspect of free-est generation life I described above), "the more common manifestation is a shared perspective between parents and their children, which actually serves to facilitate greater and less contentious parental authority in the relationship." Yankelovich called this very recent phenomenon "Zapping the Gap." When I discussed these findings with Yankelovich's John Page, he was heartened to find validation in the anecdotal data I offer here. I was not surprised, because I'd clearly seen that with a lack of rigid greatest generation- or boomer-style certitude coming from their parents, kids did not need to angrily rebel against an authoritarian adult regime. Post-boomer parents, though logistical tyrants, no longer represent the authoritarian presence that once organized entire towns, neighborhoods, and everyday family life. For better or worse, there simply is not enough authority there to rebel against!

Despite the x-rated exchanges that pass for normal dialogue in many twenty-first century households, and the lively world behind the wall of silence, many parents are now considered by their children to be their "best friends," as Barbara Hofer, an associate professor of psychology at Middlebury College, reports.

If you have at least one child in college, as my wife and I do, who regularly calls during those "boring" moments walking from class to class, you know exactly what I mean about this new kind of connection. Writing for *The New York Times* online, Rick Pearlstein described this new parent-child relationship, as he seemed to yearn for "the good old generation-gap" days. In Pearlstein's words: "As I write this article at a coffee shop near campus, a kid picks up her cell phone: *"Hi, Dad!"* and chats amiably for fifteen minutes. "When we went to college," says Pearlstein, "a guidance counselor who was a freshman in 1971 tells me, you called on Sunday—the obligatory thirty-second phone call on the dorm phone—and you hoped not to hear from them for the rest of the week."

"The point I'm trying to make," Pearlstein continues, "is that the adventure of going to college consisted of a kind of freedom that you couldn't imagine until you turned eighteen. You were no longer under adult control, and you made your own schedule. . . . This is the most liberating moment Americans have in life."

Who in the world is he talking about? The free-est generation hardly has to wait for college to feel liberated. If anything, they want more connection across the parallel, divided-self lives we live today.

While "friendship between equals" is not what I suggest, it is extremely hopeful that there is now far less of a generation gap or the intrafamilial warfare there was between the greatest generation and its rebellious boomer kids. For the most part, today's post-boomer parents are on the same page as their children in this respect. Almost all mothers and fathers at every presentation I give admit that they pray for exactly the same kind of engagement that today's kids would like with us—they are eager to share intense debate, edgy cultural events, and intimate confidences with their children.

While kids certainly act out and say lots of harsh things to parents, their back-talk and swearing are not really rebellious behavior of the kind from earlier periods. It is striking that almost none of the children or even teens I've more recently seen in my practice express rage or resentment toward their parents. How different this is than when I first began. In fact, it takes a lot of work for me to move kids' focus off the social world of the second family in order to get them to talk about life inside the first family at home. By and large they no longer "rage against the machine" of adults.

The subtle, "generational-divided-ness" I have described: adults ever managing, but not always truly felt by children who secretly *hunger* for them, is fixable, especially given how receptive children are to connecting in more authentic ways. They may lash out at us, ignore or obsessively demand from us, but underneath the bluster, mind-numbing busyness, the pop culture obsessions and seen-it-all bravado, kids are looking for genuine contact with their parents.

This engagement-hunger for their parents can be seen in many current trends. Multi-generational concerts are one of its most obvious manifestations. At recent world-wide concerts young and old lined up together to watch Red Hot Chili Peppers, Bruce Springsteen, U2, Sting, and edgier groups such as Green Day. Kids and parents flock to sexually explicit, box office hits together that would have drawn a values-line in the sand for previous generational dyads. Just think how comfortable you would have been watching *Borat, Knocked Up, The 40-Year-Old Virgin*, or *Spring Awakening* with your mom or dad! If you're a young post-boomer parent, you might have some experience in this department. But, if you're any older than a late boomer, chances are that an afternoon with mom, dad and Borat would have been an unthinkable humiliation.

One doesn't need to look at these somewhat dicey events to recognize this relatively new hunger for intergenerational connection. We all live in the same sea of pop culture that turns parents and children into family-room buddies. Kids and parents spend significant time on pop culture rituals. They religiously watch smash TV shows like *Extreme Makeover, American Idol, Lost, America's Next Top Model*, and *High School Musical*. Children and parents raced through *Harry Potter* side-by-side in the tens of millions, and read books in parent-child discussion groups, which would have been almost incomprehensible to the greatest generation and its boomer children. In comparison, post-boomer parents, having swum in the same cultural sea of change, are equipped to respond better than any generation before them.

HISTORY UNBOUND—UNBURDENED BY THE PAST

My own mother and father died quite a long time ago, so, like snowflakes driven on a winter's wind, my children and my parents never touched. Moments of history that never converged—I felt sadness about this aspect of my life I thought I would always carry.

I was wrong. A few months ago, my wife Stacey happened upon a treasure-trove of family-history buried in some boxes. Until three in the morning, all four of us stayed up going through passport pictures from generations ago, letters my father wrote to my mother while he was a traveling shoe salesman in the South, a New Year's Eve invitation my parents received from the parents of the same group of friends with whom we still spend New Year's Eve, announcements documenting births and deaths endless decades ago—the list could go on and on.

I watched how our kids lit up. Leah could see herself in the pictures of my mother when she was seventeen, a short-skirted flapper, the life of the party. And Sammy could see in my father's photos and my pictures as a gangly adolescent his own awkward body almost traced from my stick-thin frame.

Families are my life, right? I'm supposed to be a big expert, right? But even I was unprepared for how much these few hours of shared family history meant to all of us. I don't know if I ever felt so three-dimensional to them or so soundly connected as through these delicate, sepia-toned reflections of our family.

Another reason kids hunger for adult connection is the double-edged sword of "history-unbound." Today's parents are not just one step removed from their kids by the over-scheduling imposed on them, but what's even more important:

Mothers and fathers are also one step removed in terms of children understanding who they are—where they came from—and post-boomer parents are so used to their own historical irrelevance they hardly even notice. They would rather not fill kids' minds with stories of their own wild acting-out anyway.

Because of this, children today are more historically untethered than past generations. They do not define themselves as much as we and our parents did by the story of their parents' lives or a longer-term family saga. History is as long as a sound-bite takes to be made and to be forgotten, as permanent as an ever-changing MySpace profile and as fluid as the ebb and flow of messages on a Facebook wall. Generally, kids have no more time for the history of family than they seem to have for the history of the world, if declining scores in this academic area are an accurate indicator. The distant past is yesterday or last week.

Many teens during the sixties and seventies vehemently disagreed with their parents on social and political issues, leading to much conflict. They heard endless oral lectures of parental odyssey they came to resent: "Please, not *that* story again!!!" But there was glue: identification with or rejection of who parents were, and where they came from.

In addition, with families so scattered across the country, kids today generally don't have the time or inclination to stand for a regular ritual of sitting still on a sofa (not even hooked up to an iPod) for several hours at Aunt Bertha's house, as I and millions of others did weekly with their respective grandparents, aunts, uncles, and cousins. Geography permitting, can you imagine this kind of forced ritual without the free-est generation wreaking family havoc, mightily resisting, and probably being saved by scheduling mayhem anyway?

The other side of the coin is that this lack of historical "baggage" has a liberated feel. Kids are predominantly free from the overwhelming fears and chronically traumatized lives of those who lived through the cumulative horrors of the twentieth century. While we face deep financial challenges, the free-est generation and its post-boomer parents are no longer haunted or driven by distant shadows of the Great Depression, the Second World War, and the Korean conflict, McCarthyism, and the Cold War. Even Vietnam is too far gone for most kids today to have internalized. Our daughter's peers now travel to Southeast Asia and casually mention names of towns that constituted nightmares and deep wounds to many in previous generations.

At the same time, they are also free from the inter-generational conflict that exploded during the sixties. As late boomers and post-boomers were coming of age, this period of national turmoil was finally being put behind us, and many of today's parents are absolutely determined not to impose our views and life struggles on our children in ways that once led to so much conflict.

So, the stage is set for a less ideologically driven and martyred retelling of the past. If we go about it in the right way—explained later in the book—twenty-first century kids are open to hearing about their parents' lives and family stories. If we learn to recognize adult-centered communication as not only a parental right (we *should* hog the spotlight every once in a while) but a necessity, more parents will find willing audiences of kids.

When viewed outside the divisive political context, there is another fact of post-boomer life that bodes well for anchoring kids in a sturdier sense of their heritage: the explosive increase of immigration. Twenty percent of the population now has at least one parent from another country. Over time, this will also encourage kids and parents to share their personal, historical journeys as they define themselves in an increasingly pluralistic society. Understanding who one's parents are and where they came from is essential to creating deeper tolerance, empathy, and a solid sense of self, especially when compared to the moment-to-moment shape-shifting that has taken the place of "identity" these days.

I know that millions of other families will spend more time like the magical night my own family enjoyed looking through those precious photos—when the past and the present converged. No parent will be unmoved by the look of surprise and deeper understanding they will see on their children's faces.

DO THE KIDS KNOW WHAT YOU DO EVERY DAY— NOT SO MUCH EITHER

I grew up in my mother and father's shoe store. I saw exactly how hard they worked in order to make a very modest living; how many times my father had to climb up and down a ladder for just one sale. I saw how many people my mother had to greet, always with a smile, while she worked the register filling out thousands of handwritten receipts.

A double-edge sword also applies to kids understanding the sacrifice that parents make in order to provide for their children. Ask kids now what their parents do for a living, and they'll most likely mention job titles they don't understand. Many have no idea at all. The majority of children today haven't got the foggiest idea of what makes it possible for them to buy the iPod, MP3 player, and cell phone that are so vital. This isn't because twenty-first century kids are craven and selfish. This is yet another kind of freedom they have been afforded: the freedom from guilt about how hard their parents work. So many mothers and fathers today are putting in extremely long hours, but we are determined that our children not feel guilty about those struggles.

The desire to instill in kids deep down gratitude for efforts made by the adults who provide for them has been sacrificed to a widespread fear of inflicting pathological guilt on children.

Every time I bring this up at parent presentations—that parents might consider letting kids know what they must do in order to make ends meet—someone challenges me. Mothers and fathers insist that they do not want *their* kids to be burdened by guilt feelings. Surprisingly, when I address groups of urban poor parents and grandparents, despite their even more stressful financial struggles, they too do not want to burden their kids with the details of sacrifice that could lead to "unhealthy" guilt.

The down side is that children do not easily develop a deep appreciation for how hard working life is. Instead, kids develop unrealistic notions about how much money they will need to have when they grow up; the kind of commitment that's required; the endless pursuit of buying "stuff" without a sense of where the money actually comes from. This disconnection from work reality is also part of twenty-first century celebrity culture, expressed every week on shows like *American Idol.* Many kids think that if they want something badly enough, it will come to them magically. Believing deeply in oneself has replaced the grind of trying hard to become competent, a challenge that parents face every day. And, another *very* twenty-first century phenomenon is that, compared to celebrity, how can kids admire what their own workaday parents do for a living? Truthfully, as I've learned, too many don't.

The hope is that an increasing number of beleaguered post-boomer parents are far more open to the message that a realistic understanding of their efforts to make ends meet, perhaps even invoking guilt, is worth it in this pervasively consumerist world. If such awareness can be made more clear to endlessly demanding kids, the result may be mutual understanding and ultimately stronger children. So many parents are beginning to think that a bit of guilt is well worth it. The question is how to do this without turning ourselves into martyrs and creating burdensome resentment or pathology.

The answers are surprisingly simple when parents give up their unfounded fear of pushing kids into becoming lifelong patients on some future's psychotherapist's couch. In our intensely child-centered world, the free-est generation is hardly in danger of being overwhelmed by pathological guilt—nothing could be further from the truth, and many mothers and fathers are beginning to sense this.

Also, as in no other time in our history, businesses are beginning to creatively address work-family disconnection. Bring Your Daughter/Son to Work Day or even child-care arrangements feel so twentieth-century compared to the innovative programs such as flextime, extended maternity and paternity leaves, and staggered workdays now springing up around the country. As I will describe in Chapter Seven, corporate America is recognizing just how much the split between children at home and parents at work ends up taking a toll on everyone. Parents who feel burdened by kids who don't know or appreciate their efforts enough amount to a productivity and personnel cost that must be addressed.

Therefore an opening now exists on several levels to heal this kind of dividedness, to help kids authentically engage with parents by understanding exactly what mom and dad do to earn a living, as well as the everyday sacrifices parents willingly make to enrich their kids' lives.

We have a wonderful opportunity to build bonds with our children, and to better prepare them for life by practicing a new, authentic engagement in which it feels natural to share our workaday lives and family stories. The question of how to do this will be provided in later chapters, but the good news is that parents are almost chomping at the bit to become more appreciated, to not remain invisible, held hostage by fears of creating pathological guilt.

FREEDOM OF EXPRESSION— THE (SLIGHT) UPSIDE OF BACK TALK

Dawn says to me: "We were hanging out in the schoolyard. All of a sudden Perry started screaming at me that no one in the grade wants to be my friend; she said I was obviously 'bi,' my best friend was a 'man-whore' and, anyway, how could anyone want to be friends with a slut like me?" "Did anything go on just before, between you?" I ask. "No, it came out of nowhere. This is what happens all day—don't you know that, Dr. Taffel?"

I do know. Watching these sudden bursts of "total honesty" by kids has made me young despite my years and old before my time. While parents do logistical somersaults on the margins of connection, or hover above managing moments, divided-self kids *surf* their consciousness, often unloosened from their internal world or conscience. Listen to the dialogue between twenty-first century kids and you can't help but be affected by both their freedom of expression and their quick slide down the slippery slope of casual cruelty.

A parent of an *early elementary school* girl recently reported the following conversation: "We don't like Harley—she's fat." "Why? I think she's nice," objected my client's daughter. How did her grade-school pal respond? She said without hesitation and with instant ferocity: "Make your choice and you'll have to live with the consequences. It's your funeral!" immediately turning her back on this stunned girl. Not surprisingly, the same freedom of expression goes on at home with mothers and fathers; record the everyday exchanges between parents and kids, and much of it would need to be censored on MTV or VH1.

Still, there is a hopeful upside to all of this freedom of speech as well. Decades ago boomer parents themselves raised by the greatest generation and still living in the shadows of Victorian sensibilities could not even imagine what would have happened had they dared to address their mothers and fathers with this kind of talk. But at the same time, these generations simply didn't speak about uncomfortable things. The price of rigidity was an almost complete lack of candor.

Now parents, giving in to a cultural sea change in acceptable discourse, hardly blink an eye. And not without reason, regardless of the popular view that "kids have gone wild," many parents today would rather hear *something* from their kids, rough talk and all, than be entirely out in the cold. They refuse to be left outside that wall of silence and know absolutely nothing about their kids like their own parents from previous eras. A few nasty epithets seem like small potatoes compared to the high-risk dangers kids face every weekend in a post-boomer world.

As one mother speaking for many barked at me, when I raised an eyebrow about the raw cursing she tolerated, "Don't look at me that way. I know it sounds terrible, but, unlike my own mother, at least I get to hear some of what's happening with her friends. I feel my daughter's language is a small price to pay. I have no intention of changing how she speaks to me!"

Another post-boomer parent did not mind that his kids every so often would come up to his face and with finger pointed right at him, shout out threats—as long as it allowed them to talk together more freely afterwards. "I don't want emotions festering inside them. I don't want the kind of dangerous explosions from my kids that we see in the news on TV. No, it's worth a few harsh moments! I'd rather it be toward me than anyone else."

And just this week, Ann, the mother of Phoebe, an eleven-year-old, made me squirm with discomfort as she described her daughter's unrelenting rudeness that lasted a couple of hours. I kept trying to point out that mom didn't need to listen to all this, and that she shouldn't! But Ann persisted in believing that behind these harsh-sounding outbursts lay some real truth she thought was critical to know—something Ann knew she'd never have shared with her own mother.

In fact, Ann was right. After the barrage subsided, mom took Phoebe out to the nearby beach for a seaside snack. ("Are you insane!" I thought, "Now you're going to reward her for this?") But Ann remained patient, and all of a sudden Pheobe whispered her real concern: after having spent such a wonderful time together over the weekend, the "queen bee" and the rest of the girls would now have "too much information on her." "Why would this be a problem?" mom asked. "Because," Phoebe explained, "the queen bee always hated someone who hosted a good sleepover, and she had the power to forever turn the entire group against anybody within a week." The two then quietly plotted together how to avoid such a turn of events, a wonderful outcome that had started with a burst of childhood venom. Ann sternly reprimanded me, "Don't be so judgmental. I'll go through this forever if it keeps the lines of communication open and I can help her in the end."

This kind of thinking *is* something new under the sun. Many parents today intuitively recognize the potential danger of a split-off inner world within kids and the even greater danger of being entirely disconnected from them. While their acceptance of abusive talk runs against my own grain (we barely allow cursing in jest, let alone angry swearing in our house), I've learned to understand what post-boomer mothers and teachers are responding to. In Chapter Five I will offer more constructive ways to stay authoritatively engaged, while dealing with the problems raised by freedom of expression.

ELEMENTARY SCHOOL T & A—AND THE NEW RESTRAINT

The New York Times *borrowed Alanis Morissette's line "friends with benefits" to describe a new phenomenon among young teens: sexuality that comes along with friendship. The* Times *was on to something. Although I don't think they fully understood that "benefits" were becoming less a result of connection through friendship than simply the result of sharing the same space at a party, where sixth grade (and younger) kids might randomly hook up, at least talking about it more explicitly than ever before.*

Sex is another way that the free-est generation is freer at earlier ages. Sexual dialogue and behavior is often as casual as answering an IM. Sexuality pulsates through middle and high school and increasingly elementary school life, with such speed you quickly realize that casual sex or graphic talk is no longer reserved for "bad" girls and boys. In the past five years, the same sexually explicit exchanges I used to see in middle school are now making their way down the corridors of elementary school and on the internet highway every night.

There is no question that the degree to which kids have been experimenting with sex in recent years at ever-younger ages is shocking, and very worrisome. Elementary and middle school kids show me astonishingly explicit text messages every day. Middle-school "cum parties" have been endlessly reported in the media; "rainbow contests," however, might require some introduction: girls wear different colors of lip gloss and the boy who ends up with the most colors on his penis is declared the winner. "HJ" is a commonly used elementary and middle school term for hand job, and is gradually replacing quaint bumping and grinding on the dance floor. Same-sex permutations, mostly girls experimenting with the "L" word (for teen boys, homophobia is more rampant than I've ever seen), are becoming a common rite of passage in middle and high school. This phenomenon has been described in several recent publications by teens themselves.

Celebrity hunger is also showing up in this area. Encounters are visually recorded, discussed, and blogged in cyberspace, making a once slightly more intimate experience (secrets and kids were rarely synonymous; some things never change) now the realm of MySpace, YouTube, and mass-marketed public property. "If it's okay for them, why not me, and I may even become a star in the process!"

The good news is that I have also seen the explosion of sexuality balanced by a new restraint: kids of all ages have begun to show an increasing awareness of the risks of engaging in sexuality, and they have started to talk more to parents about previously off-limits topics and to police one another's behavior in impressive ways.

Despite the headlines, many kids are not entirely reckless in their sexual behavior. After listening to so many children and teens, and speaking with parents, teachers, and national researchers on trends in sexual behavior, I have seen that kids are openly discussing a wide range of sexuality a lot more and a lot earlier than their parents did with *their* mothers and fathers. I am getting used to hearing graphic descriptions of sexually explicit discussions reported by parents at almost every workshop. I am repeatedly told by teachers and sex researchers that if given a forum, kids always catch them off guard by how much they are willing to share with comfortable, confident adults who simply ask. Also, I am still surprised by how much kids talk to each other and to sympathetic parents and counselors *before* a weekend party, asking for guidance in ways that would have made even Woodstock Nation blush.

While good statistics about the specifics of this sexual activity are hard to find (researchers have told me that funding would be withdrawn if they asked children about oral and anal sex, due to fears that they might "put ideas into kids heads"), all the talking and teaching seem to be having an effect. By all measures since the nineties teen pregnancy is down dramatically, the age of first sexual intercourse is up as well as condom use, and the number of kids who are still virgins by high school graduation has been increasing over the past ten years. Non-intercourse sexual behavior is no longer a promise or line that cannot be retraced, nor is it considered a prelude to "going all the way."

This ease with things graphic serves kids well; it slightly raises the "I-don't-want-to-hear-this" threshold of most post-boomer parents, so that they can be a little more open to the ways kids see sexuality now. Children may be redefining sex in ways that drive parents crazy, but at least they feel comfortable enough talking that parents know more about what children are thinking—enough to guide their kids better than they ever could have without the explicit details.

This reality was brought home by the Midwestern mother of a fourteen-year-old who sent me a note. Mom wrote that her daughter had come to her afraid she might be pregnant because she'd let a boy ejaculate near her vagina. The two then got into an (almost) non-hysterical debate about whether this action should be considered as sex, with the daughter insisting it was absolutely *not*, and that her friends who were "going down on boys or engaging in anal sex were still virgins." What is significant and hopeful (if one can get past the shock) is not only the openness here, but the facts that mom could then discuss—in an ongoing way—why waiting until her daughter was older and in a long-term relationship would be better. Perhaps the advice worked: a year and a half and a couple of boyfriends later, this high-schooler is still a virgin.

I've seen the same semi-comfortable openness between post-boomer fathers and their children. One father I knew had many conversations with his sixteen-year-old son about the importance of *not* pushing his girlfriend for oral sex, even though it seemed like *everyone* was doing it. And I've increasingly heard that when fathers get together for "a boy's night out" they actually ask each other for parental guidance about how to handle these life issues with their children.

Of course, sex at any young age is nothing to condone. But confiding in adults and parents in open discussion was almost unthinkable before post-boomer times.

In addition to parents taking a more active role in guiding sons and daughters, another hopeful sign is the degree to which kids have been policing each other. I hear weekly from adolescents and even preteens about no-holds-barred "interventions" that both boys and girls perform with their friends who've gone "too far." One group of freshman high school girls confronted a boy in their class who'd taken advantage of a friend, engaging in alcohol-soaked sex. I can barely print the language used in their intense reprimands, but they literally backed him into a corner, defined him as a "male-slut," threatened to put him off limits to any other girls in the grade, and then imposed the ultimate punishment: sending emails and text messages about his small penis around the school.

Boys can be just as affronted when they feel a girl has crossed the line from casual hooking up to out-of-control sexuality. Many middle school and high school boys have told me about angry exchanges between themselves and girl classmates. One boy recounted telling a girl in his class: "I wouldn't touch you—you've 'given head' to practically every boy in the grade. What's the matter with you?"

Don't apply a double-standard to these free-est generation kids. I am equally heartened to see high school boys counsel each other to wait for a different girl or relationship to come along before taking the sexual plunge. Numbers of times during the past half decade, I have been impressed by boys who were literally asking me for permission not to engage in sex with their girlfriends at that point in their lives. This is an event almost unheard of for the red-blooded greatest generation or for many of their sex, drugs, rock 'n roll boomer kids.

It must be said that some sexual restraint is also being driven by the harsh facts of twenty-first century life. For example, girls would rather not remove their clothes to go "all the way" and reveal a far-from-thin-enough body. Commitment-phobic boys loaded down with the lessons and paraphernalia of safe sex also flock toward non-intercourse behavior they (incorrectly) believe requires no clumsy and time-consuming protection. And, the increased use of SSRI's (i.e., anti-depressants such as Prozac and Zoloft) by preteens and adolescents may inadvertently inhibit sexual drive, just as it does with many adults.

Now, where exactly does this leave these kids' mothers and fathers? I believe in that classic, double-edged post-boomer position: a scary but surprisingly hopeful place. Parents are right to be concerned about the way too early sexualization of kids and the provocative, detached manner in which many sexually approach each other, as well as the vicious, hard-core gossip that pollutes the hallways and airwaves of elementary school through high school.

Compared to a time of pre-AIDS awareness, however, their own kids today are actually doing far *less* than many boomers and post-boomers did decades earlier, and they certainly define themselves with far fewer self-esteem crushing labels.

The willingness to discuss sexual issues with mom or dad is hopeful, even as graphic elementary school banter about sex is mind-boggling. Because of the new freedom of expression, we are far better equipped to guide our children about sex than the generation of parents I counseled a decade or two ago.

ANGELS IN OUR MIDST—
THE FREE-EST GENERATION AND GIVING

One of the little-known secrets of the free-est generation is that it is becoming the most philanthropic on record. This does not make headlines; it is not about "friends with benefits," Columbine or Virginia Tech violence, "mean girls" or "lost boys."

But it is a fact that has flown mostly under the radar, because until recently, the importance of generosity has been hidden from other kids (and even onself) out of typical kid embarrassment. Doing good deeds has never been considered "cool," so a divide between external cool and the internal drive to do some good has, until recently, prevailed.

This is changing. As more and more celebrities and megabillionaires make headlines with their commitment to change the world, kids are beginning to equate philanthropy with power. The internal divide against owning one's goodness, being afraid to make a public statement, is ready to be bridged. Don't knock Angelina. "Heart" is finally becoming hip, even for teens.

Yes, youthful generosity may be encouraged by the necessity of adding service points to one's academic resume. Indeed, I have heard children even in middle school refer to community work as forced on them by the need to keep up with their peers. But for whatever reason, the fact is that over the years, kids of all ages inspired by celebrities, elementary school programs, religious and community centers, have become increasingly generous. It's a growing service mentality I will describe more specifically later in the book.

Their generosity can, however, be seen in just one astonishing phenomenon, the rise of the Kids Care Clubs. A number of years ago on a "boring" Saturday afternoon, Deborah Spaide, a mother of five in Connecticut, asked her kids to help their elderly next-door neighbor with her backyard. Deborah's children enjoyed this newfound philanthropy so much that they agitated for a repeat performance the following week. Soon other kids demanded to be involved and after just a few years Deborah's tiny group had turned into the Kids Care Clubs, an organization with over 400 chapters around the world, complete with newsletters and a web site. Schools over the past decade have also managed to begin challenging the notion that parents and children cannot do good deeds together. Especially after the twin disasters of September 11th and Hurricane Katrina, schools have increasingly asked mothers and fathers to create programs *with* kids that help surrounding communities. I've personally consulted to yearlong lunch programs for homeless shelters staffed by parents and kids. I've also seen an increase in the number of serviced-based efforts that do the once-unthinkable: send teens and adults off to poverty-stricken areas to help rebuild communities *together*.

These volunteer projects are wonderful initiatives that cross the divide in kids and allow them to be known as good *and* provide real world initiatives between parents and their children to do good side by side. Despite the coarseness of our culture, the tough talk and wild acting-out, it is becoming a signature of free-est generation kids that they are more open to philanthropy, to being part of the larger fabric of humankind than we'd ever expected of children and teens in the past.

How parents and communities can foster this inspiring kind of authentic engagement will be the focus of Chapter Seven.

THE EVOLUTION OF FOCUS—
NECESSARY TWENTY-FIRST CENTURY SKILLS

The headmaster of a well-known school admitted to me that when they began computer-based homework, no one anticipated what they were unleashing—kids whose definition of focus included being interrupted by a continuous stream of incoming IM, Facebook, and text messages. "You're right to be concerned," I responded, "but this is the direction of the world to come. They had better learn how to concentrate with interruptions, because it's never going to stop. I can't be sure, of course, but I'm beginning to believe that unbroken concentration may be a thing of the past."

The very nature of consciousness has been redefined over the past two decades. Focus is being liberated in ways that often unhinges older adults, but thrills post-boomers and children by allowing them constant mental motion and unlimited horizons. Kids of all ages experience a crazy quilt of digital connections every single moment of every single night.

As I described earlier, a typical preteen or adolescent's evening (this is now happening in elementary school as more education becomes computer-based) can be spent at a screen engaging in five online discussions at once. Talk about free flight! And, in case one thinks of this as a "price of privilege," with the spread of technology cyberdriven multitasking is not simply a middle- or upper-class phenomenon, nor exclusively in the province of adolescence.

It feels both familiar and startling to recognize the astonishing increase and widespread use of technology by our children and preteens. The numbers change daily, but here are just a few points to consider: 64 percent of kids have downloaded music from the internet; 48 percent have streamed a radio station through the internet; 66 percent use instant messaging.

About 16 million teens and younger kids have cell phones; roughly 60 percent of American teenagers own a cell phone, and spend an average of one hour/day talking on them—about the same amount of time the average teenager spends doing homework. By 2007, some 6.6 million of the 20 million American preteens had cell phones; it is projected that by 2010 there will be 10.5 million preteen users.

Almost 70 percent of all 8 to 18 year olds have a TV in their room; on any given day almost 70 percent of all 8 to 18 year olds watch cable TV (often uncensored), while almost 49 percent watch broadcast TV, a nearly exact reversal from 1999, when 69 percent watched broadcast, and 50 percent watched cable.

And if you think the use of technology is just associated with older kids think about these two facts: 42 percent of kids ages 6–8 use the Internet; 67 percent of kids ages 9–11 and 82 percent of kids 12–17 use the Internet, as well. For children between the ages of 6 months to 6 years, the average "screen" use is over one and a half hours per day—the average time spent reading or being read to, is 40 minutes.

Though kids vehemently claim otherwise, all of this online chatter surely has a profound effect on their definition of focus. *"Hey Mom, don't get all crazed, can't you see I'm doing my work . . . don't worry about it!!!"* says twelve-year-old John, looking very comfortable as he effortlessly moves from one screen to another. But talk to John the next morning, and he is depleted by his conversations from the night before. Trying to return every IM, he has gotten into several discussions and arguments with friends that will need to be tackled throughout the school day. It happens so fast, John doesn't really know what hit him. He is both liberated from the constraints on socializing common just a few years ago and exhausted by that liberation. And he'd have it no other way, even as his computer-literate post-boomer parents find themselves slightly behind his fast-forward focus and unlimited reach for the horizon.

I am totally sympathetic to the concern parents and teachers have

about how unfocused and depleted by online socializing kids are these days.
But in this, too, there is a positive side—if it is managed forcefully.

Having discussed earlier how technology has so undermined children's empathy and ability to travel to the inner world of the imagination, it may seem contradictory for me to now point out anything positive about their frenzied online lives. Certainly, the super-charged multitasking they engage in, even as they supposedly do their homework, is troubling.

What is positive, however, is that technology is yet another post-boomer way in which our lives and the lives of our children have been dovetailing, allowing for greater, not less guidance and supervision. We adults have been forced to become ever more plugged in and must endlessly multitask to manage our busy work and home lives. We may not be instant-messaging or connecting with hundreds of "friends" on Facebook, but we're on our cells and smart phones more and more of the time.

Post-boomer parents are to some extent fellow travelers with their children and are well prepared to help set limits. More and more post-boomers I meet are sophisticated; they're unafraid to guard against the dangers of the web, while eager to share its benefits. Many I've met have developed effective techniques—setting limits on screen time, sharing online sites, and understanding, enjoying, and monitoring the worlds of YouTube, MySpace, blogs, and so on. Later I will describe how to limit time online.

GOOD NIGHT AND GOOD LUCK—THE FREE-EST GENERATION AT BEDTIME

Surprisingly, another great hope for authentic engagement is the dreaded "bedtime struggle." Hundreds of parents have told me how hard it's become to get their kids to go to sleep. Many need mom or dad to come and lie by their side. For some, as soon as mom or dad leaves the room, they head toward their cell phones or watch TV, or sneak laptops under the sheets and

get right back online. "It seems like my kids have no ability to soothe them-
selves, even for a few moments," says one parent after another.

Why do so many mothers and fathers as well as children of all ages
tell me every week about bedtime struggles? Selma Fraiberg's notion
of an internal world that I mentioned earlier has great relevance for
the free-est generation at bedtime. Kids have been split off from the
self-soothing potential of their internal imagination, and bedtime is
when they could use it the most.

They are now trained at such young ages to interact to external
stimulation that imagination without interaction has become hard for
them. With so many electronic devices and interactive images to play
with throughout the day, traveling to the world of imagination and
self-soothing fantasies, so helpful for drifting off to sleep, calls on muscles in the brain that kids no longer learn to easily use. This is a topic
recently covered in a Sunday *New York Times* article.

I can't get out of my mind the picture of one of our close friend's
children. As a one year old he had a complete grasp of the TV remote,
knew how to turn on the complex cable system, and, at 18 months
moved into the realm of handling a Blackberry. As much as this puts
smiles on all our faces, his imagination ultimately may be a victim to
the thrill of interactive competence.

From the moment kids put down their heads, then, they don't
know what to do with themselves. *They are bored!* Of course, they are
bored. This is the first time that they have had to endure a moment
without external stimulation to fill their minds.

The flip side here is that, in keeping with the new openness, in
putting off going to sleep, children of all ages are talking more freely
to mothers and fathers at bedtime now than at any other time in my
work as a child-professional. While parents often complain that the
day never ends, and sound like Al Pacino, in *The Godfather III*—*"Just
when I think I'm out—they pull me right back in again!"* these same parents absolutely *love* those intimate, bedtime moments of engagement.

With no logistics left to manage, with the lights dimmed, the sheer boredom of kids who can't sooth themselves often turns this moment into the most heartfelt exchange between a parent and child.

This is a time for engagement and a time to quietly encourage imagination that doesn't receive enough attention during the day. Relaxed connecting is a wonderful skill for harried kids and parents to learn at bedtime—one of those twenty-first century headaches that can be turned entirely on its head and into a time of authentic engagement.

TOWARD AN ENLIGHTENED ERA IN CHILD REARING

My father died when I was 22, still an adolescent in today's terms. His passing was so sudden that I went cold, so numb I did not shed a tear. One night several months after his death, I dreamt about him. "Ronnie," he said to me, "do you remember when I sculpted circus animals for you?" He reached out with his hand, tenderly giving me the soft clay it held. I could see his heart in his eyes, and I touched his face. I woke up in tears, a crying that continued every morning for months after.

The next day, I bought some clay and began sculpting. Two months later, I fell in love for the first time, with a girl who mysteriously came over to me offering a sip from a container of milk. The sudden connection I experienced in the dream and the burst of creativity that followed were no accident.

It is also no accident that the majority of kids engaged in the ways I will describe, discover an enduring passion, make a best friend, or if they are older, fall in love. Authentic engagement is the essence of what we must create between adults and kids. These fragmented times call for nothing less than relationships filled with life, rather than only logistics and technique. The most essential goal for parents in raising today's kids is not to be cowed by the freedom of their lives. We do not have the power to alter the techno-pop culture that defines so much of experience today; but focusing squarely on how to engage kids will make an enormous difference and help heal their divided-selves.

This engagement does not conform to the old rules of engagement. As the following chapters will show, post-boomer "loving" is different. "Limiting" is different. "Listening" is different. "Community" is different. We must stand up for our true-selves as parents, to go far beyond what twenty-first century mothers and fathers are *officially* encouraged to do, and move closer to what we *secretly* say and do—often beyond the gaze of friends and even family members.

By learning how to engage the free-est generation in ways that fit the here and now of life, we will allow them to fulfill the exciting potential of their know-no-bounds twenty-first century lives.

We will help them reach under that façade of cool and bring out their best-selves.

4

ENGAGEMENT THROUGH LOVING

Parental Love that Brings Out the Best in Today's Kids—and Us

AT FIRST GLANCE, love may seem unnecessary to discuss when it comes to parenting, since it is such a given. But for many of the reasons I described in the previous chapters, nothing could be more central to engaging the free-est generation. As I listen to children of all ages and parents around the country, it is surprising to me how much the topic of love comes up. Children know they are loved and cared for, to be sure. They are actively involved in the logistics of daily life with their mothers and (increasingly) their fathers, but it is still often hard for them to actually *feel* our love.

In order for kids' true, best-selves to be touched by us, we need to show love in ways that match today's realities. It is time for the kind of parental love that can be felt through the frenetic din of a post-boomer world, a style of expressing love that has the powerful authenticity twenty-first century child rearing demands.

LOVE MEANS DRAMA—
SAY IT WITH FEELING OR DON'T BOTHER

Maggie, mother of eleven-year-old Ali and six-year-old Tommy, reported this (very familiar) story of a family outing to me. She had planned a nice day for herself, her husband, and the kids, driving into the nearby city and going to a museum:

> "We had a busy schedule, maybe too busy—I'll grant you that. But Ali and Tommy were bickering enough to totally get on my nerves. Like I've done a thousand times before, I tried to maneuver around it. I used every technique I've seen on TV, in the magazines or online: ignoring them, letting them settle it on their own, and finally that '1-2-3 Magic' business—you know, giving them a warning and then if they don't listen by '3,' a consequence.
>
> But I couldn't help it. I got on a nagging jag. What had started out with the intention of showing them a wonderful time on this special trip ended up being just another day on the conveyor-belt. And, instead of good feelings, I bet the only thing they'll remember is my nagging and what we bought for them at the museum gift shop."

We've all been through this. Maggie's real disappointment was that her loving gesture did not get through; despite her determined use of pop-parenting techniques, the outing together didn't feel much different from their normal days on the run. Frankly, since kids today are continuously being shuttled around, I'm pretty sure neither Ali nor Tommy even registered that Mom was nagging all that much, and they certainly had no idea she was terribly disappointed.

DID YOU FREAK OUT TODAY?

Seven-year-old Adam has been told to come to the dinner table five times now. His mom, Evelyn, comes in and gives him one last chance before the food gets cold. He's into *Webkins* and his trance can't be broken. Suddenly and understandably, Evelyn screams at the top of her lungs, thinking this will finally get through: "Can't you ever listen to me? You're a space cadet. If you don't get off the computer now, I'm disconnecting it for a month!!!" (This is hardly a credible threat, since the whole family needs that screen to survive). Adam barely looks up and hasn't even registered she's been talking to him, or that she has been trying to get him to the kitchen table, even though she's served his absolutely favorite meal, chicken nuggets and pasta.

To put it bluntly, popular parenting techniques, as well as equally predictable "freak-outs" leave us way too boring to be noticed by the free-est generation, let alone remembered once they leave our presence.

Like Maggie, most over-scheduled post-boomer parents feel a lack of the easy engagement that seemed so natural in previous eras, although not without its problems. Because today's parents don't have as strong a structure of neighborhood and kinship ties, and because our kids are distracted by nonstop cultural noise, adults often feel a lack of traction with their kids.

In order to feel "whole," kids need loving engagement from an equally whole adult, not a two-dimensional, technique-wielding manager. Authenticity breaks through the façade and reaches children's true-selves, their best-selves.

Unfortunately, we parents are often our own worst enemies and don't come across as three-dimensional enough to our children. A lot of the time, we're a mirror of the twenty-first century culture all around: a fragmented collection of this or that parenting technique currently in vogue and a stream of quickly-moving moments that need to be managed. Worse, when we're not screaming or rushing

everyone along, the modulated quasi-therapeutic parenting techniques so popular now are destined to make even the most well-
meaning mother and father shrink into a tiny speck on the multiplex
screen of a child's mind. Check out the box below and you'll see why so
many kids today tune us out, well-meaning though we may be:

IT'S 10 PM—DID YOU BORE YOUR CHILD TODAY?

Mom: "How was school?"

Susan: "Not so good, Cassie wouldn't talk to me."

Mom: "That must have really hurt."

Susan: "Yeah, all the kids played with her except for me."

Mom: "It probably felt bad to you."

Susan: "Yeah, whatever . . . what's for dinner?"

Neither version—the latest psychobabble or freaking-out—
works with the free-est generation. In a special effects world you've
got to be a bit edgy for your love to get through.

HOW TO BE "EDGY" ENOUGH
FOR YOUR KIDS TO FEEL LOVED

With twenty-first century kids of all ages, there's no escaping it: The
"edge of relatedness" (as psychologist Darlene Ehrenberg calls it in
her book), meaning the place where two people feel and touch each
other with the kind of "authenticity" one can't forget, must be *edgy* for
today's kids to even register our presence. And edgy is not the same-
old, same old, whether it's the latest faddish technique or nagging or
losing-it in order to get their attention.

I discovered this fact of modern engagement in my interviews
with children. Those parents, teachers, coaches, and clergy whom
they described in loving ways were the ones who spoke with intensity
and drama—not over the top, but with obvious authenticity that got
their life-lessons and caring across:

- "Boy, the way she talked and explained things you could never forget her. One day she totally stopped teaching class, sat on her desk, and started speaking so low, telling us a story about what it was like when she grew up in the South—how you had to be polite—we could hardly hear her. All of a sudden everyone stopped calling out. She was tough, but she really loved us."

- "The way that Coach said things, I knew he cared about me. He took me over to the side after a game and whispered without anyone around that he could get in trouble for telling me this, but he said that he cared more about us having fun than whether we won. I loved that guy—he was different than my other coaches."

- "That mom was so fun, but she had strict rules about keeping the kitchen and the rest of the house clean. She got real mad when we didn't. Once she stood on top of a kitchen chair and read us the rules from a paper. I don't think they were actually written down, but I did back then. She was a riot. We always *loved* being there!"

In a reality-TV world, where every emotion of the human palate is on display every single night, the need for children of all ages to feel authentic emotion from parents has only become more pressing. That's the trouble with predictable psychobabble or nagging or over-the-top screaming: to these kids it's actually *boring*; it hides the subtlety of human emotion they're used to dealing with every day in their pack of peers or in the world online.

AM I A TWO-DIMENSIONAL PARENT?

It is a paradox of rushed, modern living that the people kids know best, we parents, are often the people in their real or screen-lives who show the least varied range of emotion. As both a parent and professional, I too feel the confusion about how to react on a daily basis, even when I hear the most shocking stories.

During the course of a few days' consulting with schools or in my practice, I learn that an early teen, Peter, is planning "a date" in an abandoned garage with a complete stranger he met in cyberspace. Theo, who's ten, is teased relentlessly in school for being too "gay." Erica, an elementary-school girl, is subtly demeaned by classmates because of the "ambiguous" way her mother died—was it from natural causes or a suicide? Louis and friends regularly smoke pot in the bathroom at his middle school, next to kids who purposely make themselves vomit, as a group activity. Anna is threatened online to stay away from school because she stepped forward to the guidance counselor about one of the other kids.

It would seem impossible *not* to react to descriptions of such extreme behavior. But every fiber of my being is caught up in the dilemma we all face: to show love and concern without being entirely predictable, as in: "How does that make you feel?" or, instead, launching into a rant or a lecture. I know that parents face the same challenge at home most evenings, starting when their children are in kindergarten, as they begin hearing the details of ordinary kid life: fortresslike cliques, onetime friends who are now enemies, unfair authorities, academic worries, dramatic triangles, "stuff" envy, and much more.

We experience all kinds of feelings about the regular but deeply upsetting things our children (sometimes) share. But, way more than we think, we come across as two-dimensional. Too many of us either use what have become psycho-babble mantras, "from the can" techniques that kids read as being programmed, and therefore inauthentic, or explode with frustration rather than seizing the moment to have a more heartfelt, attention-getting exchange with our kids.

Kids will not even notice parents' most intimate feelings unless we "say it with feeling or don't bother saying it at all." When parents express the full palate of human emotions—love, hurt, disappointment, hope, elation, worry, determination, fear, and so on—screaming or nagging pale in comparison. Mothers and fathers are almost without exception profoundly surprised by their kids' responses: "I finally got my kids to hear me, and to feel my love at the same time."

HOW TO STOP BEING SO PREDICTABLE AND BORING

Communicating with kids fully is much easier said than done. Until you pause for a moment, you probably won't realize just how constrained or predictable your usual responses to your kids are. We have an endless variety of emotions in our human repertoire. Stop for a moment and consider how many you leave out of your daily interactions with children, in order to manage the logistics of a fast-paced twenty-first century day.

Eminent family therapists such as Salvador Minuchin and Harriet Lerner, and thousands of other clinicians, have videotaped interactions in therapy sessions, as well as around the house, showing the predictable nature of communication between family members, dubbed "the family dance." Think about your own reactions to a child dawdling just before school or bedtime, or angling for that maddening impulse item at the checkout counter. What about those "dances" you get into visiting your own parents for a holiday weekend? No matter how successful, independent, and grown-up you may be, chances are that within a few minutes the parent-child interaction you were stuck in as a youngster can crop up before you even sit down.

These dances discovered by family therapy pioneers decades ago have recently been substantiated by researchers such as John Gottman, who carefully follow subjects' physiological responses during ordinary interactions, as well as the recent wave of brain-imaging which shows us what parts of the brain are activated along with different behaviors and experiences.

Patterns between us and our kids, then, are deeply ingrained. And, here's the kicker: our smart-as-a-whip, free-est generation kids pay attention to every interpersonal nuance. As a result, they know our dances perhaps better than we do and certainly as well as any scientific observer. Just about every four-year-old I've met can do a spot-on imitation of the dance their parents get into regarding just about every ordinary issue.

If you want your message and love to get across, then it is imperative you know your dances, so powerful they limit access to our full range of emotions. The good news is that these patterns are also open to change, once we become aware. Finding our "true-self" parent, not that managerial, two-dimensional, or out-of-control parent, will bring out kids' better-self from behind the harried disconnection and dividedness of twenty-first century life.

Here is an exercise that will help you to get a fix on this. Before bedtime or during the in-betweens of your schedule, write down some dialogue from that day between you and your child. "He said," "I said," "He said," "I said." Keep it short; I know you don't have a lot of extra time. *Also, do your note-taking in private, not in front of your child.* Any sense that he or she is being observed will change the way you both express yourselves. After writing down just a few dialogues, you will find yourself struck by what narrow, predictable exchanges you have been engaged in: either the nonemotional logistics of time management or interactions that quickly escalate into blow-ups.

One of the most striking skills I've learned over the years is the ability to almost instantly, within a few sentences, pick up on a constricting dance that can hide a parent's full range of emotions and true love. In fact, when I am presenting to an audience of parents, no matter how large the group, and a mother or father asks a question about an issue at home, I can spot the dance they are caught in with their kids *just from the way they ask the question.*

For example, mom or dad may use "too many words" in a question (during which I lose focus), adopt a lecturer's tone toward me (which triggers boredom), sound angry just beneath the surface (leading to a sharper response from me or audience members), take on the stance of a victim (which can lead to impatience on everyone's part), and so on—all within thirty seconds. When I respond by asking parents whether their kids tune them out, fight back, bargain, and so on, I come across as a mind-reader which, of course, I am not. The exercise invariably brings home the point: The dance rules! Know your dance, or your love will become a victim to boring predictability.

So, I ask you to write a couple of "stories from home" tonight. You then can compare your artificially-limited repertoire to the range of emotions you are capable of, and that the free-est generation needs to experience from you in order to feel engaged. To get kids' attention and your love across, you must go against invisible constraints and, in a responsible way, *using your own beliefs, style and words*, respond in a fashion your child absolutely cannot miss. Anything less is just static in a fiber-optic, high-tech world.

BECOMING MORE DRAMATIC

I have worked hard in my practice, and with our own children, to find genuine emotional flexibility, to explore the terrain between being an inhibited parent or a "freak-out" over-reactor. I am often still surprised by what a positive, true-self response I get when I more authentically express feelings. Consider how I responded with each of the kids I described above—and notice their far more engaged reactions.

When Peter first told me cavalierly about his plan to meet a date he'd hooked up with online in an abandoned garage, I yelled, "*Are you out of your mind!?*" All of a sudden he looked at me with real attention for the first time, hearing my caring and, thank God, he was ready to listen. To Erica, who was tormented, but numb, about the way friends had spoken so harshly to her about her mother's untimely death, I responded: "*I feel like I want to cry when I hear what those girls do to you.*" She finally did cry then, because she could feel my emotion. My caring allowed her to express her own buried sorrow.

To Louis, who mindlessly "smoked up" in his middle school, I expressed my exasperation this way: "*Are you trying to drive me insane?*"

Far from shutting him down, this forthright response initiated the first thoughtful discussion between us about the provocative behavior he'd allowed to spin out of control. To Ernie, who hesitantly told me that he really liked a girl and that every adult he knew had warned him that "first relationships" are doomed, I almost whispered, *"With all my heart, I believe there's a chance for you and Chloe to make it. It really is possible."* These dramatically delivered words helped Ernie muster the courage to go against the group ethos and fall in love.

With one of our own children, Leah, I gave in to my own tears. For the first time in our relationship, I told her how "hurt I've been feeling" by so much endless TV, online activity, and door shutting. *"I miss you, Leah,"* I said, *with pain clearly expressing itself in my voice, "even though you're growing up, and I know I'm not supposed to be talking like this."* All of a sudden a wall broke down and Leah began crying as well, admitting what had been obvious to her, but not to me—that she missed our time together, too. It was the beginning of our "recovery" from the painful distance of adolescence.

KNOW YOUR AUDIENCE—EVERY CHILD IS DIFFERENT

Keep in mind as you expand your emotional range that you can't authentically engage without taking into account your child's temperament. This is another way in which two-dimensional, "from-the-box" parenting advice is so ineffective; kids have distinctive personalities from the get-go and will respond to parental emotions accordingly. Unlike Leah, when it comes to our younger more sensitive child, Sam, we can't be very dramatic. The idea that kids have different temperaments, that there are shy kids, fear of first-time-experience kids, highly adaptable kids, tenacious kids, sensitive kids, loud kids, active kids, and so on, is a concept we have known about since Alexander Thomas' and Stella Chess' pioneering book forty years ago, *Temperament and Behavior Disorders*. However, the concept has only recently been accepted in the mainstream child-rearing world.

Understanding the powerful effect of a child's temperament on parents, rather than focusing exclusively on parents' impact on a child, will, I predict, become standard thinking over the next decade. In the near future, child rearing will officially validate every mother's or father's experience: "Our family has never been the same since Johnny was born" or "I did very little with Jenny; I just didn't stand in her way."

So it should come as no surprise that with our younger child Sam, expanding our emotional range has had its limits. In his case, since he was by nature, "hard-wired" to be more sensitive, we can never really yell. We have needed to find other ways of being dramatic, because Sam's temperament could not easily metabolize intense emotions. He was far better off with heartfelt, but very quiet expressions of love. That's Sam.

You need to look at "*your* Sam" and what dramatic display of parental emotion he or she is temperamentally suited for.

Figuring out how to raise the quotient of genuine emotional drama in interactions with your kids will take some trial and error. Don't be concerned, because in my experience it doesn't take long to break out of the patterns of our dances and to discover the manner of engagement that works best. The better-self response from your child will be unmistakable, and this is your guide to whether you've hit the right emotional note.

Consider this exchange in my office to get a feel for how drama, attuned to a child's temperament, helps our children experience us as three-dimensional beings. While not always apparent instantly (as this example shows), it almost always leads to more authentic engagement and a greater expression of kids' (and parents') best-selves.

Jolie, a single mother, is raising her youngest child alone. Amy is a junior in high school and is supposed to be thinking about college. Mom has very little money, and careful planning will be necessary. But, meanwhile, Amy's close to failing in school. She's dyed her hair jet black, gotten her tongue pierced, adopted a Goth wardrobe, and become part of a wild crowd. In addition, she's coming home later and later, some nights not at all. They have been arguing a great deal about Amy's curfew. This is part of the dialogue from a session I described in *Breaking Through to Teens*.

Jolie: No matter what, I still love you. But why do you get into so much trouble all the time? I don't understand you. You promise me you'll be home by two, and then there's this big excuse when you show up hours later.

Amy: Yeah, well, if you paid more attention to me you would understand what's going on.

Jolie: You're always so busy. You never have time to talk, anyway.

Amy: Well, I am busy because I don't want to turn into a slug like you. Mom, you're so dull, nothing ever goes on around the house. So, sure, I want to be with my friends [Jolie says nothing]. If I go away to college, what are you going to do? You don't have a life. What are you going to do?

Jolie: [With a burst of feeling] Okay. You know what? I like it when you're here. But to be honest—and I don't want to hurt your feelings—here's the truth: I also like it when you're gone. It's me time. I can focus on me. It's quiet; I play the music I like; I watch my shows. I don't just think about you. So, if I'm going to be honest, sometimes it's okay when you're not home. . . . in fact, I actually look forward to it.

Amy: [The glare on her face suddenly disappears. She gets tears in her eyes.] But you always act like you don't have a life at all.

Jolie: [Clearly thinking hard] Look, Amy, I can't promise you how I'm going to feel. But in my heart, I know I'm going to survive. I've been through much worse. And, I know I'm going to be okay. [Amy looks skeptical]

Jolie: Listen, I've been through the divorce. I had no job. I got a job. I went back to school, and I got a degree. The business closed down, and I found another job. [She's now crying.] I'm going to make it no matter what happens with you. You've got to stop worrying about me!

For the first time, Amy is listening with rapt attention. She's temperamentally resilient and is taking in her mother's dramatic expression of love and determination. Jolie has never talked to her this way, and because Amy can hear direct, even blunt emotions, her mom's finally gotten through.

Like Jolie, break the dance while keeping your values and your child's temperament in mind; don't be afraid of mistakes or creatively expanding the range of your emotions, so that your children or teenagers can hear you through all that cultural noise, and *feel* you there with them. The best parts of kids, filled with love and compassion, will more likely come your way.

"DANCING WITH THE STARS"

Recognize your child's in-born temperament—have fewer ineffective dances.

Today's parents must learn to appreciate the long shadow of temperament, as Jerome Kagan puts it. Children's hard wiring can guide your footwork out of clumsy, frustrating dances. Temperament, or basic characteristics, are noticeable to every parent from early on, and remain fairly consistent through the teen years. If you recognize this and try to match your moves in the dance with your child's basic temperament, you'll have a greater chance to authentically engage, and spend less time

(continued)

fighting. Here are some of the main temperamental con-
stellations to watch for and how to approach each:

1. Sensitive child—tone of voice, pacing of questions,
   much less yelling.
2. First-time fearful child—practice, go slowly, let child's
   reactions guide.
3. Tenacious child—offer a "limited choice," either one of
   which you can accept.
4. Active child—allow fewer choices, talk small and quick,
   arrange a lot of everyday physical activity to burn off
   energy, and be on the look-out for food allergies.
5. Difficulty with transitions child—simple, but harder
   than you think: cut down on the number of transitions;
   one less per day can make a huge difference.
6. Low frustration tolerance child—anticipate escalations
   ahead of time, and always try to attend to biology:
   not enough rest, hunger, and over-stimulation. Physiology always wins.
7. Clingy child—prepare your child for transitions, more
   one-on-one time, try to make sure there are fewer surprises for this kind of temperament.
8. Scattered and disorganized child—ask kids to repeat
   what you said, help with gentle reminders and break
   tasks into smaller chunks. This "executive functioning"
   will get somewhat better with age, but not as quickly
   as you'd like.
9. Quiet or low mood child—mind-set is critical: low-
   grade moodiness is not a rejection of your love, which
   is how it feels to many mothers and fathers; much
   more down time is needed, as well as reassuring
   rituals.

LOVE MEANS ADVICE—
CLEAR OPINION WITHOUT CERTAINTY

Fourteen-year-old Mary reported this exchange to me with a great deal of anger: "I went to the guidance counselor because there are these kids who keep saying horrible things about me . . . I can't avoid them; they're on the school bus, they're in my class, they're online sending me gross messages. I wanted to know what I should do. So, what does the guidance counselor say? She says, 'Tell me what you think you ought to do.' Do you believe that? Why does she think I asked her in the first place? Is this supposed to be helpful? What is it with you people, anyway?"

I've repeated this story often because in my workshops, school consultations, and counseling sessions, it has been shocking to learn how little post-boomer adults guide kids with clear opinion. As described above, we lost a bit of our authoritative parental voice and wisdom moving toward and into the twenty-first century. I also have discovered that kids feel our lack of guidance as a lack of caring.

Mary is right. The hesitance to give serious, thoughtful advice is another way in which too many adults fail to lovingly, authentically engage with children. One of the most challenging aspects of the freest generation is that it faces endless choice from early on, whether to become part of the kindergarten clique; to seamlessly lie because they know they won't get caught; to hang out in unsupervised houses; to go to weekday night concerts; to visit porn sites in the elementary school years; or speak to strangers online—just a few issues among many, many twenty-first century realities.

Has there ever been a time when children of all ages needed more engagement through commonsense and unapologetic direction, from adults who are unafraid to say what they believe out of love and concern?

Yet at earlier and earlier ages, kids turn to their peers or to the pop culture for that guidance. Why? It's not about a lack of parental love, it's that some post-boomer mothers and fathers feel dwarfed by kids who know no bounds and are uncertain about whether advice is useful in a world with rules so new and ever changing. On top of this, many parents still buy into old, anti-establishment theories that telling kids what to do will short-circuit their need to find out for themselves. Finally, as if these reasons weren't enough, there's a widespread sense of relative isolation among families today diffusing the collective voice of adult authority in most communities.

So kids address problems in their fragmented lives too often between themselves. Indeed, children are much more skilled at giving each other advice than we ever were. The director/writer of the 1995 movie *Clueless,* Amy Heckerling, was way ahead of the curve in perceiving the growing phenomenon of kid-to-kid guidance. Interestingly, that was the same time I was noticing the rising power of second family culture. But peer support is not all kids need. In the jagged social world children inhabit, they face issues every day that intimidate, and they do it without enough adult maturity, wisdom, or experience to engage and guide them.

Kids, anxious under that façade of "cool," feel a lack of parental advice as a lack of love and caring.

Mary's outrage expresses what many youngsters feel when they finally do cross the subtle divide between the child and adult world. What we haven't understood enough is that unlike kids of previous, more authoritarian eras, the free-est generation accepts adult opinion as an expression of love. But advice must be offered wisely, in a manner that fits today's kids' expectations of being listened to and being able to express their own views, and in a manner that matches their idiosyncratic temperament.

DO YOU KNOW HOW TO GIVE LOVING ADVICE?

Unfortunately, whether it is the guidance counselor Mary approached or parents themselves, almost nobody teaches adults how to give effective advice. Just like you, I've had to learn the hard way, through trial and error, from the thousands of kids and families I've spoken to and worked with.

My hard-won lessons have helped me understand that when it comes to offering clear guidance, many of us undervalue our own life wisdom. This is especially troubling because today's parents, veterans of vast social change themselves, have so much experience that relates directly to the post-boomer realities of their children's lives. And, even if you'd like to be a more outspoken parent, you're up against a not-so-subtle constraint: advice is discouraged by the widespread use of pejorative labels such as "helicopter moms" and "Little League dads," phrases that inhibit by pointing a finger of blame at highly involved parents.

Contrary to this popular criticism, one of the most surprising observations from my travels around the country is that far from being over-controlling, too many parents today are practically bullied into under-parenting.

By this I don't mean the cliché that we are friends to our kids rather than authority figures or that we are pathologically child-centered or relentlessly controlling. While there is truth to all these, far more crucial is that we undervalue our life wisdom and the need to effectively use it.

We are so worried about making mistakes that we parent the way malpractice-fearful doctors too often practice medicine. We are ever-vigilant not to be blamed, for whether our kids are popular or accepted into a good nursery school; whether the phone rings for play dates; what teams and college lists they end up on. We over-manage all the *peripheral* events we can possibly manage (like those extraneous tests doctors sometimes order to protect themselves), rather than get to the heart of the matter, putting our opinions on the record to ensure kids' safety and their character development.

Clear parental advice has become an increasingly rare commodity for just about everyone, regardless of socioeconomic status. I have done countless family consultations with highly successful people. I've done virtually the same number of consultations with poorer parents dealing with very different day-to-day life challenges. But when it comes to effectively advising their children, just about *all* are unsure of themselves.

Then, just to make matters worse, let's not forget all those TV commercials that sanctimoniously remind parents to start talking with their kids about the "tough" things, and early! But no one actually teaches parents how to offer our opinion, which might be pretty good advice, since it is born of experience much closer to these kids than our parents' or our grandparents' experience was to ours'.

This cannot go on. Besides a dangerous "guidance vacuum," it creates too much subtle division between children and their mothers and fathers. What looks like over-involvement on the surface belies an under-involvement with the direct guidance children need to feel loved and held. Regardless of their bravado and seeming sophistication, kids simply do not have the cognitive abilities, literally the brain development, until young adulthood with which to make reliably sound judgments. They need us to help them sort through conflicting messages and competing views.

Longitudinal research, which by the late nineties started to finally put some meat on the bones of parenting theory, has shown that clear, authoritative parental expectations and guidance are not just preferable, but necessary. As I reported in "Nurturing Good Children Now," that "clear expectations create strong connections between parent and child ... moreover such a connection is a strong indicator of whether or not your child will engage in high-risk behaviors." Likewise, the Johnson Institute, in Minneapolis, which followed tens of thousands of children, found that "kids of all ages need clear guidance and absolute rules to safeguard them from impulsive behavior."

As the research supports, kids need to know what you believe might happen due to their behavior—the natural consequences of making choices *before* an event occurs. They need clear, life-wisdom advice because, as the new wave of biological research and high-tech imaging has shown, the part of the brain that controls executive functioning, i.e., the ability to think ahead, plan, anticipate consequences, and organize isn't fully developed until the age of about twenty-five. So your guidance is something desperately needed at all ages, at least until kids go off to college, and probably continuing for a while after. In the face of this, post-boomers need to value how much their experience growing up in a fast-changing world mirrors that of their children.

The first step toward offering advice that helps kids feel lovingly guided is to understand the relatively new concept of *learning temperament*. Knowledge of learning temperament will open up a channel to your precocious or jaded or even stubborn child, regardless of age. If we offer advice without accounting for this, it is likely to fall on deaf ears and cause irritation both for our kids and for us.

SIX STEPS TO LOVING ADVICE

Step One: Do You Know Your Child's Learning Style?

There is a basic similarity between the learning that occurs during advice giving and a child's "learning style" in school. It is ultimately the responsibility of adults to grasp a child's unique way of processing information. Learning specialists, particularly since the nineties, have influenced schools and parents throughout the world. Their message is simple: Instead of fitting all kids into wholesale teaching models, we must fit some of what we are doing to match kids' specific learning needs.

The *learning temperament* perspective, recently introduced by educational experts like Dr. Rebecca Mannis, takes the learning style approach one step further and I believe deeper. We need to meld the latest work on temperament with the concept of learning style. Understanding how a child best learns and that temperament doesn't change much with age increases the chance your opinion will actually get through and be felt as love, rather than a boring reprimand or lecture.

Let's say you have a temperamentally tenacious child. Once she puts her mind to something, she cannot let go. This is a fact of her personality you've been dealing with forever. For advice to get through, you will need to offer a couple of options (both of which are acceptable to you), rather than go head to head. This highly effective and well-researched "limited-choice" approach is a method proposed by Dr. Stan Greenspan, author of *The Zero to Three Foundation,* and can be used with kids even in the toddler years.

For example, "Do you want to get dressed by yourself *or* with me, so we won't be late and hurt Grandma's feelings?" "You can share that toy with your brother without a fight and then instead of me needing to watch you guys, I'll have more time to read to you before bed, *or* you can play by yourself; either is ok with me." And later in life: "I don't think you should smoke at the concert tonight; I believe it's not right and not good for you. If we even sense you've smoked, there will be no concerts for awhile. But, since we can't be there to supervise, it's up to you."

By granting your tenacious child some degree of autonomy, your words will have a better chance of getting through, rather than creating a toe-to-toe battle.

On the other hand, your child may be a temperamentally active type, one who learns best on the move. For such a son or daughter, as odd as this may sound, advice will need to be offered in the midst of another activity, like dancing, doing the laundry, or driving to school. Our own highly active daughter, Leah, learned best while she was practicing her gymnastics moves on our coffee table. Kids like Leah are much more psychologically receptive to advice when they're not made to stop moving around physically.

Or perhaps your child is temperamentally fearful, thrown by new situations and challenges. With this kind of child your views—which are processed by them as jarringly unfamiliar—will need to be offered gradually, in a step-by-step fashion, especially when they are not agitated.

The idea that you should match your style of advice-giving to your child's learning temperament may come across as indulgent or too child-centered, even precious. You may think that part of the job of parenting is, after all, to teach your children to listen in whatever way is comfortable for *you* as the parent. Sounds good on paper, but the research is clear that we can't remold our children's basic temperament, so why swim upstream?

The legendary investor, Warren Buffett, advises using the tail wind that already exists instead of trying to fight against the resistance of a strong head wind. It's exactly the same when it comes to learning temperament and advice giving.

So, if increasing the chance that you can guide your child toward safer and more values-based decisions is your goal, then this kind of temperamental matching is the way to go.

LEARNING TEMPERAMENT IN ACTION

Following are a couple of real-life teaching examples from my practice using learning temperament to tailor the manner in which guidance is offered. This matching may lead to a break-through in your child's acceptance of advice.

Twelve-year-old Ryan, extremely intelligent, was having terrible difficulty with a boy in his class, Jeremy. Ryan had been imposing himself on Jeremy, who just hated being "pursued." Jeremy picked on him until Ryan would lash out, ironically making Ryan look like the "bad guy." Many times I explained to Ryan why it was not wise to approach Jeremy and, for example, ask him a silly question like "Hey dude, what time is it?" Or even a sensible question like "What did the teacher say about our reading assignment?" Even though Ryan is smart as a whip, he couldn't understand why his behavior was annoying to Jeremy, and how his persistence set him up for further abuse. I finally realized that my advice was falling on deaf ears, because he had a hard-wired *sensitive* temperament, which made him tend to hear others' opinions as personal criticism.

When I discussed my observations with his parents, they confirmed that Ryan had always been extremely sensitive, equating just about any attempt at guidance with fault-finding. Recognizing his learning temperament was the turning point for me and his parents. I soon realized Ryan was so guarded he had entirely misinterpreted my advice, translating it into less critical terms that he preferred hearing. As hard as it might be to comprehend this, when I told him "Don't ask questions of this kid" he actually thought I meant "Yes, sometimes it's okay to approach Jeremy" or "Approach him with a smile on your face" or "Phrase the question in a way that's friendlier."

The more I "got" this, the more I tuned in to Ryan's learning channel. Slowly, his parents and I learned to give him advice with the gentle, sensitive tone of voice he so desperately needed to stay open. Sure enough, Ryan became less touchy about direction and more adept at schoolyard politics. The unnecessary questions lessened. He accepted that he should leave Jeremy alone, especially when Jeremy was with other friends. Gradually, Ryan stopped chasing Jeremy and found his own group to hang out with.

Ryan's true-self, a better, more tuned-in side, emerged. And it showed. Several months later, Jeremy and Ryan found themselves talking around a lunch table after play-practice for several hours, and having a blast—unthinkable at an earlier time.

Here's another case example of adult advice matched to a very different learning temperament. Marlena was an attractive, street-smart young adolescent. For a variety of reasons, the most important being her learning temperament, Marlena craved crystal-clear advice. She'd always been thrown by ambiguity and would rather hear a hard-nosed opinion than anything fuzzy, which made her nervous. In fact, taking written tests, she often misinterpreted ambiguous instructions. Statements that could be construed in different ways drove her crazy.

Marlena needed clarity in order to hear loving advice from her parents and from me. The worst kind of opinion would have been something hedged or "balanced" or laissez-faire, such as: "Well, it could make you feel better about yourself on the one hand, or maybe worse, if you hooked up with that boy you just met." This would just upset her. Instead, her parents and I learned to say, "Think about this fact: everyone in school is going to know exactly what you did with that boy. You're going to feel bad afterward, because of what you'll hear about yourself."

Marlena had a great mind; but if advice was presented more vaguely than this, like so many kids with her learning temperament, it would never get beneath the facade.

Step Two: Say Exactly What You Think

One day in late elementary or junior high school, my father took me aside, looked me straight in the eye and said, "Ronnie, I'm going to tell you something I don't want you to ever forget. I won't be around to make sure this will happen. But when you decide what you want to be when you grow up, make sure it's not all about money or what other people are doing. Make sure it's something you really love and that it will make a difference in the world. Learn it, and then use it to help people. What you have in your head and heart can never be taken away. I can't make you do this . . . but if you don't, that will also stay with you forever.

He didn't realize it, of course, but my dad was being very "twenty-first century," tapping into my idiosyncratic learning channel. Like our son Sam, I absorbed best as a kid when a person was quietly firm, direct, and noncritical. My father had found a way to effectively tell me exactly what he thought, based on his own life experience of not having gone to college. I never forgot his perfect-pitch directness.

You don't need to tell all your dark secrets and private matters; your beliefs about what is right or wrong to share should always trump any experts' advice, including mine. But you must convey your values and your insights about the consequences of problematic behavior. Using a sense of how your child learns best (remember, for some kids too much information is considered "brain-dumping"), you have many, many life-lessons at your disposal. Times have changed dramatically; parental clarity is tolerated by children of all ages today, because in most situations you can't possibly be putting ideas into kids' heads—they've already learned it in school or seen it online and on TV many times before.

As with our emotions, and using your own personal values to anchor you, there is far greater freedom than we realize in engaging our kids and helping them benefit from direct guidance and the personal, painful, and productive lessons we learned along the way.

But, if you're like so many pop-culture, dwarfed parents in a post-boomer world, you may need a booster shot about the value of adult experience. Check out the "life-wisdom questionnaire" below to encourage confidence in some of the opinions you have collected from hard-won life lessons.

LIFE WISDOM

You Know More than You Think

Many parents take for granted how much we know about life that can guide our children and teens. We grew up in a time much like our kids and have a lot we can teach them. But this can't happen if we don't take some stock in what we do know. Check out a few examples that are still relevant from your early years to almost every 21st century child:

- Are there such things as secrets in school, online or will just about everyone find out-fast?
- Is it easy to face someone you 'hooked-up' with the next day?
- Do substances affect school performance and motivation?
- Is sex without friendship better than friendship without sex?
- Is it wise to talk about a friend behind his or her back, or will they find out—by tonight?
- Can boys and girls be best friends? Can girls lead? Should boys be caretakers?
- Does shame last forever, will it eventually pass or should you do something about it?
- Should you approach the 'coolest' kids in front of their closest buddies?
- When your intuition says something isn't right—do you trust it?
- Are certain video games more addictive than others?
- After more than a couple of hours of TV how do you feel?
- Can you tell pretty quickly when a person isn't "right" for you?
- How many best friends does anyone need to have?
- Do you need your friend's permission to go out with his or her ex?
- If you see an adult do something wrong, should you step forward?
- Should you get into a car when the driver looks slightly out-of-it?

(continued)

- If someone is "bossy" or a "bitch" by nature, do they usually change?
- Do most teachers respond to being cool or to respectful trying?
- Should you blindly follow what adults say—or wait to be sure they are responsible?
- Will joining in on dissing someone else make you feel better about yourself?
- Did it ever hurt to say "I'm sorry" or to try to make amends?
- What are the most important characteristics of a best friend, in school and online?
- Will it be comfortable to smoke-up with people you're not comfortable with?
- If you drink quickly will you be able to control it or to tell how it will affect you?
- If a friend won't share, is he or she going to be a good friend?
- Does complaining about a grade work—or does asking for help make a difference?
- When an extra-curricular doesn't feel right, is it ok to find something else?
- Is your trust something that should be given away or should it be earned?
- If a friend or an adult won't forgive, are they really a friend?
- When you regularly feel badly being with someone, is that a signal to notice?
- Should you go to violent movies when you know you won't easily forget what you see?
- Does trying hard make you a nerd, geek, freak or loser?

- Is keeping a ledger-list of hurts and slights going to make you feel better or worse?
- Can you really read peoples' minds and know exactly what they think of you?
- Do 'floaters' survive in school or must everyone be in a particular group?
- Are "players" happier than those who find a real friend?
- Should you go after your passions or go for a well-padded, but theme-less college résumé?

Step Three: Now Leave Room for Some Back-and-Forth Dialogue

As I've learned the hard way, with the free-est generation, it is essential you give kids the latitude to air their opinions about what you've just told them. You must be open to back-and-forth discussion. Children of all ages feel more entitled than ever to disagree, as if they were guests on Chris Matthews' Hardball, *and many parents find this infuriating. We must not interpret their push-back as a sign of disrespect; it is just another characteristic of the free-wheeling, free-est generation.*

Even younger kids today expect to be given their turn to speak, and when we're not in the midst of being annoyed about this, many of us admit that we're impressed, even proud. Take the case of seven-year-old Emmy, whose mother Nicole had tried to tell her the rules of fair play with friends. Emmy wouldn't listen. As she put it to Nicole, "Mom, you need to take me seriously. I have my reasons too!" After some coaching from me, Nicole realized that Emmy was committed to a Dr. Seuss notion that "A person's a person no matter how small." Emmy wanted her time on center stage to share her own points of view. And to her credit, she had already formulated rather complex ideas about the do's and don'ts of second grade friendship.

I'm not at all suggesting that letting your kids express their differing views will be easy. Take the case of Megan, who discovered that her fourteen-year-old son, Amos, was drinking. Amos insisted that he would not tolerate mom's advice until she listened to *his* views; this was difficult because his views were both clichéd and pretty outlandish. He asserted that every single kid in the school drank (unlikely—not even close to what statistics bear out); that the research of the impact on kids' brains showed no harmful effects (not true); and that teen experience would lead to more restrained drinking in college life (actually, alcohol dependence in high school kids begins startlingly quickly). Megan, a boomer mom, had a difficult time keeping herself from being triggered into a lecture about the evils of alcohol. She was so inflamed that she almost found herself recommending marijuana, as a better choice.

As soon as Megan listened to Amos' request that his views at least be heard, they began to have the back-and-forth dialogue necessary, during which mom could express herself. Her life wisdom on the subject included many tips on how to not feel left out if everyone around is drinking and you don't happen to feel like it. Tips like how to nurse a drink for hours without actually drinking a drop, how to find a party buddy who is not getting soused, and so on. The approach worked because with her opinion she always left room for Amos' views. Not only did mom get through to her son; slowly he became one of the kids in his grade who moved away entirely from drinking. And just lately he's been trying to help a high school buddy find help for his substance problem. When given the right combination of direct opinion along with give-and-take dialogue, Amos' better-self emerged, and he felt cared for.

Megan's experience is far from unique. It is almost always surprising to parents how much kids will talk about dicey matters once the door is opened. Researchers in early adolescent and teen sexuality have the same experience out in the field that you will have at home. They've repeatedly told me that they underfund expenses for interview time, because they don't expect kids will want to talk for so long and reveal even the most personal matters to "nosey" adults. In a

YouTube world, today's children and teens are rarely bashful once given the opportunity.

Step Four: Can You Repeat What I Just Said?

I have wasted endless time and energy by not following this simple guideline for effective advice: after tailoring your style to your child's temperament, clearly expressing your beliefs, and opening the door to back-and-forth discussion, you need to restate what you believe and why.

The reason is that given kids' normally scattered attention today, they often cannot be counted on to recall (even if stated just a few minutes before) what your opinion was in the first place. So with children of all ages, be forewarned: by the time you've finished the give and take, there is a real possibility your views will have floated off somewhere to the outer edges of their consciousness. Therefore, keep the following in mind: *Repeat your position and remember: listen long, but keep your explanations short.*

Crisply and clearly, your kids need to understand *why* you believe they should not be picking on someone else, *why* ostracism is so hurtful, *why* it matters to be polite, *why* you think sexuality should be delayed for as long as possible, *why* you will not tolerate them going to an unsupervised house.

The list of topics is endless, but the rationale behind your expectations should not be. Keep it to one or two sentences, or your show will be ruthlessly cancelled. There is no kid audience out there for complex or lengthy points.

Step Five: The Power of Impotence

Now it's time to admit to something that may seem counter-intuitive to parental authority: your inability, even impotence, to control your child's behavior.

In order to convey that you understand the realities of their lives, and therefore to make the kind of authentic connection I am advocating, it is essential to say: "*I can't control you; in the end, it's your choice.*" The most critical aspect of giving advice to the free-est generation, then, is not only the content of your opinion, but a statement about your limitations as a parent.

Thinking back on it, my own father was being incredibly modern in admitting his limitations about my future decisions, but even then, it was precisely this admission that helped get his message across to me.

Recognizing *our* adult limits (we always focus on limits for kids) allows children of all ages to hear advice more readily, because they realize that you have grasped a fundamental reality of kid life. Compare "You *can't* make fun of Jenny" vs. "I know I can't stop you, I won't be there; but I don't believe it's right to make Jenny feel bad." This is a simple twenty-first century truth: no matter how closely we manage every logistical detail of our children's lives, we can't be there to control their choices and behavior at every moment. Through a spate of wonderful books such as *Real Boys, Reviving Ophelia, Another Tribe, Lost Boys, Schoolgirls, Queen Bees & Wannabes,* and my own book, *The Second Family,* we may know a lot more these days about what is going on in the peer group, but kids are still living much of their lives outside of our control.

This Zen moment in child rearing, the paradox of being as clear as you can about what you expect and then admitting your limitations is perhaps the single most important moment in getting both your love and advice across to children.

It may seem "way random," as kids love to say, but when I think of the power of accepting this simple truth, I am reminded of a golf tournament that Tiger Woods was (no surprise) in the process of winning. His lead was dropping with each hole, but he seemed to be in control of his emotions. The announcer said something that relates exactly to this point. To paraphrase: "Watching Tiger, one can't help but be impressed with how he's in control, not because he's trying to be in con-

trol, but because of his acceptance of the moment. It's like he's surren-
dered to what he's been given, the here and now—and it allows him to
stay in charge."

This powerful Zen moment of accepting one's limitations is as
true for parents of kids in kindergarten as it is for the father of a teen
who proclaimed, "You absolutely cannot smoke up at the concert—I
forbid it!" His, son, Ramon, said nothing at the time, but told me the
next week, "Who does he think he's kidding. At a concert I can do
whatever I want." Ramon reacted entirely differently in words and
action after I counseled dad to subtly change his message: "I don't
want you to smoke at the concert—here's why—but I also know I
won't be there to stop you. It's going to be your decision, although
there will be a price to pay if you do."

Some parents who come to my presentations tell me they think
this is taking a weak stand. I'm well aware that it could sound like this.
However, recognizing our limitations is not the final step of the
process. The "consequences" part of advice giving will follow.

*What I am saying is that free-est generation kids feel anxiety about our
ignorance regarding how easily they can go against parents' commands.*

They are reassured to hear mothers and fathers who are aware of
this reality—aware of how clueless we can actually be. I cringe when
I hear parents in our own circle of friends claim that their children
"tell them everything" and they know "exactly what's going on." They
are in for rude, rude shocks. Being realistic, especially when it comes
to parents who normally seek to micro-manage every moment (which
gives the *illusion* of control) is a loving kind of power that kids welcome and respect.

Take, for example, Aura, the mother of seven-year-old Meredith.
Aura was an adoring, highly competent mother. Her guidance on
classroom politics, however, was totally ignored by her strong-willed,
second-grade daughter. We spoke several times about the advice-
giving process I recommend, which went totally against Aura's managerial grain. But, finally, out of frustration (and probably to prove me

wrong), she took me up on it. Very quickly Aura discovered that after she told Meredith her view on handling ostracism, then let Meredith voice her own opinions on friendship, *then* (most difficult) admitted she wouldn't be there to monitor Meredith's behavior, Meredith began to open up to her.

Suddenly, the conversation moved on to how hard it was for this second grader to balance her ideas of right and wrong with the mean group leader's popularity. It boggled Meredith's mind that a girl so cruel could be so in demand. For the first time Meredith let Aura in on her thinking, as well as the dynamics of the second-grade pecking-order, and she actually listened to her mother's astute observations on handling this group's "mean girl."

The same thing happened with Kathleen and her teenage son, Stephan, who was drinking. When she admitted her inability to control whether Stephan took that extra shot of vodka with his buddies, his pinned-back ears perked up. Stephan actually began to "name names" of kids he was drinking with and describe what it was like to be with his second family of peers. It wasn't that they pressured him to drink, he explained (the old-think myth of peer pressure is something I've described in *The Second Family*); it was more a question of not wanting to miss out on the "bonding experience" if he didn't participate. For one thing, it was hard to laugh at his best buddies' stupidity if he wasn't a little buzzed along with them. No one, Stephan assured his mom, would hold it against him—he'd just feel more alone.

Within minutes, instead of Kathleen's clueless belief in her power to control him and Stephan's equally clueless belief in his power to control six shots of alcohol, they were engaged in a new-frontier conversation about the meaning of teen drinking and bonding. What's more, Stephan's views about how much he hated the way some of his friends' personalities changed when they drank started to come into the open. His more honest, better-self emerged as mom followed my lead.

The "take-away" here, as many twenty-first century kids like to call it, is that admitting to your limitations vastly increases your strength in the interpersonal equation. Stark frankness levels the playing field substantially with real-world free-est generation kids, and opens them up to loving advice. But you must also include the next essential step.

Step Six: Now for the Consequences

Finally, you absolutely need to say in your own words, from your own values, and using your own life experience as a guide, something along the lines of: "If you decide against what I've suggested, here is what will happen . . . ," articulating not only how your kids might get hurt or hurt others, but also consequences that you will enforce.

This is where the entire range of boomer and post-boomer parents (myself included) have the most trouble. The concept of consequences is not a slam-dunk, partly because the whole notion of "limits" has changed so much for the free-est generation. Yet laying out consequences along with advice is truly essential to guide and create loving engagement. I've heard from principals, teachers, and camp directors across the country that no form of guidance, whether it is a "social-emotional" teaching module or a value/ethics program or a responsive classroom initiative, works without some form of enforceable consequences.

The same need for enforceable consequences, to give some teeth to your guidelines, is as important at home. Consequences help kids to feel that we mean what we say and say what we mean; they help distracted kids to remember when it is so easy to forget; they help children feel connected to us across the divide of our harried lives; to feel "held" by the adults around.

Of course, given all I've said about how much goes on behind that wall of silence and the ability of children of almost all ages to pretty much do what they want without us finding out, how in the world are we going to know whether they do or don't follow our advice? Will you actually discover whether your child has engaged in hurtful ostracism at the playground or gone to another's house without anyone there to supervise, or "smoked-up" at the concert?

The good news is that despite the wall of silence, kids almost always leave signs of what they are up to. You'll spot them if you keep your eyes open. Since the free-est generation is so unafraid of getting caught, one can almost always count on lack of focus and lack of attention to every detail. There are often far more signals than you would think, but only if you allow yourself to see your child clearly. I will devote an entire section to "seeing clearly" in the next chapter, in which you will learn that it *is* possible to figure out a great deal of who your child is, even when you are not around.

LOVE EQUALS EFFECTIVE ADVICE— PUTTING IT ALL TOGETHER

A couple of real-life examples will illustrate how to combine these steps I've suggested.

Five-year-old Ian had trouble on play dates. He needed advice about how to handle the touchy issue of sharing. During the past few get-togethers with his best friend, the two had had several fights over sharing toys. If this wasn't solvable, these boys might not be able to maintain their friendship. Adult input was called for.

Ian's learning temperament was that of a sensitive child who needed to be in control of his environment and heard best when there were no other distractions. I coached his parents to say the following during a quiet in-between moment: "Ian, you need to learn to share, but this is a skill that comes with practice, so you can start small."

At five years he already had his own opinion about sharing, which mom and dad needed to make room for—free-est generation kids learn their "rights to free expression" very early.

So a good, twenty-first century, back and forth exchange followed. Ian said that he thought the fights were the other kid's fault because it was unfair to have to share if they were in *his* house. Ian believed he should be able to be the boss as well as the host. They listened respectfully, repeated their views, and then said that maybe play time with his friend would go better if he put away some of his favorite toys, ones he knew he couldn't share easily. Even with a child this age, I asked mom and dad to make it clear that his mom wouldn't be in the room to monitor every second, so cooperating was ultimately up to him. And then of course they needed to follow their advice with consequences: if Ian didn't learn how to do this, he might well lose the friendship (a bit of life wisdom), and they certainly would schedule no more play dates with this boy for a long time—a cooling-off period.

Ian got the message, reluctantly shelving several prized items for the next play date. Much to everyone's surprise, the get-together went extremely well. Ian's better-side showed up, and he actually hosted with a lot of grace for such a young child, even asking his guest if he was hungry, and sharing some of his favorite snacks.

Ian and his parents learned an important lesson about advice: authentic engagement had a powerful, concrete impact; it encouraged the boy's best-self to eke out a victory over his competitiveness.

Here's another example. Middle schooler Eric was extremely angry with his English teacher. He had not been calling on him in class, and Eric believed he had graded his last presentation "unfairly." When Eric talked about this with his mother, Lindsey, and then with me, it was clear that his reaction to the teacher was to withdraw even further, refusing to participate in class at all. This only exacerbated the situation, with animosity growing between the two, which was a serious situation since Eric was not performing well in a number of his other classes. He'd been doing a great job at primarily one thing: alienating the school staff.

Eric's learning temperament (he was tenacious, not particularly sensitive, and, in fact, loved a Socratic argumentative approach) told me that advice directed to him needed to be presented in a way that challenged but let him come to his own conclusions. With this in mind, I coached his mom, Lindsey, about offering guidelines. Lindsey advised that Eric's withdrawal would not only push away the teacher, but that he would have to live with the consequences: an angry faculty who had power over his class placement the next year. Despite Lindsey's confrontational style (which Eric needed), she made it clear she couldn't control Eric's behavior in the classroom. Lindsey also left a lot of room for Eric's predictable opinions, views on teacher-student relationships, fairness, etc. Mom listened, but then went back to her core belief that growing up meant finding ways to deal with responsible adults. She then offered him a limited choice (fitting his tenacious learning temperament): He could figure out how to cooperate or he could end up in a class he didn't want, with kids he didn't like the next year.

Eric left the discussion angry, saying that he didn't think any of her approaches would work, that the teacher was "hopeless," and that nothing would help. Lindsey was not happy with me about this outcome.

Several weeks later, however, the picture had become completely different. Eric went ahead with one of his mom's suggestions: he approached the teacher and talked to him privately after the class, saying how unhappy he'd been about not being called on more often, and apologizing for being so "quiet." Much to his surprise, the teacher said Eric was right—he'd been upset about how the boy openly criticized other kids in the class. This was why he wasn't calling on him as much. He even reminded Eric that he'd mentioned his tone to him several times early in the year.

This change in direction, stemming from well-delivered adult advice, transformed the course of the entire school year. Eric even applied the advice to several other teachers. By the end of the term, he had, as I predicted, moved from being on the "watch-list" of the guidance counselors to being a contender for advanced classes in the following grade.

Unexpectedly for Lindsey, Eric also began approaching her for more advice, opening up about the difficult territory of girls and drugs, a closeness she could never have imagined before.

Not all situations work out so smoothly. Kids dealing with far tougher issues take more time and unexpected turns. Sierra was an extremely anxious kid in my practice, who drank more than her body could absorb. Emphasizing my own and her parents' inability to control her behavior, I was also very clear about how much I thought she suffered from her decisions. I helped Sierra to remember how she felt following a weekend of drinking. After a number of failures even recalling my words, Sierra recognized that for the next three or four days after hard partying, she was much more anxious than usual.

Over time, Sierra began to see that my adult advice had the *slightest* merit. During one meeting, she suddenly muttered a line I'll never forget: "I hate that I'm so anxious I can't just let loose and drink like everybody else. But I also can't forget what you've been saying or what I've been feeling."

Sierra did not stop drinking entirely, but clear advice offered in the way I've described led to surprising changes. One night Sierra bumped into her father at three in the morning as she weaved her way into the kitchen. The two began one of those middle-of-the-night discussions about life and the real choices she needed to make about alcohol, friends, and boys. This first-time exchange did not lead to Sierra's *never* drinking again, but their breakthrough talk had legs. She began to tentatively discuss a lot more with her mother and father, whom she had previously labeled as completely irrational and a bad source of commonsense advice. Gradually, as she heard about her own mother's messy experiences and what she'd learned growing up as a post-boomer, Sierra developed a slightly different view of hard partying— an outcome that did not completely stop her acting up, but led to some restraint and an openness that had seemed impossible just a few months before.

A similar sequence happened with another adolescent, Harris.

After mom offering advice about other life issues, out of nowhere Harris suddenly emerged from behind his teen façade and opened up to his seemingly prudish mother for advice about sexual decisions. Using the paradigm described here, mom was able to rein in her reflexive impulse to lecture as her son described the real-boy pressures he felt to *demand* that his girlfriend, Mattie, participate in oral sex. His mother offered her clear opinions (to wait), admitted to her limitations (not in my house, but I can't be with you every moment, so even though I don't agree with this morally, it's your decision), listened to his views (without interrupting, as she usually did), and told him the consequences she'd learned through her own life-experience (Mattie will probably expect a lot more contact with you after sex of any variety—a realistic argument that got Harris' male attention where he lived).

These unexpectedly frank mother-son exchanges between two loving, but heretofore distant, family members even threw me. So did the outcome. Like many free-est generation kids I know, Harris and Mattie delayed and delayed, so that it became clear they would not be together long enough to make going farther sexually worth it.

Both youngsters, whom I followed for years afterwards, began to turn more to their parents as a source of advice and life wisdom. For these children of the free-est generation, life did not miraculously turn into smooth sailing. There were many ups and downs along the way.

But both stayed safer by discovering that they still had lots to learn from their parents, mothers and fathers who were less afraid to show love through clear guidance.

LOVE MEANS DEMANDING EMPATHY—
A PARENT'S BASIC RIGHT

It was stunning for me to learn how much insensitivity parents (everywhere in the country) absorb from kids in the name of enlightened parenting or the rush of frazzled living. It took a while, but I learned that another way in which mothers and fathers can forge bonds of more authentic engagement is to hold children to higher expectations, in terms of showing them empathy.

Many boomer and post-boomer parents believe love means kids should be allowed to "get off their chests" whatever they need to. This encourages anger, recrimination, and criticism from children so "feelings won't fester beneath the surface." Unfortunately, accepting verbal abuse divides parents and kids, erodes authentic engagement, and buries kids' best-selves further out of reach.

It is an outdated notion that empathy trumps a need for consideration from children toward adults. Parents must be recognized as human beings whose feelings also can be hurt. The free-est generation is often fierce toward mothers and fathers, not necessarily out of rage and rebellion, which once might have been the case, but because they're so uninhibited they genuinely seem oblivious to the impact of their actions and words. They've never been taught that what they do and say matters, and that their one-liners can deeply wound. The on-line culture reinforces a kind of disconnection from their own actions: words are like high-altitude bombing—deadly, but one rarely has to see the victims.

Expecting that kids emerge from their self-involvement and learn what it means to empathize with (even) their parents—contrary to popular child-rearing notions—is experienced by children of all ages as an expression of love. Asking kids not to be casually hurtful toward those who care for them the most prevents a great deal of unnecessary anxiety and self-hate in the free-est generation. Demanding empathy challenges a child to summon his or her hidden best-self, the one that parents deserve to see more of.

The great British pediatrician D.W. Winnicott believed that increased empathy, especially toward one's parents, is a hallmark of mental health. Psychologists as well as child educators have recognized Winnicott's insights about empathy for a long time. But the emphasis has been "horizontally," toward children's peers. Schools, for example, focus on encouraging empathy through anti-bully, tolerance-building and social-emotional programs, which stress consideration toward one's classmates and buddies. An equal emphasis on empathy toward adults and parents has largely been ignored—yet this child-to-parent compassion is essential to authentic and loving engagement.

We need to be more aware that the parent-child relationship represents the most powerful opportunity for nurturing empathy in children, and is a means for kids of all ages to recognize the buried compassion of their split-off, true-self. Viewing parents as a different life form, as two-dimensional beings without feelings, is detrimental to kids' emotional well-being. It leaves them feeling mean and out of control, unhappy with themselves after having been obnoxious to their parents. They feel far more connected to the coarse façade of the pop culture than to their better side.

Today's parents must learn that love is strengthened by expecting empathy from our kids, and that we must stand up for our own humanity.

My wife Stacey and I experienced this with our children, Leah and Sam, many times, but two occasions come to mind. The first was after Leah's six-year-old birthday party, a neighborhood and family bash. Suddenly Leah expressed the following sentiment, in the midst of a whining jag (one familiar to many parents after this kind of high-octane event). Within minutes of the party ending, she screamed out: *"You never do anything for me!"* This was mind-boggling. After all, we had just arranged a party for fifty of her friends, along with our immediate family, and her friends' mothers and fathers. We had rented a modest community space, cooked most of the food ourselves, and landed a popular "sorceress" children's entertainer, to boot.

Our initial reaction at Leah's burst of anger was to focus our empathy entirely on her; she must have been wired-up and over-tired, we thought. All of a sudden—I really don't know what spurred this—we responded in a way that shocked us. We demanded *her* empathy: *"How dare you say this after all we did for you today . . . we want you to sit there, not move, and to listen to everything that we did for your birthday!"*

We then began describing all the behind-the-scenes planning that went into making her fun day happen. Doing so was an eye-opener, not only to our free-est generation daughter, but to us. Leah started to cry, and we realized that she was tearful neither out of anger or frustration, but because she was actually feeling badly about how she had taken our efforts for granted. It was a stunning moment. And we all felt better instantly. Her wonderful, though tired, side emerged again, and we sat together recounting the best parts of the day—as well as some of her disappointments.

The second example occurred when Sam and I were on a ski lift. Sam was then about ten years old. He and I were headed up the mountain, which was no small accomplishment for me since I suffer terribly from a fear of heights. I spent my time praying silently that the bar on the chair would come down; I was shocked when it got stuck in the upright position and absolutely panicked when the ski lift stalled near the highest point on the slope. Now, Sam was well aware of my fear of heights, and as I was sitting there clinging to the chair and to the loss of my mind, he casually leaned back and crossed one leg over the other in a display of carefree nonchalance. I looked at him and could see a certain twinkle in his eye.

Being in what felt like a near-death situation, I surprised both Sam and myself by turning the tables on him. *"How could you not take care of me at this moment, Sam? You don't have to show me how comfortable you are . . . you really need to pay attention to how scared I am."* Panic overrode twenty-first century discomfort about "laying a guilt trip" on him. This burst of parental need got through and almost the next second he took my hand. Sam's heart had broken through a mocking *South Park* moment. Many years later, this upside-down experience remains: a spark of regard for my feelings as a parent he has brought up on several occasions since.

Whom do you want: the false-self of the façade or your child's better, true-self? Mutual compassion brings out the better side. The free-est generation needs to grasp that empathy is a two-way street. Parent after parent has come back to me invigorated after I've counseled them to demand empathy at home, with the same profound sense of liberation and love when their children and they have connected in this way.

Years ago, one mother, Barbara, reported such a tipping point when her six-year-old daughter, Abby, fiercely balked as she asked the child to be patient and let her get some office documents copied. "This happened after I'd spent the whole day taking her from one activity to another. Suddenly I found myself saying with real feeling: 'Hey, *I* have needs, too. Not only are we getting *my* errand done, we're not going for your ice-cream later!'" Barbara continued, "Abby looked at me and for the first time she seemed to understand that something was actually bothering me. I was shocked it had taken me this long to demand empathy from her. She apologized, waited patiently, didn't even ask for the ice cream, and we spent an incredibly close evening together. I couldn't believe the change in her demeanor."

Even *teens*, those we naturally expect the least understanding from, benefit from being reminded that empathy is something to be offered to parents, not just the other way around. Here's an example I've reported several times, it was so dramatic: Mike wanted his graduation party to be held in his home. His mother, Emily, initially agreed, but as the day got closer, Emily began freaking out, picturing so many people in her modest house. She started talking about renting a cheap space in a nearby community center. This infuriated Mike, because he was afraid his friends wouldn't think it was cool.

In our meeting, I told Mike that I agreed with his mother. Not unexpectedly, he howled about the "unfairness" of it all. But then I shifted the focus, surprising myself by saying, "I want you to understand what this feels like from *my* side."

Mike initially considered my demand for empathy a violation of twenty-first century kid rights. "What about my side? You're not getting it!" he yelled at me.

I responded with unexpected intensity, "I *do* understand. I was so self-conscious about how I looked that I didn't want pictures taken at my graduation from grade school, even. But I lost that one, just like you're going to lose this one too."

Mike responded: "That's totally different. You can rip up pictures afterwards. I'll have these memories my whole life."

"Look," I insisted, "I want you to try to see it from my perspective; what it felt like for me." And here's where I really moved away from outdated parenting beliefs and the training I still held sacred, both emphasizing one-way empathy: "Hey," I said to him with real feeling, "it's never just about your feelings—mine count, too!"

Remember, kids may not show that you've gotten through to them right away; and, as often happens, I didn't have a sense that I'd made a significant impression on Mike, or any impression for that matter. A couple of days later, however, I received a surprising call from Emily. "I don't know what you did," she said, "but for the first time, Mike let me explain how frightened I was; that I just couldn't handle this party at home. He didn't agree, but at least he tried to hear me." The party was moved to the community center, and Mike had a great time; so did Emily.

The free-est generation is waiting for us to demand the empathy that is part of loving engagement. Kids' best-self is there to be touched, and our heartfelt efforts deserve nothing less.

LOVE CAN BE IMPOLITE—
BEING RUDE AND STAYING CONNECTED

Some of what I learn about kids today drives me a little crazy. According to children of all ages, their favorite American Idol judge is Simon. As a well-meaning adult with the conviction that kids need to live in a more compassionate environment, this originally offended me. "How," I asked one kid after another, "could you like someone who is that nasty?" The response was always pretty much the same: "Just because he's rude doesn't mean what he says isn't true or won't help." Finally I got it; for the free-est generation, rude, crude, and impolite does not always cancel out love—or squelch their best instincts.

Sometimes our emotions, no matter how dramatic and sincere, aren't enough. In this hyperkinetic A.D.D. world, unpredictable and even rude responses are often necessary to get kids' attention. Again, pop-parenting constraints make this easier said than done—most of us are frozen by the child-rearing myths of total acceptance and consistency—except, of course, when *we* explode!

The rough and tumble world of twenty-first century life teaches that if we want to get kids' full attention, sometimes we shouldn't shy away from rudeness.

It took me almost a decade of working with post-boomer parents and their kids to realize that, in fact, the best conversations were often ones with an almost impolite feel to them. I believe this is because such exchanges are more genuine, more spontaneous. Children value and are inspired by authenticity, often more than boring and unconditional positive regard, a holdover from mid-twentieth century parenting advice. Much needed after the crushing constraints of the Victorian era, respectful communication found its expression in the genius of Haim Ginnot in his book *Between Parent and Child*. Almost every child-rearing expert from then on echoed this concept, in wonderful books such as Adele Faber and Elaine Mazlish's *How to Talk So Kids Will Listen and Listen So Kids Will Talk*, Lawrence Balter's *Who's in Control*, and Nancy Samalin's *Love is Never Enough*, to name just a few. Their views held sway for decades and were entirely consistent with mid-to-late twentieth-century family life, that is, until our free-est generation kids arrived.

In doing treatment with twenty-first century children and teens and listening to many thousands of parents in schools across the country, I finally understood that we needed to move beyond this brilliant but constrained heritage. Given the coarseness of life in the fast lane with today's kids and the acceptable range of love, what we consider impolite vs. polite, is far greater than we realize.

LEARNING TO BE LOVINGLY RUDE

When I asked kids what matters from parents, they regularly brought up the kind of adult who speaks his or her mind—those whose responses you could never take for granted.

Some of the most successful parents I've known make it their business "to let themselves be," warts and all. Nancy, the mother of two girls, is a master at semirude interaction. When her daughters begin to talk, instead of immediately pouncing, she often makes them (Mom!!!!) wait their turn. When she interrupts or moves temporarily on to do something else, her kids do not shut down—as many parents would fear. When they tell a story, Nancy responds with sharp emotion and rarely gives pap-sounding answers. Whatever she says, whether it's "I have no idea what you're talking about" or "How could you say that to her, it sounds so mean!" or "You're behaving like you're a two-year-old, not a ten-year-old!" Nancy seems to get her daughters' attention. Sure they may get angry for a moment, but since they know she will eventually try her best to listen, they easily drift into those back-and-forth discussions that create genuine traction.

"RUDE" DISENGAGEMENT CAN CREATE
LOVING CONNECTION

Staying stuck physically often reflects a stuck conversation. In the heat of the moment and the battle of wills that seems to go on endlessly during our harried lives, body and mind can get caught in a kind of brain freeze. Kids and parents dig in and literally nothing moves except skyrocketing blood pressure.

Despite this familiar experience, suddenly changing location (if possible) or walking away (if safe) is one of the most difficult suggestions for some parents to accept, but it is powerful. Parents ought not stand on ceremony. Get up from the couch, move around the house, or leave an angry child's room. Thousands of parents have told me that a bit of distance helps loosen a stalled or negative interaction. It pushes a pause button and creates punctuation in the endless run-on sentence that is a parent-child argument.

Stacey and I discovered this firsthand when our daughter, Leah, was about four or five years old. She was in the middle of pushing every button we had, and we remembered reading somewhere how important it could be to take "a parents' time out." So we suddenly walked away from Leah, went into our bedroom, and shut the door. Believe me, this was no small feat for two progressive parents, and Leah didn't make it easier on us. She squeezed her little fingers into the space between the bottom of the door and the floor, and through her cute-as-a-button "kitten paws" we could feel her imploring us to come out for another round of complaining. Pretty crafty for five years old! But we stood firm. We stayed the course. When we finally opened the door—ten seconds later—instead of acting like a child broken by this more-than-rude display of parental behavior, Leah suddenly asked, "Was I doing something that was bothering you?"

The world-famous European family therapist, Maria Selvini Palazzoli, suggested to parents that they *suddenly* leave the house (even with the most troubled kids), putting an ambiguous sign on the door that read, "We will be back sometime later." Pallazoli's advice is not an ethical possibility here in the United States, nor should it be. But the underlying concept has validity: the idea that if a child is safe, parents should take the impolite route of escaping from dug-in kids, if only for a few moments, to calm down and to get their child's attention.

Here's an example from my practice. When Brian repeatedly told me with a grin on his face about prank calls to older people, I said: "Brian, you seem unable to think about the effect you're having on these people. You know what? I have to take a break from you for a minute," and I walked out of the room. When I returned a few minutes later, Brian was finally willing to talk about the extremely childish and mean way he often treated his parents and friends. He and I were then both open to a more honest and kindly exchange than before my rudeness. I had actually never seen this slightly more compassionate side of Brian before; it was hidden behind that seamless façade of sarcastic humor.

Parents, too, should consider the option of taking such a moment away. I cannot overestimate the number of mothers and fathers who have admitted how, *if it's safe,* they take a parent's time out by leaving their kids in the lurch with mouths open. After sticking for years with the boomer and post-boomer theme of "I've got to be there for them!" many have come around to another view. They'll do anything to calm down by suddenly breaking away for the moment: walk around the block, close the bathroom door, listen to *their* music, call a friend, meditate, deep breathe, or find a few moments to sit alone in the car out in the driveway. Almost every time, they report how kids discover from these jarring behaviors that something was on an adult's mind.

"Rudely" leaving often creates mindfulness for the free-est generation, whose process is so fast-forward, their thoughts are like one long run-on sentence that focuses primarily on the "me." This is a mindfulness that can lead to the heart buried inside, instead of just the façade that covers it.

IRREVERENT HUMOR LEADS TO ENGAGEMENT

While humor occasionally comes up in the parenting literature with an emphasis on sensitivity, irreverent humor is a tool mostly unexplored in child-rearing guides. This is unfortunate, because with today's kids, irreverence can provide a lightning bolt of connection.

Given the endless menu of coarse comedy in pop culture—*The Simpsons, Family Guy, South Park, Borat, Superbad, Sarah Silverman, Def*

Comedy Jam—and the nature of everyday banter in the schoolyard—it shouldn't be surprising that edgy humor is a *must* to loving engagement. As reported to me by a spokesperson for the Yankelovich Youth Monitor in 1996, twenty-first century kids began rating humor as one of the primary characteristics most admired in adults.

This trend continues and repeatedly comes up in my workshops. It can be a certain face, a snide expression, disdainful body language, or the tossing off of a self-deprecating remark; anything that breaks the moment with a laugh can open up a channel of connection with our kids. When it comes to humor, what the free-est generation actually hears and remembers is almost always the irreverent. And, you're the guys to be doing it: as boomer or post-boomer parents (with *The Simpsons* now nearing its third decade), you've been raised on a steady diet of comic irony. Irreverence is a lot more ordinary than it was several decades ago before the exponential expansion of cable TV and *Comedy Central*.

I still learn every day how powerful the right use of irreverent humor has become to this generation of stand-up comedy kids. Take the example of middle schooler Adam, who was deeply glum when he came to see me. It turned out that he'd just returned from the doctor, who'd said that one testicle was enlarged. Our conversation wasn't making much headway, until I wondered out loud whether an enlarged testicle might require a change in his TV-viewing habits, since he was such a dedicated couch potato. Maybe he'd need to switch to a new kind of couch, I said, with a cutout section so he'd feel more comfortable. Instead of getting angry, Adam seized on this with delight and began to speculate that he might soon require a wheelbarrow to move through the wide hallways of his suburban school, or might even need to call ahead to announce his arrival. I joined in and we were off to the races, with Adam jumping up and down, doing improv about how everyday living might be affected by this new challenge—routines that had us both rolling on the floor.

The emotional and health crisis passed. Once again, I learned that much of the time (see box on p. 132 for when a parent should *not* use humor), stories of mothers and fathers who leaven tough situations with humor are worth remembering. For example, I saw a good friend of our family do this *Cops* bit in front of everyone when his daughter returned home from a sleepover: "frisking" his daughter down, obviously sniffing her for tell-tale signs, and reminding her of the jar she "should pee in before going to bed." What was striking was the laughter from this fourteen-year-old, instead of the embarrassment or anger I would have expected.

Take-offs on commercials are becoming a good source of parental shtick, as described by a mother in front of hundreds during one of my presentations. To her ornery, tight-lipped daughter whom mom suspected of having engaged in some high-risk behavior the night before, she quipped, "A new dress . . . $50. . . . an expensive haircut? . . . $25. . . . but being honest to your mother about what happened at Adelaide's house last night, when no adult was around—*priceless*!" All of a sudden, laughter and their distance turned into an intimate discussion of some random hooking-up.

Discussions about serious issues can spontaneously emerge with the most politically-incorrect, but hilarious spontaneity. Witness a mother I know whose nine-year-old son indignantly said, "Mom, I don't care if you want to know what happened in school—my private life is *my* business!" Her response: "Hey, don't give me that—*I am your private life*!" a line delivered with such a blend of authenticity and comic relief all around fell down with laughter, as did her ornery preteen, who then went on to describe the trouble he had gotten into that day.

I've gotten busloads of parents to spend time with their kids watching TV comedy shows just to have mutual, funny reference points. These shared moments provide parents and kids with scripts to talk about difficult matters without actually having to "own" the words, a twenty-first century variation of the old therapeutic practice of talking through puppets. Indirect communication humorously bridges the divide and touches the irreverent side of kids' true-self that is reserved only for their very, very best pals—or the entire world on Facebook.

WHEN *NOT* TO BE FUNNY

Kids Can Be the Toughest Crowd

Different children and teens have different capacities to hear your jokes. Even with this "stand-up" comedy generation, there are temperaments that cannot tolerate the snappiest, funniest responses—especially from a parent. Follow these guidelines (and your own intuition) to gauge:

1. Sensitive kids cannot joke about their areas of sensitivity—a reality that now begins way before the teen years.
2. Most children and teens will not accept humorous jibes in front of other kids, friends or siblings. This timing will almost always turn a humorous moment into a sour one.
3. You can't joke about a child of this generation if you can't make fun yourself—peer group repartee teaches kids that 'dissing' is a right of childhood and adults are fair game.
4. When kids are tired, hungry or frightened humor feels like the sound of chalk on a board. Don't fight biology, you'll lose.
5. Many children react more to the tone of a joke than to its content—figure out whether your tone is what's turning off your child.
6. When you, mom or dad, are tired/resentful, humor

> will often be felt by kids as aggressive. A joke may relieve you, but your child won't take it lightly.
> 7. Once a child says "not funny," saying it again with different delivery will only make him or her angrier.
> 8. Never make your child's friend the butt of jokes, even if he or she already has. You are not the peer group; this is not your "right."
> 9. Most times funny is good, but be ready to apologize if your joke bombs.

Love in the twenty-first century needs to be redefined. It can be expressed in many ways, and some of them are not the warm, fuzzy, or mindful styles of communication so many parenting guides have urged. The free-est generation needs to see us as three-dimensional beings; and expressing the genuine outrage or disappointment or confusion we feel with them, in dramatic, clear terms is a much better way of communicating than the use of pre-programmed mantras. Spicing our interactions with a dose of irreverent humor and some rudeness when justified, is also an important means of conveying that we value authentic connection. This kind of loving I recommend does not dispense with the warmth and compassion parents naturally express toward their children; those are never out of fashion. But often children need for us to be tougher in our responses, more direct in our advice, and much more open about the ways they make us feel.

As we begin to redefine how we express our love to fit kids in these times, they feel genuinely engaged. When this happens, the response is almost always the emergence of a truer-self, one that is smarter about life, kinder toward others, and more honest with us.

Really, what else is love about than helping to bring out the most authentic parts of ourselves and the very best in our children—the heart that is waiting to be touched, just beyond the divide of twenty-first century life?

5

ENGAGEMENT THROUGH LIMITING

Crystal-Clear Wisdom to Guide Children and Teens—In a World Without Limits

WHAT DO I WANT? I want to have all the fun and freedom that goes along with being a kid today. It's not like it was in the old days—we can go anywhere, do any stuff we want. It's tough sometimes, but it's great. And I wouldn't want to change places with any other time."—a typical preteen's or early adolescent's view of twenty-first century kid-world.

Notice the confidence, the certitude of this statement. No longer is freedom or having fun something a child expects to gain by maneuvering around or rebelling against adult authority. It's just another rite of passage, a right of childhood, an entitlement that comes with the turf. With kids who know no bounds, fun is endlessly accessible, like a Visa card—anywhere they want to be. No wonder one of the most difficult issues between parents and kids these days is the problem of setting limits on children's behavior and privileges. In a post-boomer world the task is utterly daunting, and whenever this comes up in my talks around the country, and it always does, parents throw up their hands, rail about the power of the second family, and generally believe that "it's me alone against the entire pop culture."

And they're right to be a bit dismayed. For one thing, mothers and fathers used to be able to lean more on a community of adults who also participated in the disciplining of children. When the parents of the greatest generation made a threat or set a limit, more often than not their children understood that serious consequences might follow if they didn't heed adult commands, weren't careful enough in their subterfuge, or didn't cloak themselves in an entire counter-culture movement. The force of kids conforming or rebelling was met with the equally determined voice of adults who did not usually feel alone in this process. With neighborhood or kinship systems around to back them up, and perhaps also the reinforcement of church and other community groups, they were not alone.

As Bob Dylan wrote in his 2000 song, *Things Have Changed,* and when it comes to setting limits, things have changed *a lot*. For better or worse, most parents today feel far less held by a blanket of authoritative security. When parents do threaten a punishment, free-est generation kids often feel just that—free to ignore, free to speak their minds, free not to worry too much about it, and certainly free to try to talk their way out of any consequences.

The free-est generation simply does not respond as readily to the setting of limits. Kids feel free to say the most outrageous things to their parents, to teachers, and to other adults (backtalk once unthinkable is now ordinary). They feel entitled to use cell phones at all times (seamlessly engaged in text conversations under the table while "participating" in family dinnertime). They have TVs in their rooms (and expect to watch what they want on cable TV with its thousand stations). They go anywhere they want online. When they are younger, that might mean Webkins (one of the major training grounds for later interactive online experiences). And as early as mid-elementary school, porn is an easy destination. Witness second-grade girls, who, looking for the nude pictures of *High School Musical*'s lead star stumble on to absolutely graphic, sexually explicit websites. In high school, online social networking games like *World of Warcraft* team up strangers from across the globe. By college at the latest, gambling entices and lures both *Heartland Poker* folk and ivory-tower students. (The parents of an Ivy Leaguer I know discovered their son's thousand-dollar nocturnal gambling extravaganzas had entirely replaced his daytime studies.)

Let's not forget offline activities, which are expanding as quickly and frenetically as the internet. Extracurricular adventures, going on play dates two to three times per weekend day, and concerts and parties (once kids are a bit older) are taken for granted birthrights, certainly not privileges to be earned.

Yet, despite our young friend's "declaration of independence" at the beginning of this chapter, it is helpful to know that during my interviews with children and (yes) teens, they repeated over and over that they very much wanted their parents to set limits. How could this be when freedom is such a staple of their lives? Because, surprisingly, even twenty-first century kids need the security of what I call the "family envelope" around them in order for their best-selves—their non-jaded, true-selves—to feel safe enough to emerge. Without a firm envelope at home it's a wild, hard-edged, universe of excitement and danger that waits.

The free-est generation is not stupid. It is excited and scared enough by all this freedom to know that someone needs to help rein them in just a bit.

THE FIRST PRINCIPLE OF LIMITS:
GUARDING YOUR FAMILY ENVELOPE

In discussing the issue of loving limits with parents, I always use the concept of the family envelope. Imagine an envelope or container around your family. This envelope is made up of *your* beliefs and expectations, *your* ability to understand your children accurately, and the kind of together-time *you* hold sacred. Too many kids of this freeest generation believe there is not much of a family envelope around them. They certainly don't think the container is firm, expanding only if they prove themselves capable of handling privileges.

Given that they do not feel this protective envelope, it should come as no surprise that children at earlier and earlier ages drift out to the second family in search of the container they secretly yearn for—the security of boundaries, rules, bonding rituals, and comfort. This, after all, is what a peer group is all about. The second family has its harsh rules: "do as we say or you'll be out." It has its empathic, understanding side: "we kids know what you feel like." It provides extensive bonding time: every kid everywhere in the country (and increasingly the world) is tuned in to exactly the same sites, TV shows, pop music, and movies. So even if the peer group carries its own freight of anxiety and meanness, kids would rather have something holding them securely than no feeling of a "there" there.

Even progressive child professionals, such as teachers who have been in the classroom for decades, are beginning to recognize that firm limits on freedom are necessary. Take the example of a sixthgrade teacher whom I knew, who taught me an unforgettable lesson. She got so fed up with the rudeness toward her and between kids that she suddenly halted teaching and said she was finished getting the curriculum across until she could get her students to lose the insults.

For the next three days, she stopped anyone from calling out or interrupting or even slouching in their seats. Some parents were at first outraged. This seemed way too authoritarian for these boomer and post-boomer veterans. But, surprisingly, the kids had a different take. After several days of their teacher not letting up, they began to wait their turn and to actually respond with some kindness toward her and each other. Far more dramatic, they approached the teacher privately and started to open up about the things that were making them anxious and fearful in the jagged dynamics of the classroom and the second family. Suddenly this forward-looking educator began to hear about covert alliances, kids who were being picked on, sneaky bullies, and silent victims; and she could also begin to teach about life, not just the formal curriculum.

Every one of her students and most of their parents recall that this was a turning point they would never forget. I never did.

So keep in mind that our children are yearning for us to effectively create a safe envelope for them, even though they are often outraged about it when we do. This is another crucial way in which they want authentic engagement from us in the form of parental authority.

But they do not want it in the dictatorial manner previous generations tended to use; they will absolutely never want to return to the rigid certitude, comforting though it may have been, of earlier eras.

The good news is that when we set limits in ways that fit the freest generation, kids not only listen, their better-selves emerge. Using this perspective to anchor us, I will introduce effective ways of enforcing limits that won't cause family warfare or make you feel like an authoritarian dictator (not that you'd allow that anyway). Rather, what will follow is an approach tailored to this new era of child-parent relations.

We'll begin by focusing on what I consider to be the most pervasive problem just about every parent in a post-boomer world faces. Not one workshop I give for parents of children of all ages ever passes without this issue being brought up. And whether we deal with it has profound implications on how kids treat themselves and each other every day.

LIMITS AND THE FIRST AMENDMENT— CURBING FREEDOM OF SPEECH AT HOME

A mother I was counseling many years ago described her seven-year-old son verbally berating her in front of his whole class about being five minutes late picking him up: "Mom, you're being stupid, you're not thinking. I saw on Oprah *how bad this can be to a child. They could end up seeing a psychiatrist." She didn't know whether to feel proud of his precocious verbal pyrotechnics or whether he should be punished for his language and public disrespect.*

That the free-est generation knows few bounds is hardly an accident. Most post-boomer mothers and fathers, having grown up in a stew of social upheaval, have few hard and fast rules and allow kids to say just about anything that comes to mind. Many also believe that their kids' cleverness and facility with argument will help them in the cutthroat, competitive battlefields of today's schoolyard and tomorrow's career worlds.

During every workshop I give, parents complain about their astonishingly adept and relentlessly brash kids at home, starting with four- or five-year-olds. The only problem is that from the distance of where I am standing on stage I can actually see, hear, and feel their "secret" pride.

I also know most parents are held hostage to a concern that if they don't allow kids to express themselves, communication and connection may be threatened entirely. I have hardly met a mother or father in any part of the country who does not flinch at what they hear at home, even from elementary schoolers. At the same time they are scared to death that kids will cut them entirely out of the communication loop. It is striking how early a fear of being iced from future communication begins.

The fact is, however, that these kids are perfectly able to learn when they are out of line, and to respect parents who draw that line with them. Unless a child has a diagnosable non-verbal learning disorder (i.e., being unable to pick up social cues like talking too loud or too close, asking unnecessary questions, or saying random things), kids today are interpersonally sophisticated and highly adept at being able to learn when they've crossed a line of respect.

An essential part of authentic engagement through limiting, then, one that encourages kids' better-selves to see the light of day, is for adults to rec-ognize that kids' freedom of speech must have its bounds, especially toward mothers and fathers—the fundamental teaching relationship for all that is to come. Without some minimal respect toward parents at home, very little else can be accomplished.

THE END OF BACK TALK (ALMOST)

Today's kids respond when we do not allow them to cross the "honor one's parent" line, no matter how clever they are.

Learning what to do is relatively simple. The problem is that given the whiplash change over appropriateness during the past few decades, parents really don't know what to allow anymore. As movie and social critic David Denby wrote in a *New Yorker* article after at-tending one of my lectures, parents almost as much as their kids live in a *sea of crud* pop culture. With *The Real World*, VH1, *Dance Your Pants Off, Entourage,* and a slew of cross-generational hit movies like *Borat, The Forty-Year-Old Virgin, Wedding Crashers, Knocked Up* and *Super-bad* for them to watch, who knows what's right anymore in the con-sideration department?

WHAT YOU NEED IS A LITTLE "RESPECT!"

Why Consideration Still Matters as Much as Free Expression

Contemporary parents often have a hard time grasping that respect is not old-fashioned, a throwback to another more rigid era. Instead, we now know that demanding some degree of deference from pre-school through high school protects your child's emotional well-being. Learn-ing that you have feelings, that certain lines are not to be crossed, gives kids a blueprint of interpersonal wisdom from you—the most important person in his/her life. And don't worry. In this wild culture, your children still won't be shy about expressing their views. Respect teaches kids and teens:

1. To put off instant gratification—kids and teens can't always have what they want, in that exact moment. This recognition builds patience towards you and the world.
2. You also have feelings that need to be taken into account—you are not simply a source of supplies or there when needed—a necessary lesson about personal limitations that will generalize to friendships and love relationships later in life.
3. Small considerations towards you represent the beginning of genuine empathy—that checking out another's social cues and responses encourages kids to recognize their impact on others.
4. To understand that rules and expectations are essential, even from those who love them the most, and not necessarily unfair. This is a mind-set that translates into school and other settings where authorities' feelings must also be considered.
5. To feel better about themselves—less mean towards those they love; less guilt often means less negative acting out in the rest of their world, as well as opening up more to you, because they feel secure and more in control in your presence.
6. To be appreciative and loving towards you—makes parenting more joyous, less adversarial and more fun.

(continued)

> According to many surveys on the lack of satisfaction of today's parents, this is a critical need for mothers and fathers nationwide.

YOUR BODY KNOWS WHEN YOUR
CHILD'S BEEN RUDE

The truth is *you do know when you've been assaulted*! Almost every parent I've ever spoken to, even if their core values vary wildly, knows exactly when their child has hurt them or has been inconsiderate. Regardless of the child-rearing approach or what we've been told is acceptable or what treatment we have become used to, we feel verbal abuse physically. In fact, research by those who have studied interpersonal communication, such as John Gottman, has tracked our underlying physiological responses as we go through being upset, angry, or anxious. The body can't be fooled. When kids cross a certain line, it hurts, and somewhere in your body this fact registers. "Where" is entirely determined by how you're wired; it could be in your stomach, your tone of voice, your jaw, or your heart rate, but it *does* register and you *do* need to pay attention. This is the best way to come to a clear, firm conviction about whether kids have crossed the respect line, no matter what you may hear all around or what kids tell you "everybody" is doing.

Mary Anne, a mother I know, was in the park with her two children. She said to both that it was time to go home. Four-year-old Jen suddenly screamed loud enough for absolutely everyone to hear, "Not now! Shut up, Mommy, you fat butt-head!" Mary Anne told me that instead of responding to this verbal assault, she felt herself almost lose conscious thought, and reflexively looked down to see if four-year-old Jen was right—*whether she'd gained any weight*. Then she became confused: should this be ignored and just treated as a youngster expressing herself? Suddenly hearing my voice, mom remembered to listen to her body (instead of judging it). Mary Anne realized her jaw was beginning to clench and immediately snapped out of her trance. She told Jen she would not tolerate that kind of talk, and then lifted her outraged daughter and put her in her younger sib's stroller to leave the park.

Within moments, Jen had morphed back into her more human and wonderful self. Mom could now verbally deal with her offensive outburst, naming exactly what line had been crossed.

ACT NOW—TEACH LATER

After recognizing your own bodily signals, the key to curbing destructive freedom of expression is to name what has just been said as wrong or unacceptable.

The fact is given the coarse culture we're living in, children of all ages often blurt out something that crosses over that line of common courtesy or good sense or empathic consideration. They live every day in this sea of crud, and as the saying goes, *"The fish is the last to know it is swimming in water."* So chances are the exact comment and tone that angered or hurt you did not even register with your child. Like so much else in this "just do it" post-boomer world, "stuff" pops out without thought as to its impact on the other. This is unfortunately the style of everyday conversation within the second family. As one of the typical preteens I spoke to reported, "Hey, we're supposed to rag and dis each other, that's what friends are for!" and too often, I guess, parents as well.

Just once in another era, in another time, I yelled "shut up!" at my mother and father, when they were getting on my thirteen-year-old nerves. My mind had been corrupted by a month away at camp living an *Animal House* existence with forty other thirteen-year-old boys. For a moment I think we all actually lost the capacity to speak in the face of this heretofore unheard-of sign of disrespect. "What did you just say?" my mother finally responded in a hushed voice, usually reserved for the gravest of tragedies. "Nothing," I murmured, ready to crawl under the kitchen linoleum.

Not today! Too often, parents simply skate past such moments, by now used to the coarseness of daily interactions to notice or not wanting to spoil those rare times together with "useless" bickering. The result is that kids haven't got a clue about their real impact. So the key is to be unmistakably clear with your children. I won't proclaim what crosses that line for you, but your body will register it. Pay attention to what you're experiencing and then name *exactly* what was said that doesn't feel right, in order for your jaded-too-early child to grasp that something unacceptable just happened.

> "Brit, when you said 'get out of my face,' it hurt my feelings, especially since I was trying to arrange a play date for you."
>
> "Jason, calling me a name like that may be fine on TV, but it's completely unacceptable here."
>
> "Deron, I don't care if I am your dad, we're not best friends, and you'd better not use that tone with me!"

You will immediately see a light of recognition go off in your child's face. As if a circuit had been closed, an interpersonal disconnection will now have just been re-wired.

"JUST SAY YES!"—TO SETTING A LIMIT

It is now time to create a consequence, a clear result you will enforce if your child repeats the behavior, and one that you'll really be able to follow up on. We've heard all kinds of notions about appropriate consequences such as: they ought to be *compassionate*, they need to be *creative*, they need to *fit the crime*, they must happen *immediately*, you must be *consistent*, and you ought to *teach* something about character building.

All the research, though, shows that despite these ideas racing through your mind as quickly as you might click on to multiple web sites, the truth is you need to keep only one question in mind:

Is this consequence enforceable?

When I do presentations around the country it is striking how few parents answer the question "What do you think is most important about consequence?" with the idea that it simply be enforceable. There is a wonderful scene from *Everybody Loves Raymond* that shows Ray trying to "lay down the law" to his twin sons. As he fumbles around for the right consequence, Ray escalates to familiar heights, finally grounding them "for life" and making them shut their eyes and go to bed right then—before noon. Deborah, his far more pop-parenting sophisticated wife, intervenes. She dismisses him with a brazen "I'll handle it!" and the spotlight then focuses on her own mind-bending confusion about doing the right thing (the show does aim to be balanced).

Now this is broad comedy to be sure, but it strikes a nerve and actually underplays what I hear on the parenting circuit, which is far more exaggerated. When both mothers and fathers create consequences in the heat of the moment, they threaten things like: "No TV forever"; "we're never going on a family vacation again"; "you have to break up with your boyfriend tonight"; or "I'm never cooking another meal."

Frankly, with so many considerations going through the post-boomer parenting mind, it's no wonder we become paralyzed and spew threats that even four-year-olds can parse out. As many of the youngest kids I've interviewed have reported to me: "I can tell from how my mommy says it, if she means the punishment or not!" And when I get those parents and kids together in the same room and watch them interact, even the tiniest tots' predictions are surprisingly accurate.

So the key is to quickly think whether the punishment you are threatening is enforceable, because if it is your child will know and the negative interaction will more likely than not end quickly.

SLOW DOWN—YOU'RE MOVING TOO FAST

Sometimes, Thinking Is Better than Acting

As parents have told me in numerous workshops, an important stop in coming up with realistic consequences—especially in the super fast-paced, twenty-first century world we live in—is to slow down the action.

1. Stop for a moment to think whether it is realistic and whom it will hurt more, you or your child.
2. Take a few deep breaths, which often encourage time to reflect.
3. Reduce your immediate threat by half before it leaves your lips.
4. Often it's best to delay giving a punishment until later.
5. Stop the interaction and (if safe) walk away from your child to cool off.
6. Come back later, when you and your child are calmer—and you've had time to think about a more realistic consequence.
7. Don't be afraid to replace an impulsive consequence for another, enforceable one—children learn more about the process of responsible reflection than they are damaged by 'inconsistency.'
8. Try not to give in to relentless pressuring and negotiating, no matter how clever. You are only teaching that if children nag long enough they will get their way.
9. Despite all these suggestions—with these sophisticated free-est generation kids—we all are provoked into unenforceable consequences.

> 10. In my view and increasingly according to law and changing mores—corporal punishment should be off limits. If you've run out of other consequences, it's time to seek out counseling.

None of these is avoiding the issue or giving in to your child, because whatever you chose to do, remember that teaching will come later.

Mary, who attended one of my workshops, reported that she had stopped the whining and humiliating public back talk of her daughter, Stephanie, on a play date by immediately declaring the play date over. Interestingly, Mary found that within a few minutes her daughter had moved on to feeling very loving and good about returning home. In fact, her freedom of expression had been nothing more than an expression of over-stimulation and fatigue.

A dad in an audience of elementary school parents reported that he actually stopped the car enroute to an amusement park after being called a "dork" by one of his kids in the back seat. With the car in the lot of a drive-through bank, he turned around, repeated the offensive word so there could be no mistaking what was so wrong, and then demanded an apology before he would move an inch closer to where they were headed—that new *Superman* ride at Six Flags the kids had been all hyped-up about for a month.

Again, the offensive child didn't even realize he had said something that crossed any line whatsoever, especially given the sib-dissing going on in the back seat, until dad named it and declared what the consequence would be: one he was absolutely prepared to enforce. Within seconds the entire tone of the trip changed, and everyone went on to have a pretty cooperative day. Not without its moments, but much, much better.

I am still a little taken aback after meeting with one mother, who'd attended several of my workshops, and hearing about the consequence for disrespectful talk she was willing to enforce. Mom told us all she'd actually brought her family home *one day early* from a vacation to follow through on her statement of what she would do if her kids didn't stop their unnecessary roughness toward her in the verbal department. Mom drew a gasp from the audience of parents. Her determination in the moment and the results were stunning to her as well. For the first time her kids actually "got" that freedom of expression did not include the freedom to wipe their feet on her like a doormat. It wasn't the last time any of them ragged on her again, but far less divisive talk occurred in their home until adolescence, when the battle over obscenity on the family's airwaves needed to be rejoined.

Once parents feel permission to set a limit on the free-est generation's freedom of expression, I am astonished by how creative post-boomer parents can be. I am not suggesting that any of these particular choices would be right for your family—*remember you are the expert of what's safe in your house*—but the following examples gave me something to think about.

In audiences from different parts of the country, numbers of mothers reported that they literally removed the doors from kids' rooms after their children continued to cross the verbal abuse line. In doing so, these parents were saying in effect, "Privacy is a privilege. If you don't respect me, for now I will not respect you." In another family, a dad actually disconnected the part of the circuit box in the basement that led to the kids' entertainment-center side of the house. He was stunned at how suddenly his children adjusted their way of speaking to him.

And in several other families, parents would not even disclose what sort of consequence they had in mind, violating all rules of post-boomer fair-play with: "If you call me that name one more time or keep pushing at me when I've said I can't take it anymore, some huge consequence will follow!" The kids, of course, would instantly stop all action and start badgering mom or dad about what this consequence might be. Interestingly, none of these successful parents would give an answer. Instead they actually escalated their purposeful vagueness: "I'm not saying anything yet, but it will be much more severe if you don't try to understand that what you said is off-limits."

The first time I heard this was from a father in an elementary school I visited almost every year. Each time the same audience of parents would ask him if this vague "non-consequence" was still working. Each year, much to my surprise, he'd nod his head. Most telling, his wife, who disapproved of this "unfair" tactic, grudgingly admitted that it did get their kids' attention, no matter what was going on.

There were no miracles in any of these houses (although I was taken aback that some of the preteens whose doors were removed actually preferred to keep it that way). But in almost every situation, kids finally "got" that their parents would not allow them to cross that line from free speech to trash talk.

Listen to your body, find your personal line, make clear to your child what he or she just said, or they won't know what you're talking about. Then create a consequence you can enforce. This is not enough, though; in order to engage your child's better, more considerate-self you must also take advantage of these opportunities to teach your children in a fuller, deeper way about why their backtalk was inappropriate.

Remember, in this post-boomer world they often really don't have a clue, and Bart Simpson isn't going to teach them, either.

CALMED DOWN?—TEACH NOW!

For the truly progressive and fair-minded parents out there who might be thinking that consequences alone are what I have in mind for backtalk, don't be concerned. Consequences are not always about punishment, but about opening up a possibility to teach values. Why? They create a pause in the action, one that offers an opportunity to talk and teach later, strengthening the hidden, more considerate-self of your child.

So, after the transgression, when everyone is calmer, and I mean physically calmer, not just emotionally, this is the time for you to teach and get across the message you'd like to communicate.

Such a moment of relative peace may occur ten minutes later, or it may be a few hours, since everyone's hard wiring is so different. But sometime after an event, and preferably before the evening ends, try to sit down with your child and very briefly review what happened earlier. Repeat again what words or tone or phrases crossed the line of acceptability. Explain briefly how this was connected to ending the play date or the vacation or not allowing the concert that weekend.

Then ask the following question: *"How can we do it differently next time?"*

Once the kids and you are calmer, it is quite amazing what kinds of creative ideas parents and children come up with. For example the father who described his explosion with his kids on the way to Six Flags reported that afterward, one of the boys suggested that they change seating arrangements every few minutes or hours, depending on how much they were getting on each others' nerves. This active problem solving is not only helpful to family functioning, but is also great for character building. It has been used with children as young as two-and-a-half to strengthen their skills at solving interpersonal situations and thinking before acting.

Why would this free-est generation, who seemingly "know no bounds," be open to consequences on their freedom of speech? The truth is that they *expect* a response to inappropriateness. Many kids have told me that they find it odd (even disconnected) when parents don't react! In their second family lives, out-of-line comments get an immediate response. Whether it's in the schoolyard, the classroom, during a play-date, or online, kids do not allow offensive comments to go unnoticed; in fact, this is part of the glue and connectedness they feel with each other.

And, this is why after parents draw a line in the sand, rather than their kids closing off communication, they sit up, take notice, and are able to hear what mothers and fathers need to say. As these examples illustrate, when parents speak in immediate, no-nonsense ways, kids' better-selves emerge, and they are more willing to "own" their unacceptable behavior.

Addressing the central issue of backtalk is vital (though, realistically, given our free-wheeling times expect no miracle of ever-considerate kid-speak) as you establish a foundation of expectations about communication. Without this basic civility it is impossible to move on to the more general realm of setting everyday limits that are effective with the free-est generation.

EVERYDAY DISCIPLINE: WHY LIMITS ALONE DON'T WORK TODAY—AND WHAT YOU CAN DO

When I was in middle school, my mother and I had a parent-teen standoff. As a child I was never spanked or beaten, but along with almost all of the kids in my greatest generation neighborhood, I was sometimes slapped, more as a reflexive reminder to pay attention than to hurt. In fact, all my close friends' mothers seemed to have slapping rights whenever we got out of hand. On this one day in my early adolescence, my mother and I were engaged in an argument over God knows what. She raised her hand in midair and suddenly without thinking, I grabbed her wrist and said, "That's it—don't ever do that again." The force of my clenched hand made her thin wrist seem terribly frail, turning upside-down the rules of engagement in our house forever.

When it comes to everyday limits, twenty-first century parents often complain that they feel frail on a "who's in charge" level, and these days it happens way before adolescence. As I've heard in many workshops, parents complain that they've taken away everything they can, but are overwhelmed nonetheless by kids' outrageous attitude and larger-than-life sense of entitlement. Why, ask so many mothers and fathers, do we have such trouble being in charge and creating consequences that count?

There is a fundamental and often overlooked reason very much connected to what has changed for parents and children of all ages in a post-boomer world. Follow me for just a moment down a seemingly random path. But with some patience, this idea will open your eyes to one of the main reasons today's mothers and fathers have trouble generally staying in charge of our children—and what you can do—without squelching your child's spirit or potential in any way.

THE POWER OF INSTRUMENTAL LEARNING—
A.K.A. VIDEO GAMES

The story begins with the difference between "classical" and "instrumental" learning. Classical learning, or as most of us think of it, "Pavlovian" conditioning, is a fundamental, very twentieth-century and greatest generation concept. It is linear: about cause and effect, behavior and response, crime and punishment. You might picture an animal being trained to salivate for food upon hearing a bell, or in reverse, someone being punished (probably zapped by a jolt of electricity) for engaging in a prohibited action. This theory of classical conditioning prevailed in both parenting and education for much of the twentieth century. There were rigid rules, straight-line desks (chalk and board instruction, as teachers call it), immediate consequences (regular spanking was the consequence of choice for almost nine out of ten American parents), and the most extreme consequence of all: the ultimate threat of ostracism from family and kin.

Then instrumental learning entered the scene. In this "Skinnerian" model (popularized by B.F. Skinner in the United States), learning happens in a process of discovery about cause and effect. In my graduate school psychology classes, for example, a pigeon would accidentally touch a horizontal bar and, *voila!* a pellet of food appeared! Nothing might happen for another few minutes while the pigeon just walked around in circles, until it accidentally hit the bar again. Then once again, a tasty morsel would instantly appear. Within a short period of time, just about every pigeon would move itself right near the bar, madly pecking away for more pellets.

Now, think about your children's experiences playing video games. The creators of these games know exactly how powerful instrumental learning is, especially combined with a dose of classical limits; they also know how important it is for today's kids to believe they are creating their own rewards, even if the expectations are designed by someone else.

Video games are so appealing, then, because they are designed to give kids a touch of disappointment (limits—you "die") and then an unexpected, but sudden burst of special-effects, positive reinforcement (bells and whistles, and being allowed to move on to the next level). Though a game may take a while to master, the reward keeps kids coming back for more. Both the most benign online games, Webkinz and the original SimCity, as well as the much more outrageous Grand Theft Auto and World of Warcraft, use this combo plan. Online poker could be the poster child of how classical and instrumental learning is as strong as Crazy Glue in getting kids' (and adults') attention.

For free-est generation children and teens, especially, yearning for some limits along with self-expression, a balance of classical conditioning and a dose of instrumental reinforcement is a remarkably effective combination.

A TOUCH OF 'CLASSICAL' LIMITS— A HEAPING OF INSTRUMENTAL CONSEQUENCES

Given the social fabric of a post-boomer world in which children's love of freedom constantly vies with a need for basic security, it is quite understandable why today's kids respond so well to the combination of classical limits and instrumental rewards (which should be mostly nonmaterial in nature). It may not seem "tough" enough to view consequences in this way, but it is realistic, it fits this era. And, most important, this approach will allow you to get across the expectations and the values you hold dear far more powerfully.

Now how does this look in real life? *First,* as I've indicated in the previous section, we need to spell out our expectations clearly. *Second,* we need to create consequences we can enforce, those we are willing to "go to the mat" for. This classical part of learning will never change.

Actually, unlike what we read in the popular press, my workshops around the country tell me that expectations truly matter to post-boomer parents who get a bum rap for being way too lenient. It's not a question of lenience, it's just that they are on the frontlines and viscerally know how much is changing—and how little of a collective adult voice they have to back them up.

Third, we must also reward genuine effort. It is essential to recognize when your children are doing right, not just impose consequences when they are doing wrong.

Parents often take for granted exactly those character-building behaviors that they most want their children to learn. When I ask mothers and fathers whether they've mentioned anything about a moment of "good" behavior, such as sharing with a sibling, being kind to an older person, exhibiting politeness toward a parent's friend, being immediately honest about a school grade, or showing restraint during a frustrating play date, I get the same response. Parents generally admit to me that they were glad when something like that happened but swiftly moved ahead managing the logistics of the day, usually without mentioning or acknowledging the good their child had done. We are just that busy!

The key to harnessing the power of instrumental conditioning is helping your child recognize when he or she is behaving according to expectations and to use positive reinforcement in irregular doses (remember, being too predictable means being tuned out by special-effects kids). This way you will "grow" more of that behavior. If we turn our rushed, managerial style of parenting into one that also notices the good, this leads not only to more effective parenting but to kids who develop a true sense of agency, i.e., self-direction and gen-uine self-worth.

But change takes time. In trying this out, it is important to be pa-tient. Kids will likely travel on roundabout and unexpected paths to-ward positive change.

PATIENCE REQUIRED:
MOST KIDS' MINDS ARE LIKE SLIPPERY WALLS

In workshops I've found the following image to be very helpful in developing patience as a parent, which is essen-tial to the process of changing kids' unwanted behavior:

1. Picture your child's mind to be a room with four slip-pery, bare walls. This is the state of kids' attention span in our fast-paced world. Slippery walls also reflect the sense you probably have that no punishment or teach-ing seems to stick with your kids for long.
2. A whole lot is thrown up against that wall by you—encouragement, reward, punishment, lectures—and sadly, just about all of it slides down the wall and is quickly forgotten.
3. When you adopt a balance of classical consequences and instrumental rewards, somewhere along the way a moment of clear limits and acknowledging the good sticks to that bare, slippery wall, and they learn.
4. Then before long, another lesson catches the edge of that first one. Two things have stuck to your child's developing brain. Now there's enough to build on: past lessons that stop future lessons from sliding into oblivion.

(continued)

> It takes longer than you would like. It's much less linear and more chaotic than you'd prefer. But sure enough, a substantial degree of what you wanted to teach finally sticks to that wall.

In fact, this is a fair description of the way many kids learn. We now know from brain imaging that the actual "hole" in the prefrontal lobe of kids' brains starts to fill in during adolescence. Kids' analytic, planning, and executive functioning gradually develops as a patchwork of connections, a slow leap forward in the evolution toward an adult mind.

EXAMPLES OF COMBINING CLEAR EXPECTATIONS— AND OCCASIONAL REWARDS

Damien was a boy who got on just about everyone's nerves. His whiny, complaining tone made him the butt of derision and name-calling by his siblings, parents, and kids in school. But Damien often did kind things for his parents or his brother and sister that were ignored. After some coaching, I got mom and dad to do two things: first, walk away from any interaction in which he was being annoying; second, every so often notice (with a smile or a few moment's "hanging" together) when Damien spoke in a less whiny tone, went out of his way to help his younger sister, or said "thank you" to his mom and dad. Within a few weeks, Damien's demeanor was starting to change around the house.

But this was just the beginning. Suddenly one day in school after this relatively peaceful time at home, Damien yelled at one of his bully classmates, "This school is supposed to stand for decency. If you can't treat me well, what in the world are you even doing here?" A teacher nearby heard Damien and said to his long-time tormenter, "He's right, you don't have to like him, but you have to tolerate his presence without putting him down." The two boys certainly did not become friends, and for a while Damien was ostracized, rather than overtly abused. But the teacher's standing-up for him felt good—just as being acknowledged at home felt good.

This change then unexpectedly morphed into something else, a sense of effectiveness that developed into a passion: Damien decided to join the swim team. Another few months passed, and this whiny little kid gradually developed patience, determination, and a newly "ripped" body. He still was occasionally annoying, but now he had a sense of accomplishment and self-worth that counterbalanced his behavior.

Randi wouldn't take showers, a habit her late-elementary and middle school friends noticed every day. Her mother was constantly making snide comments and unenforceable threats about her hygiene and hair. Night after night, they struggled around showering and freshening up, all to no avail. This swirl of bad feeling spread into Randi's willingness to do homework and increasingly was affecting her performance at school.

Again, I emphasized that mom not abandon her expectations for cleanliness (two showers a week was her minimum acceptable standard), but that she lose the threats and replace them with a positive, instrumental approach. Hearing me in the background, mom began noticing and acknowledging small moves by Randi to take care of the little things. At first, it might have been something as simple as taking her plate and putting it in the sink. No big fuss, no hyperbolic praise (we'll get into the uselessness of overpraising later), just every so often notice by mom of Randi's good behavior around tidiness.

Pretty soon Randi was picking up on these comments, and one night, independently and without any encouragement, she stepped into the shower for perhaps thirty seconds. Her hair was barely damp, but mom mentioned it in a positive way nonetheless and allowed a few extra minutes for watching TV together. Little by little, Randi began to take it upon herself not only to shower but to take the time to wash and "do" her hair and clothes in ways that actually created positive responses from her classmates.

Once again, this change opened up unexpected paths. Randi made a best friend who was an excellent student. They began to study together, spend time online together, and treat each other well. This is a big deal, of course, in the transition from elementary to middle school. Randi's standing improved both socially and academically, enough that she and her mother had to learn to deal with far more complex issues of "chilling here and there," as well as first curfews.

Finally, I consulted to a third family with two children, one kindergartner, the other in third grade, who regularly got under each other's skin. The kids seemed to bicker about absolutely everything. Their mother came to me after having taken away just about everything she could possibly think of in her attempts to classically condition them into more kindness toward one another—especially her older son. Key to the boy's attitude was his free-est-generation-style of ruthless negotiating every time mom tried to lay down the law. He knew every button to push until finally she would snap and send him to his room (which turned into yet another power struggle). He then would lash out with vengeful spite toward his younger sibling.

I encouraged mom to immediately end those negotiating escalations rather than join in, and to talk to her son in a quiet moment later about her expectations for some sib kindness. Just as important, I asked her to notice any slightly more positive interactions he might have with her or his younger brother. When he demanded a little less toughly or spoke to her with a slightly less strident tone, mom should occasionally acknowledge the difference. She might show her appreciation by a simple touch on the shoulder or by making sure to spend a moment or two of alone time with him. Note that mom did not resort to material goodies. As she realized, expressions of love and acknowledgement are most often much more powerful reinforcement for our kids than any other kind of reward. Soon, her son began engaging with her differently, not through endless negotiating, but through arts and crafts projects, one-on-one together.

Within months, the need to see me for consultations ended, as the tone between the siblings dramatically changed and he had stopped his relentless assaults to get the upper hand on mom. Instead of spending time complaining about each other, they were spending time doing crafts together. Of course, sibling spats didn't forever disappear. From that point on, though, this boy stopped pushing his mother toward the point of sudden explosion.

As each of these examples shows, balancing clear expectations and instrumental reinforcement helps kids develop their hidden true-self, their better sides of being more responsible for their actions and knowing right from wrong. After some kid blow-back, then moments of calm teaching, the confidence that results allows children of all ages to unexpectedly zigzag into new competence and even new passions.

Note that when I suggest that we balance limits with occasional praise, I truly mean it. In our twenty-first century world, adult praise needs to become a commodity that again has value, for it to be effective with these free-est generation kids.

LIMITS AND AUTHENTIC PRAISE—HOW WE WENT WRONG

One of those turning points, when something we take for granted suddenly changes meaning, occurred a few years ago. I share this story with parents everywhere I can, because post-boomer moms and dads have all been there: Sometime back when we used to have real winters, our area experienced a wonderful "weather event" that turned into every kid's dream, a snow day. I went over to the local sledding spot with our son, Sam, and a few of his friends, later to be joined by my wife Stacey and our daughter Leah. While we were standing amongst a huge crowd of parents and their free-est generation offspring, I noticed something through the Currier & Ives-like scene all around. From every spot on top of the hill, as kids of all ages from three to thirteen came back to their parents, I could hear enthusiastic shouts of "great job!" and "that was the best sleigh riding I've ever seen!"

I couldn't help but sense that most of the kids, bundled up in their thermal outerwear and looking like tiny astronauts, hardly registered their parents' loud proclamations of endless praise. In fact, what I did see were befuddled looks on kids' faces and even some eye-rolling, as if to say: "What are you talking about—'The greatest sleigh ride ever?' I'm just responding to the laws of gravity."

Remember to acknowledge only when you mean it, and not every time you notice a change for the better. I emphasize this because child rearing went terribly awry in the praise department with our kids, turning a powerful necessity into something so cheapened it became inauthentic and perhaps even destructive. Have you ever wondered whether the past thirty years' emphasis on robotically praising our kids has actually been good for them? And have you considered that there might be a link between rote, reflexive adult praise, and the proliferation of harsh reality-TV shows laced with "brutally honest criticism," as well as the ever-edgy tone of the second family? I believe these twenty-first century phenomena of "mean" might in part be a manifestation of our decades-long love affair with praise.

For a while, I and others in the child-rearing world had been sensing that the self-esteem movement (which began in the sixties and seventies after the discovery of family violence and hidden abuse behind closed doors) was a profoundly important contribution to understanding and ensuring the safety of our children. But by the nineties it had gone way too far and created unintended consequences. Three decades after its "discovery," boomers, post-boomers, and now the free-est generation have come to consider continuous praise a staple of life and a necessary precondition for work to be done.

All those "good job," "great work," and "that was the best ever" comments filtered down not just into our families but into educational philosophies that impacted our children every day. For years, when presenting to parent groups I'd noticed virtually the same plaque in just about every auditorium built after the sixties and early seventies. Behind me on the stage was the sentiment (literally written in stone) reminding us that our children are uniquely individual and that they need to be celebrated—a statement I totally agree with, at least in principle. But in real life something was "off," as I listened to parents and teachers valiantly searching for new ways to cook up a serving of praise, no matter its authenticity, no matter the challenge:

> "I love the color of this picture," Dianne, a veteran elementary school teacher, offers. "Where?" asks her little charge. "That touch of gray, way, way back there in the painting," Dianne responds. "But that's my fingerprint." "Good choice, anyway," Dianne continues. "But it was an accident; gray paint from the last painting was on my finger." "Exactly, and it looks terrific . . . great job!"

The language of praise has been institutionalized and ritualized. Kids don't just graduate from one grade to another, they celebrate their yearly accomplishment through *commencement exercises* once reserved just for true graduation. They no longer just write a report or a paper; at the end of the project they have a *book publishing party* for the entire class. And let's not forget those *certificates of participation,* handed out each week just for showing up, like so many first-place blue ribbons at a county fair.

Yet despite all this, despite the well-intentioned reasoning that went into building our kids' self-esteem and protecting their sense of self-worth, one couldn't help but notice their lack of response, and even that jaded look of boredom as kids got older, very fast! Ever since I read researchers Edward Deci and Richard Flaste's eye-opening work *Why We Do What We Do,* it became clearer to me what those blank expressions, dazed looks, and parental complaints of low motivation were about. Deci found that the more we praise children, especially when it is inauthentic and principally a child-rearing or educational strategy, the less kids want to do.

More recent works, such as psychologist Martin Seligman's *Authentic Happiness*, and Robert Brooks's *Raising Resilient Children*, have discussed the unintended negative effects of the self-esteem movement. Dependence on a continuous, inauthentic stream of positive feedback seems to be associated with less happiness and resilience, an inability to rely on oneself for honest appraisal, and shallow reserves of self-soothing patience to strengthen tolerance for frustration.

We needed to go through this deification of praise; we needed a period of "discovery" in the sixties and seventies to learn that kids required healthy self-esteem. We adults needed to realize how this had been either ignored or crushed behind the once drawn curtains of family life in America. This was part of what set the free-est generation free, allowing them a clear path toward believing they should be treated respectfully and could accomplish anything in life. But enough is enough!

FALSE PRAISE AND THE "MEAN" POP CULTURE

I believe the increase of false praise has inspired a hunger *for realistic feedback, leading our children to seek out a kind of engagement that may be unnecessarily harsh.* Think for a moment about the proliferation of nasty and flagrantly sharp-edged reality TV. In a world of cheapened praise in which children cannot count on genuine feedback from parents and too often even the educational system, they hunger for feedback that is brutally honest. From *American Idol* to *The Apprentice, The Real World, What Not To Wear, America's Next Top Model, Project Runway, America's Got Talent, Hell's Kitchen, Top Chef,* and *Made* (to name just a few), the core of each of these shows is bluntly delivered honest feedback. This exhilarating frankness, familiar to kids in their everyday peer-life, is a key to drawing them in.

The same can be said for the increasingly sophisticated nastiness of peer group life. "Mean girls" and "bad boys" no longer just rag on each other's appearance, as was the case in earlier decades. Dialogue in the second family is now a constant stream of highly charged, brutally honest feedback about *everything*. Nothing escapes the eye of the group, which makes adult over-praise seem surrealistic. The free-est generation is so blunt because, as one child told me, "Honesty is what friends are for. Sure it's tough, but somebody's got to say it." How different from the greatest generation's defense of "constructive" criticism: "I'm your parent . . . if I don't say it—who will?"

As their pop tastes demonstrate, our kids yearn for realistic feedback and genuine praise only when they deserve it. As too many kids today report to me, they can't rely on their parents to be honest because, "They love me, so they'll never be able to tell me the truth."

The issue with praise, then, is not just whether it creates greater self-esteem or motivation, but whether it leads adults to be seen as authoritative enough to be listened to, and honest enough to be trusted. If not, we will further encourage our children to seek authentic engagement and limits in the harsh world of reality TV, and especially in the peer group, online and in person.

USING PRAISE CORRECTLY
TO STRENGTHEN LIMITS AND TRUST

Practically speaking, this is one of the most difficult areas to address in terms of boomer and post-boomer behavior. For parents who grew up in those schools with plaques extolling our uniqueness, swimming (no, I would say "drowning") in a sea of "good job" and "that was the greatest," this will not be so easy to change. But for our kids' sake, so that they can absorb our love and trust, as well as for our own sense of authenticity, it is worth a try. Here's what to do:

First, only praise when you mean it. Remember, as I emphasized above (when combining clear consequences and instrumental learning), you do *not* have to find something to praise every time your child creates a product or does something better. Keep in mind, the research that finds the more kids are praised, the less they want to produce, so *occasional* acknowledgement is really better. It's preferable to give a short "okay" or "nice" as a response. And it's okay to pass on a comment or even, if you feel the drawing or the homework was second-rate or rushed, question whether your kids actually gave it their all: "Samantha, did you really try your best with that picture? It's pretty bad—nowhere near what I know you can do."

I know these words sound harsh. However, unless your child is temperamentally hard-wired to be unusually sensitive, such a comment will not damage, no matter what you've heard from the experts. Quite to the contrary, kindly delivered, honest feedback will demonstrate that you are authentically engaged with your children and that you can perceive when they're really putting effort in and when they're not. And kids most certainly know how hard they've tried. Teachers of our youngest children repeatedly tell me that even nursery schoolers respond best to honest feedback that mirrors their true effort, and are well aware when they've exerted real determination.

In workshop after workshop, parents tell me how difficult it is for them to move toward noticing and then praising their child's true effort, only if it is deserved.

But try you must. In a world ruled by *American Idol*'s Simon, your honesty couched with love and kindly delivered feedback will *not* crush your child's self-esteem, and will help him or her feel your authoritative guidance.

Second, praise efforts to manage temperament. In some ways your ability to create limits depends on how effectively you help children manage the demands of their own temperament. Why is this so? Temperamental characteristics often push kids to act up, even in the face of your repeated requests and limits. For example, they want the "stuff" now, whining tenaciously as if the world is coming to an end; unable to contain their anger, they angrily and reflexively smack a sibling; they say hurtful things, feeling overly-sensitive themselves; they balk at requests because they're scared of new situations. All of these apparent attacks on your limit-setting are actually pushed by kids' inability to manage their own temperamental vulnerabilities.

The real challenge, then, and the place where you can get the most limit-setting bang for your buck, is to praise effort that, as I call it, runs counter to a child's basic temperament. Remember how deeply ingrained and hard-wired these temperamental characteristics are. Therefore, actions that demonstrate a child's genuine effort to go against problematic tendencies of temperament should be reinforced more regularly than others.

And, always remember: praise small, praise quick, praise genuinely.

Thad, a middle-schooler whose temperament was one of constant movement and difficulty maintaining interest when there wasn't immediate positive feedback, was about to leave his after-school club. The teacher was not giving him enough attention and was occasionally critical of his commitment, though no more so than toward anyone else. Of course Thad, a true child of the free-est generation, had the good sense to know he deserved respectful treatment, but also the bad sense to immediately disengage from any activity or adult that proved to be too frustrating.

It was a major turning point in his life when with my encouragement, his parents briefly acknowledged how he'd managed to hang in from one meeting to another, and not impulsively walk away from the club—temperamentally his natural reaction.

In the end, he managed to stick with this till the very last meeting—and even make friends with the teacher. This lesson stuck to the "slippery walls" of his mind. It taught Thad the value of working against the negative side of his temperament and led to fewer battles over limits at home. Doing more homework, keeping his room just slightly above toxic levels of gross neglect, even sitting still long enough to have a conversation at dinnertime all improved slightly as Thad learned he could deal a bit more easily with the demands of his hard-wired low frustration tolerance.

Thad's better-self began to show up more when he needed to hang in with unpleasant tasks, leading to a less hassled connection with his parents. The balance of encouragement and acknowledgement left him feeling stronger for dealing with the ramped-up demands that high school would soon demand. At the end of the long ordeal, Thad told me with a sense of total ownership that sticking with the club was his biggest accomplishment in life, ever!

In another family, fifteen-year-old Lila could only speak to her younger sisters in the haughtiest and, as the family called it, the "skankiest" tones imaginable. Her parents, who consulted me about this, reported that Lila had been tenacious and overly sensitive since she was a toddler—a child impossible to create limits for. The birth of her two younger sisters was a trigger that exacerbated her "temperamental bossiness" into almost tyrannical behavior, and she become even more resistant to parental authority.

The entire picture changed after I encouraged mom to acknowledge when Lila managed to lower the "bitchy" factor in her tone just a decibel or two. Recognizing how ingrained this personality characteristic was, it was essential to notice the smallest change toward the positive, again informed by the balance of expectations and instrumental learning I wrote about earlier.

Notice the tiny difference between Lila's: "Dorks stop talking right now!" to "Please, stop sounding so dorky!" It may sound almost indistinguishable, yet with these seemingly insignificant changes, followed by mom or dad's brief acknowledgment, Lila began to speak to her younger sisters in a more humane way. And other sources of friction around the house that had required parental limits—her siblings' understandable desire to occasionally visit her in the inner sanctum of her room, to play with some of her make-up—lessened, leaving the capacity for a few moments of non-bickering family time. Years later, mom and dad's judicious balance of expectation and praise had freed Lila from what once seemed a life-long sentence of chronic irritability unless she got her way.

The same impact of acknowledgment for behaving against temperamental type can be seen with Ethan, a seven-year-old who had been shy his whole life. In Ethan's case, unlike that of so many other kids, limits meant getting him to *do* things, rather than to *not* do them. Each new group—a different school, a new class, a different set of family members or kids and teachers, was a mountain for this shy boy to climb. But the road became considerably less steep as his parents took the time to praise the small steps toward new situations that he managed.

After a while, mom told me, "You know, it was hard for me to believe that simply saying, 'I saw the way you moved closer to those kids playing Pokemon' would even be remembered the next time and would give him courage to take another step." Gradually, with mom's notice of such small efforts, Ethan made a couple of friends on the outer fringes of the group. Those friends were a gateway into partially conquering his shyness and allowed him to enter new worlds: recess play at school, afternoon activities, and finally best friends. By his own actions, and with minimal parental support, Ethan created a bit of confidence he had so lacked.

In one of the more dramatic examples of praising effort to manage one's own temperament, I will never forget the following story:

A not-too-athletic eleven-year-old girl, Allison, had talked her parents into allowing her to join an after-school girls' basketball league. They gave in despite her temperamental difficulty adapting to competitive situations. Allison would well up with tears or break down into crying jags the moment things did not go her way. By first noticing and then quietly praising her effort to try to hold back, an astonishing thing happened. After about the third game, Allison shot the ball (the first time she'd actually touched it all season) and made the shot—*except it was in the wrong basket*. You can imagine her teammates' reaction, and this sensitive girl broke down sobbing uncontrollably.

Her mom, Denise, remembering my words, went over to Allison

for a second on the sidelines; patiently she asked Allison if she could calm down, waited, *and then pounced the second Allison began to cry just a little bit less.* At this moment, mom briefly acknowledged her daughter's toughness for being able to harness her tears just a little. Within a few minutes, the girl's crying had stopped, and a couple of moments later she asked the coach herself whether she could be put back in the game. On the way home, Allison turned to her mother in the car and shocked this post-boomer by saying, "That was the greatest game I ever played. I was about to give up like I always do, and I didn't."

Redefining engagement through limits asks that parents learn to praise appropriately. We now know that one must praise a child's efforts rather than the product. We know that praise needs to be moderate and authentic (rather than reflexive and overblown) and that kids understand from the preschool years how to separate inauthentic from deserved kudos. Lastly, we also know that *authentic praise* when balanced with clear expectations is a potent combination, especially when we acknowledge effort to rein in natural temperament. Our kids' better-selves emerge when we engage them through authentic limit-setting that fits these times.

But even as we redefine how we set limits in family life, we also know that in a techno-driven-peer-group-pop-culture-post-boomer world, forces beyond anything we could have ever imagined gather out there and invisibly invade our homes, as early as elementary school.

To meet this challenge, to expand the envelope in a manner that keeps our children engaged with us and safe, means redefining how the free-est generation comes to enjoy the privileges of growing up.

EFFECTIVE LIMITS MEAN EARNING PRIVILEGES— CURB THIS ENTITLEMENT PROGRAM

"What do you mean, I can't go over to Michael's house? It's Friday afternoon and that's what kids do when the week's over"—"But everyone is

going to the mall and hanging out! I'll miss everyone."—"Don't you dare call Samantha's mom to find out about whether she'll be there. I'll never talk to you again, and I'm going anyway"—"I can be anywhere I want on-line. What are you going to do, track me every minute?"—"Mommy, I am not too young to wear a thong! All the third graders have them."

Today's kids 'who know no bounds' believe privilege is an entitlement. "Privileges do not need to be earned," think free-est generation children of all ages. "They are a basic right of childhood."

Nothing illustrates this better than the exchange I reported to clinicians in *Breaking Through to Teens*, one I had with Kyle, a whiny adolescent, who complains that his curfew isn't late enough.

Kyle: I've got it all planned out. I'll get my father just when he comes home from work. He hasn't talked to my mother yet. Then I'll talk to my mother later. I'll say that everybody's going, so I have to go. See I don't want to make it a choice, but I'll just get her thinking about what time it should be and how I'll get there and stuff like that. It's a method called distraction. I learned it watching *Court TV.*

Ron: So you're not asking permission from either of them. Do your mom and dad strike you as the type of people who like being told what they have to do?

Kyle: Are you kidding? They never like to be ordered around . . . so what's your point?

Ron: That you're ordering them into this concert idea.

Kyle: Okay, so I'll try *this* instead. I'll blackmail them—like "if you don't let me go I won't do anything around the house anymore."

Ron: Now you sound like a three-year-old. Do you really want to go to this concert? Because, no offense intended, these approaches are pretty babyish. Why should your parents allow you such a grown-up privilege?

(Long pause. Kyle is angry.)

Kyle: Maybe I do need their permission . . . It's my first concert, so I'll make it an early curfew, like 2 A.M.

Ron: I'm glad you don't have to negotiate anything for me, because I can't believe how bad you are at this. Do you really think that 2 A.M. is something they're going to agree to for the first time? Remember, they do tend to worry.

Kyle: It's just the beginning; it's what they call a *starting point* in negotiating.

Ron: But you're going to make them so nervous that it will only backfire on you. I guess I know where I'll find you Friday night—at home. That's where you'll be.

Kyle's maddening belief system is not unusual. He expects the world to be his oyster and actually can't comprehend that privileges may require a little work. Remember the empathic envelope or container I described at the beginning of this chapter? After decades of fragmented living and relaxed social attitudes, kids of the freest generation do not grasp the concept that the envelope will only expand in response to proving themselves capable of handling privileges.

Many post-boomer parents mirror this attitude. They also believe that privileges are entitlements that come along with growing older, rather than something that needs to be earned by the children they are in charge of. We're all of us caught up in our societal context. We can't help but be, so attitudes about children's entitlement that I encounter around the country have an eerie equivalent in the wider social, educational, and financial contexts of the mid-nineties to the present time.

Until the recent credit crisis, parents' own shop-till-we-drop needs were often matched by sophisticated kindergarten-consumers with an early sense of access. In 2005 the Yankelovich Youth Monitor reported a new trend that powerfully demonstrates this: casual dining, significant family purchases, and even vacations are increasingly directed by kids, with mothers and fathers asking their young charges for guidance on all manner of discretionary spending.

The belief has become widespread that feeling good about oneself is an entitlement of childhood. Well-documented grade inflation in high schools and universities has lifted expectations to such an extent that privileged families pay small fortunes to have their kids tutored for the SAT's and private schools. Certificates of participation are handed out weekly to kids from all socioeconomic backgrounds just for showing up. And most pervasive for an entire country is the ubiquitous credo: "if you believe you deserve something, you are sure to get it," a phrase that both adults and kids repeat as a personal mantra on dozens of competitive reality-TV shows each week.

Now who wouldn't want this sense of endless possibilities for our children? There is no way in such a context that either kids or parents could possibly be immune to the idea that privileges are something of a natural entitlement rather than being earned through trustworthy behavior. How can parents, living in a sea of entitlement, put up much of a fight when their kids proclaim with great authority: "This is what I want—and, as a kid, this is what I'm entitled to."

Speaking to thousands of kids and parents, I've learned that most four-to eight-year-olds expect play-dates on-demand. Nine- to twelve-year-olds expect to go to the mall with their parents and then separate for brief periods to wander off on their own. Early teens believe it is a right of passage to be dropped off and stay at the mall alone, as well as to "chill" at someone's house after school whether a parent is around or not. Fourteen-year-olds negotiate to go to parties without adults present; fifteen-year-olds start agitating to be allowed to go to rock concerts, first with their parents and soon without. As they move through high school, *week-night* concerts are all the rave. Sixteen-year-olds expect to be enrolled automatically in driver's ed, and a license is the next inevitable privilege, along with the use of a car, or even in some cases a car of their own.

None of these privileges is inherently wrong. But they are not earned or tailored to a child's particular temperament or learning style or to the developing trust of a parent, just attached to reaching a certain age—by far the most invisible entitlement program that exists in the country.

In my practice and during my workshops I see the results of the family envelope expanding without a child gradually earning privileges. Much like an economy that rapidly expands, when the envelope opens up too quickly, "bubbles" form. To paraphrase Alan Greenspan, the former head of the Federal Reserve, kids experience "irrational exuberance." The popping bubbles we hear all around us are not only corporate catastrophes, but the sounds of these kids, their horizons expanded with unearned access, exploding and imploding. When raised with an envelope that can't contain them, the free-est generation explodes through high-risk behaviors, through substance use and abuse, through sexual precocity. They implode self-destructively by cutting themselves, purging themselves, piercing themselves, and announcing their foibles to the world online.

At the same time, because all these issues worry youngsters, not just adults, they secretly yearn for their hidden-selves, their more compassionate, creative, and loving sides, to be safely held by a firmer envelope at home. Kids want their freedom and fun, to be sure, but as children of all ages tell me every day, they also want to feel more secure.

This is not the "ordinary grind" of daily life, like acceptable family discourse or sibling spats or the evening routine I discussed earlier. We are into different territory here—how the limitless world touches kids and how our kids enter into that wild post-boomer world. In order to help children and teens pass through increasingly dangerous currents, we must begin to ask them to earn these privileges they've come to expect.

"How?" parents always respond. I answer simply, "By earning your trust."

EARNING YOUR TRUST

To protect our children and help them to become their best-selves, we must turn the notion of parent-child trust entirely on its head.

Instead of parents exclusively feeling they must earn their children's trust (by being consistent, fair, present, keeping our word), it is just as essential that kids understand they must earn parents' trust in order for the envelope of privileges to open up.

Many post-boomer parents ask me what "earning mother's or father's trust" means. A simple example is that kids starting in elementary school, and certainly moving forward through middle school, must learn to keep their word. If your child tells you that he or she is going to be home on time, let's say five-thirty, earning your trust means showing up at five-thirty, not six.

This exacting definition isn't about being rigid or moral. I've learned over the years that contrary to popular belief, kids expect each other to keep their word in the peer group; it's we parents who put less emphasis on establishing a track record of trust. I've also learned that those fifteen minutes actually mean something we should pay attention to: the beginning of playing with the edges of trust or signaling just the kind of behavior we should be on the lookout for.

Johnny is fifteen minutes late, because he is copying someone else's composition, exactly the reason he was referred to me in the first place.

Selma has arrived home twenty minutes after her curfew because the kids were in a friend's unsupervised house tormenting another child with aggressive text messages.

Herbert is late because he's had a few drinks and suddenly found himself in a dangerous, sketchy part of town.

A child keeping his or her word means something: it is a sign of reliability and not keeping one's word is often the precise moment that kids are doing exactly the opposite of what they have promised. Holding them to this standard, and being cognizant about what a child might be doing with that extra time, is another powerful way in which parents can show authentic engagement and enforce limits.

As a requirement of trust, parents must weigh whether their children are straight with them about where they're going, whom they'll be with, and what they will be doing (more or less). Truthfully, until we develop GPS systems in cell phones (something that is nearer than we think), it is hard to know where any child is, given today's connectivity and the ability of the second family at earlier ages to seamlessly cover for each other using cells, text messaging, and beepers.

This was brought home to me over a decade ago in a stunning lesson I've written and spoken about often that seemed extreme at the time, but by now has become almost ordinary. A young adolescent was able to make his way halfway across the country to see his girlfriend. Of course, in the sixties and seventies many kids hitchhiked. But what was shockingly new to me was that this boy was able to go so far afield without his parents actually knowing he was away. They thought he was in town and sleeping at a friend's house. Given all the cell phone back-up and the ability of everyone in the kid-network to seamlessly cover for him, mom and dad did not have a clue until several days had passed. I thought this was an aberration—until I began hearing tales of undetectable wanderlust many times over. Another youngster, two weeks after this first boy's adventure, made it all the way to *Thailand*, also without his parents knowing he was out of town. He relied on credit cards, his cell phone, and that cyber-connected wall of silence of the second family.

In a world that gives kids such an unruly amount of freedom and such a sense of entitlement to privileges, earning trust serves a double function. It keeps kids safer by letting the envelope expand as slowly or quickly as their track record allows; and, because privileges are tied to earning trust, it strengthens the hand of parents who so often feel overwhelmed.

BEING RELIABLE

Kids Earning Privileges the Old-Fashioned Way

Kids today like to be thought of as reliable. They are proud of being trusted and put less emphasis on rebellion than generations past. Parents need to learn signs that a child is reliable and is trying to earn your trust. These are not foolproof. There is always a chance of being fooled or unpleasantly surprised, but knowing the signals is a start. It builds an ethic of earning privileges and pride in growing up. A few basic signs:

1. Keeping one's word about the small things—time home, calling as had been agreed, being (pretty) honest about who's around in others' houses.
2. Your internal feeling that what your child says makes sense—pay attention when it doesn't add up—you're probably on to something. The truth usually flits across your mind and you ignore it.
3. Both you and your partner get the same—or at least a similar enough story. Kids can only play us against each other if we don't bother to talk to each other.
4. Giving you enough time to truly think about a decision—feeling less like a hostage to time-pressure makes you feel more trusting.
5. Owning their behavior—without torturous explanations or excuses.
6. Your child is not afraid to tell you the truth—even if it's not something you don't want to hear. This is a hall-

(continued)

mark of mutual trust—in your child and your being a
reasonable, firm parent.

7. Your child has a couple of good friends, regular play-
dates and receives calls—a sign of trustworthiness with
peers.

8. Other parents are truthful around you—and do not
hold back important information you then hear about
later. This openness usually indicates that your child is
acting within acceptable bounds when you're not
around.

9. Your own growing sense of trust—be clear-eyed,
but be open to seeing and enjoying your child's matu-
ration.

EARNING ACCESS TO THE NEXT 'MUST' EVENT

*When all is said and done about entitlement and privileges, the most pow-
erful way to create engagement around limits is to use the next big event as
something kids need to earn through their reliable behavior. Remember the
balance of consequences and rewards described above. Consequences ought
not only be in the form of taking away highly coveted privileges and events;
rather they should be used as positive instruments with which to earn trust
and the privileges of an expanding envelope.*

A surprising reality about childhood, especially as it has revved-
up with endless possibilities (a semi-nightmare for most frazzled parents), is that parents have far greater leverage than they think to ask
kids to earn trust. Let's face it, every week brings another birthday
party, a group-mall date, or as children get older, a late-night concert.
Interestingly, regardless of attention issues or learning problems, few
children have difficulty staying focused on the next "I-have-to-go-or-
else-I'll-die!" event that's about to happen. In fact, once parents sign
on to this "earning privileges" concept, they actually find they have

more leverage as their child gets older and *must* be part of whatever is going on.

A mother in one of my workshops really caught the group's fancy when she reported that if her child is twenty minutes late from a weekend evening get-together with friends, the consequence is that he has to be home twenty minutes earlier the next week. His late curfew was a privilege, she reasoned, not an inalienable entitlement, one that needed to be earned anew each week. He could "work" those twenty minutes back with future punctuality. From my vantage point on the stage, I could see almost every single parent nodding in agreement with an "aha" look these tough critics don't easily express.

A father in another school reported taking a cell phone back from his eleven-year-old when she didn't use it as it was meant, to call and let him know where she was and that she was safe. She could earn it back if she used it correctly after a two-week break. "It was eye-opening to me," he said, "how quickly I got her attention when she realized the cell phone was a privilege and not something that came with the territory of being a preteen." Suddenly his daughter's better-side emerged: a first-time real discussion of where and with whom she spent time followed this exchange.

Even parents of younger kids, those in elementary school, feel empowered and engaged when we turn entitlement into a process of earning. "I never thought a birthday party was anything that should or could be a result of her cooperating with me more during a get-together the week before. By toning down her brattiness in front of others, as I'd asked her to several times at last week's event, she earned the right to attend the next party. Now my daughter looks at me with a sense of pride at having worked at the right to be going. With all her demands I didn't know she had it in her to be considerate of me."

This philosophy may also serve you extremely well down the road as your kids are starting to ("Oh no!") drive, when the difference between free rein over a car and slowly earning the privilege to one's wheels can be a *lifesaver.* As one keenly aware father told me, "In this area I actually feel like a real parent. I'm so motivated to be sure that he's okay we've made each step he takes dependent on passing the one before. And on top of this, he knows that there is zero-tolerance for any moving violation—no explanation will do."

This teen's better self, his more cautious and thinking side, emerged as he proudly earned the privilege of access to a car.

What is wonderful about turning the entitlement notion upside down is that it gives today's parents a chance to reward kids for trustworthiness. And kids of the free-est generation, as I've suggested, learn far better when they create their own independence through earning than they do when limits are entirely about "stuff" or privileges being taken away. In this new age, children of all ages feel much more agency and self-worth when the envelope of privilege expands gradually and as a result of their own actions.

By the way, remember Kyle? After our dialogue in which I emphasized the need to earn his parents' trust, he talked to them together. They flipped out, just as he had predicted, but after a while Kyle's tone softened and his parents started to settle down. The atmosphere changed dramatically and he said that since this was his first concert he would only stay out until 11:30, go with a friend his parents knew, and have his parents pick him up afterwards. Feeling taken into account, they agreed.

After a fitful start, Kyle was beginning to earn his right to privileges rather than expecting them as an inevitable entitlement. It was the first moment of his better-self emerging, one with more empathy toward others, even his parents, than had previously been seen.

LIMITING THE SCATTERED BRAIN—TURNING BRITNEY, MP3, & MTV INTO YOUR ALLIES

Finally, in our frenetic and scattered world, engagement through limits cannot be established without boundaries on screen time. As many studies show, human engagement is crowded out by screen time at all ages. Dramatically dividing parents and kids, this disconnection and loss of interpersonal leverage is vastly underestimated.

I believe we are overly concerned (though not without reason, of course) about the objectionable content so often found on these screens, and not concerned enough about the disconnection caused between kids and their equally plugged-in parents. There is no way around this fact: to feel authentic engagement with parents, the freeest generation cannot have total on-demand screen access.

This concern, the almost invisible smog of disconnection in a digitally driven universe, is one of the most intense topics in my workshops with parents and educators. From those discussions I have learned many surprising ways to limit access—and in the process create authentic engagement with kids' better, more communal selves:

Delay, delay, delay. Almost the same way one would think about sexuality and substance use, delaying kids' absolute access to screen time is essential.

The portability of laptops adds to the problem, so parents should hold off on buying that laptop until school curriculum forces the issue. Keep a desktop in your bedroom or in the family room for as long as you can. While you will surely be swimming against the tide, lobby your school that homework should not be completely computer-driven until the later grades (hopefully high school), or you will rarely see your children again. Try not to allow yourself to be lured into getting TVs for the kids' bedrooms until you can't stand it anymore. All they'll need then is a portable fridge and you can kiss them goodbye. For their safety as well as family connection, and for as long as you can, use software that allows some degree of transparency in terms of where your kids wander online.

Limit screen time through incentives. Around the world, a quiet revolution is taking place in education, one that is a political lightning rod and is flying mostly under the radar because of its controversial nature.

Dozens of programs already exist in which consequences and incentives are combined: families and their children are strongly expected and then paid (these payments are called "conditional cash transfers") to visit health centers, to keep their kids in school, and even to read books. After so much experience with so many families, I've come to the conclusion that positive changes on some heretofore-intractable issues may need a balance of classical limits and this sort of concrete incentive to gain traction. The practice also works well for screen access.

I began to understand this many years ago in one of the first schools I consulted to. One family attended a yearly workshop I gave for about a decade. At every visit they would report on the following imaginative approach to limit TV: Each child had an allowance (creating a limit) of $3.50 for screen time. Each show cost fifty cents, except for public television, which only cost a quarter. Every year I'd ask whether this arrangement "held." They and their friends, some who'd adopted a similar approach, affirmed that the kids not only watched less TV but in fact preferred the increasingly available educational shows on cable.

This once-innovative approach seems quaint by now with the exponential increase of kid access to all kinds of screen time, but the underlying balance of limits and incentives is just as effective. Consider some of the examples below and pick those that match your child's temperament, your ability to enforce guidelines, and the screen demands of your kids at home.

In increasing numbers of workshops, I've heard from parents who claim that they allow no video games at all during the week, but in return permit semi-endless gaming (a few hours per day) during the weekend. Since these parents usually know each other, I can easily tell from neighbors' reactions whether this combination of limits and incentives really works. Other parents admit that they are unable to completely banish screen time during the week. As an alternative they tape, TIVO, or DVR favorite weekday programs to be saved for weekend and vacation screen time marathons.

Still other parents, especially with kids whose computer demands seem more intense, allow a limited amount every day, including weekdays. The central question for these mothers and fathers is whether TV or online pursuits come before or after homework is done. For example, Mary finds that with her easily frustrated sixth grader, Noah, letting him spend about an hour on any screen of his choice and then insisting he move on to homework works well. Mom reports that allowing Noah to unwind creates just the right incentive for him to settle down into doing his work. In another school, Christine needed to reverse limits and incentives. With her daughter, Kat, she found that homework was best done first, with the incentive of screen time allowed when all assignments were completed. Of course, initially Christine discovered that Kat raced through her work in order to perch herself online. So mom needed to readjust and permit screen time only if she could check how much effort had been put into the assignment and how well it had been done.

I laughed when I heard about another family whose early adolescent son, Benny, made the case that he needed to "decompose" (he meant "decompress") for a while after coming home from school. This decomposing session always started with the TV on and Benny surfing from station to station until he snoozed for about an hour. Benny was right. The decks were now clear for him to begin his tasks for the evening.

Since undivided attention from parents is something the free-est generation craves, time together itself can be an incentive that limits the desire for screen time.

More and more parents tell me they offer the incentive of themselves as a reward for less time spent glued to a screen.

It is fascinating that the oldest, most old-fashioned moments together such as reading before bedtime, snuggling on the couch, or going for a ride to the mall, can be so effective in limiting the contemporary need for digital connections. As kids get older and the stakes get higher (starting in mid-elementary school), time together can take on many forms. Post-boomer parents proudly tell me of offering to go to concerts with their children in exchange for less passive time spent online. For other families, the cultural bar may be set at a different level, as in the case of the father and son I know who frequented WrestleMania together, instead of spending nights disconnected, each on their own computers. As dad told me, "Yeah, I know, it's not the most respected thing to be doing with your child, but hey, it beats never seeing him while he's drifting off online."

Finally, a pattern I've recently noticed is the number of parents and kids who join fantasy leagues and video games online *together* for a limited time every night. It may not be an inspiring thought, but the ranks of game enthusiasts now include the very parents who were supposed to be setting limits. Before harshly judging this, consider that the shared time with mom or dad on these games often proves to be extremely effective. This incentive limits the fantasy games from entirely taking over, as kids find social networking at home rather than with total strangers across the globe.

The producers of the highly acclaimed PBS documentary *Growing Up Online* have offered some of the shared wisdom of kids, parents, and experts about ways to deal with a digital world. Following are their suggestions:

GROWING UP ONLINE

Taming Your Kids' Wild Frontier

Rachel Dretzin, Writer-Producer, PBS *Frontline*

Rachel Dretzin is writer-producer of PBS *Frontline's Growing Up Online*. Through this heralded documentary Rachel's suggestions represent state-of-the-art guidelines for parents seeking to protect and guide their children. First and foremost, Rachel believes that the exclusive focus on sexual predators and the violent content of online material, while real and serious concerns, are somewhat of a distraction. Dretzin believes that most kids have managed to absorb lessons about cyber-safety. Because of this, parents need to recognize other subtle and prevalent problems kids have to face growing up online. Here are some suggestions:

- Middle school, in particular, is a danger zone for internet use. By the time kids are in high school, they're able to be far more private, sophisticated and selective.
- We parents need to know our kids online as well as we know them offline. This is especially true in the areas of social networking and too often the web-bullying that goes on in many homes at night.
- If we teach kids to love books before they reach early adolescence, it is a window of time during which they can learn to treasure the written word as well as words and images on screens—this may cut down on screen-dependence.
- Kids who have trouble online are also at risk offline. At the same time the internet does not have the power to destroy otherwise healthy kids.
- Believe in the "family computer." For as long as possible, keep your computer in a common room, dining area, in your bedroom—anywhere kids know you'll be around and walking by.
- Learn the internet along with your kids. Learn to speak online language so you can communicate with your

(continued)

> children about this area from an informed place. In other words, don't rely on authorities to handle this problem. Get in on the ground floor with them.
> - Lobby your school for classes on "internet civics" from the earliest grades. Teach kids how their words sound online, the impact they have on others, and the ways to screen out intrusions into their academic focus and their social lives.

In all these ways then, mostly by turning old assumptions upside down so they fit the free-est generation and its parents, limits must be redefined from decades past. Once kids are authentically engaged at home by a demand for personal respect, a balance of consequences and rewards, earning privileges and genuine praise, their more cooperative, loving-selves emerge with the very same parents whose demands they once dismissively opposed.

The stage is now set for a kind of authentic engagement through talking and listening that would have been impossible, no absolutely incomprehensible, for the greatest generation and most of its children ever to have imagined. To make this happen, we again must move beyond twentieth-century bromides about getting kids to open up and learn how our children are just waiting for us to enter the new world with them.

And, post-boomers are finally the group of parents who are willing, even eager, to meet this challenge. Clear the decks for some down-and-dirty coffee talk.

6

ENGAGEMENT THROUGH LISTENING

These Kids Talk to Everyone— Helping Them Talk More to Parents

*O*UR KIDS DON'T TELL US *what's really going on," says Marie, a mother in one of my workshops. "And it seems bizarre that they won't. After all, we're not crazed parents; we really do try to listen. We're not big punishers. We've told our kids: 'No matter what you've done, we'll try to understand, rather than find out later because they haven't told us the truth.' And you know what?" this mom says speaking for many, "I'm afraid they're telling me a lot less than I told my mother growing up in our pretty wild house. The funny thing is that kids talk to their friends online every night of the week. I just don't get it."*

Marie is not alone in being perplexed. After all, one of the most amazing characteristics of the free-est generation is that under the right circumstances, they *are* actually able to talk to adults, teachers, and most surprisingly, to their parents, as well. Let's face it: many boomers would have died before disclosing their adventures with sex, drugs, and rock 'n' roll to their typically more authoritarian parents. Or at the other end of the spectrum, some flagrantly threw their rebellious experimentation right into parents' faces. So whether it was a tight-lipped "don't ask, don't tell" atmosphere around the house or wild acting out, neither resulted in much constructive discussion.

My experience is that boomer and post-boomer parents, having grown up with flexible social values, can be extremely effective conversational partners for their children, but only if we understand the secrets of getting twenty-first century kids to engage with us in discussion.

On the surface this shouldn't be too hard, since the free-est generation is the gabbiest group of kids I've ever seen compared to any generation before. With endless technological access and early immersion in the language of social-emotional intelligence, not to mention the graphic discourse of reality TV, today's kids are engaged in "all talk, all the time."

Then why do so many of today's "hip," worldly mothers and fathers feel almost as much out in the cold as their far more rigid "old-world" parents were?

The answer is that important aspects of the post-boomer culture get in the way, unnecessarily dividing today's potentially accepting parents from kids, and just as important, adults from each other. First, let's look at what may inhibit your child from being the more open youngster he or she would like to be with you. Then we'll focus on the ways in which we communication-sophisticated parents inadvertently close today's kids down.

WHAT STOPS KIDS—FEAR OF RETRIBUTION

Behind the wall of silence I described above—starting from the earliest years—there are sanctions against discussing kid-to-kid issues with adults. Even kindergartners, because of their pseudo-teen attitudes and tastes (those "five-going on fifteen-year-olds") already understand the concept of allegiance to the child universe. When it comes to "private" matters, from popularity to bullying during recess, parents and adults are cordoned off by the group because they might actually listen and do something. This is a major post-boomer worry for children, becoming more pronounced at earlier ages, especially as kids reach late elementary school years. Peer sanctions include sophisticated social revenge—gossip, ostracism, even whisper smear campaigns—against kids who cross the line.

Clinicians around the country have told me in many workshops that revenge is no longer simply a theme for movies or the stage. Veteran counselors describe hair-raising stories about the backlash facing just about any child who reveals specific details at home. Anything can be said in kid-world, of course, but as a child you need courage and a very wise parent to step forward and break the code without paying a price. Thankfully, as I will discuss, this is becoming increasingly possible the more we recognize the realities contemporary parents and kids face.

I began to notice this phenomenon over fifteen years ago when I wrote about Phillip, a young adolescent who took a chance and told his mother that he and some of his friends had been drinking beer in the garage. Believing back then the "old-think" notion that kids secretly wanted to be held accountable by the adults around (rather than wanting freedom above all else), I encouraged Phillip's mother to act on her instinct, to reveal this to a trusted school counselor. Instead of calming things down, word immediately spread across the kid network. A short-lived backlash was to be expected, but Phillip was totally ostracized for an entire year. Both his mother and I had imagined some blow-back but not anything like what happened. Such was the increasing power of the second family by the early to mid-nineties.

More recently, Zack, another child in a small town, talked to his dad about petty stealing that was going on in the locker room. Zack thought about it quite a while before approaching him; then with careful diplomacy, and trying to protect the kids' identities, dad spoke to the most trusted teacher in his grade. Zack was ostracized and verbally taunted not just by the other boys, but by most of the girls too.

This is another sea change in the realm of vengeance; behind that wall of silence girls participate as well—and with great zeal.

Listen to the hard-edged realities of the free-est generation (and the tremendous potential for insight) in this exchange after a suburban middle-schooler, Drew, had stepped forward: one of the girls said to him with intense anger, "Why'd you do this? Why'd you go to the dean? You're such a pussy, Drew . . . love ya!" Drew reported this to his dad in a matter-of-fact way, and then explained, "See, that's how girls are. They put you down, and then they say 'love ya' at the end, to make them feel less guilty about how they just insulted you."

I ask you to imagine this combination of retribution and interpersonal sophistication when you were younger.

ALL-TALKED-OUT KIDS

Expecting some peer blow-back by girls and boys, while scary for sure, would not be enough to inhibit our naturally gabby kids from more talking at home with parents. Other contextual forces are at play.

Another huge factor is more subtle and very twenty-first century: the technologically enhanced peer-to-peer communication kids engage in every single night drains and deflects greater openness with parents.

As I've described, children at increasingly younger ages spend endless time "dialoguing" with each other about absolutely everything in school and online. After reading so many e-mail conversations my clients have brought in; after being shown text messages kids send to each other from the moment they get up in the morning till the moment they drop off at night; and after grasping how cell phones have become extensions of their very bodies, it is clear to me that by the time parents enter the picture kids have little energy or interest or need to talk—unless there is a real emergency.

As one child told me, speaking for many, "Sure I'd be willing to talk to my mom or dad about what happened during the day. But I've talked so much by the time I see them, I've already forgotten about it and I'm too tired to start up again."

HOW WELL-MEANING PARENTS DISCOURAGE KID COMMUNICATION—PARENTS WHO POUNCE

As if these kid factors weren't enough to create a maddening paradox—kids who feel free to talk about absolutely anything with each other, but not so much with their parents—well-meaning adults contribute to the communication gap. Unlike the more modest ways of the greatest generation, post-boomers would absolutely love the opportunity to listen to and teach kids lessons they learned growing up in a similarly chaotic and increasingly competitive culture.

However, our intense eagerness to communicate actually turns off super-cool twenty-first century kids.

As I've often suggested, most parents today feel so communication-hungry that they could be performing an operation on someone's brain and if their kid walked by offering to talk, the parents, without a second's thought, would (metaphorically) leave the patient dead on the table, so as not to lose "the moment." Kids sense this desperation, and as one kid told me many years ago: "When my mom gets that look in her eyes like she wants to 'relate,' I feel like I want to puke." Harsh words, but spot-on for boys and girls of all ages.

Over-eagerness bordering on *desperation* is bad enough. But parent-child talking has developed an edge of duty that is bound to inhibit communication. Egged on by public television spots and "responsible" corporate commercials, which implore that we "just speak" with our children about all those worrisome issues, we no longer think about talk as relaxed conversation. We feel that it is a life-and-death, community-and civic-minded chore to continuously (beyond just one "birds and bees" talk) bring up the tough topics and deliver a message. Otherwise we are culpable for the many bad things that can happen.

In response, most mothers and fathers immediately launch into a teach and lecture mode which further turns off the free-est generation. This is especially frustrating to watch since post-boomers come equipped with life experience that most closely resembles their kids'—far closer than the experiences of generations past.

IS HONESTY A GOOD THING?

Finally, post-boomer parents are deeply confused at how much honesty is a good thing. After all, many were raised on a diet of absolute frankness. Remember, they came of age in the seventies and eighties when their own mothers and fathers, immersed in a "let it all hang out" pop culture, graduates of twelve-step programs, clients in psychotherapy, enthusiastic advocates of sharing and caring groups, felt like pioneers "outing" so much that was once shameful. Having lived through such a once-in-a-lifetime sea change of the acceptable, many of today's mothers and fathers are uncertain about what constitutes healthy and appropriate openness for children.

This uncertainty makes sense. Since they don't want to put ideas into children's heads and because they can't figure out how much to reveal of their own wild past, talking and listening has become a complicated matter to parents in a post-boomer world.

For all these reasons then, creating more openness between today's youngsters and their parents represents a significant challenge as well as a wonderful opportunity. Given twenty-first century kid sophistication and the mirror-image life-sophistication of contemporary parents, there is potential for the most honest discussion between generations that we've ever seen.

Here's how to make communication with your children happen, in ways that fit this day and age.

A WELCOMING ATTITUDE

The free-est generation *wants* to stay "in relationship" with parents. Unlike previous generations, this one actually *welcomes* openness with adults if approached properly and if discussions at home don't necessarily leak out into the world of other parents (refer to the box on p. 270 for the matter of how adults can responsibly handle "hot" information). Parents do not yet grasp the relatively simple choice that finally exists: a welcoming attitude to your child's unique way of communicating invites today's reflexively open kids to embrace discussion; it protects the "flow," as kids now say.

In other words, "Build it"—a welcoming attitude—"and they will come."

This is true even for ornery adolescents. I mean it when I say to the mothers and fathers of my preteen and adolescent clients that if they follow a few basic suggestions, their kids will open up just enough that they won't need to see me any longer. I've learned this by following many children into their adult years and then asking what they remember most. I am repeatedly surprised how they treasure that one time their mother or father left their usual rules of communication aside and just "flowed," and listened to them. This was a major conclusion of the authors of the book *The Notebook Girls* (with whom I did a presentation). As these poised young women told the audience, open communication amounted to the ability of their parents, starting early on, to hear what they had to say—on their terms and without freaking out—no matter how difficult it was.

For these twenty-first century kids, judgment-laced retail formulas and bromides that don't specifically fit their consumer-driven sensibilities are immediate discussion-stoppers.

This is why the best conversations between parent and child have an unorthodox quality to them. These are discussions through slammed doors, after a major fight has just taken place, in the middle of the night, or following a profound disappointment, when all the "rules" of proper communication necessarily have to be abandoned and parents listen in exactly the manner their children need. This is not an easy skill to develop, but understanding how one's children are most comfortable talking is a *must* for mothers and fathers of kids who are used to having it their way, used to getting continuous feedback in a highly personalized and interactive world.

LISTENING FOR A CHILD'S CONVERSATIONAL STYLE— HARD-WIRED AND NON-NEGOTIABLE

A father says to me, "With one of my children, if there is going to be any talking about the day, driving home from school is when it happens. My other one loves to joke around, and in the middle of his lunacy, will get serious and tell me about a worry. Our third child is completely different. He hates any questions, altogether. With him, I'm supposed to just listen and let him get the story completely out. What's going on here? Why does it have to be so different with each of them?"

A welcoming mind will not be sufficient unless parents recognize a child's *conversational style*. Most contemporary parents have heard about learning style, but few know about the relatively new findings of speech and language experts regarding hard-wired *conversational style*. Some kids open up in the morning, some right after school, and others at bedtime. Some kids like questions and others are absolutely turned off by them. Some kids tell stories and get right to the point; others meander. By conversational style, I also mean that each child responds to a different tone and pacing from a parent; each child has a different level of comfort with back and forth dialogue or complex phrasing.

These differences are apparent from the first years of life and remain relatively intact through adolescence and often well beyond.

We must also recognize that conversational style includes a preferred manner of adult response. The free-est generation expects attuned feedback. Given the norms of the peer group, pop culture, and self-regulating video games, they are used to nothing less. To get their attention, then, parents must react in a fashion that is complementary to a child's conversational style. Anything else becomes tuned-out static in a gigahertz world. I know this may sound overly child-centered, but it is a twenty-first century reality, as the following exchange between father and son illustrates—one I reported in *Why Parents Disagree* approximately a dozen years ago, but which I only recently understood from a conversational-style perspective.

In a parent-child workshop I was running, an elementary school-age boy and his dad started talking in front of a large group. With a hundred neighbors watching, this boy revealed his unique conversational style and his need for it to be recognized. Dad asked why he wouldn't respond when he wondered how school was each day. His son replied, "Because I don't like your questions; they are too vague for me. When you don't ask me about details, it feels like—you don't even know what's going on." The heavy silence that followed was punctuated by the elementary-schooler saying, "And then I don't believe that you really love me." Tears welled up in parents as they listened. The experience made a powerful impression, and I've heard variations of the same interchange for many years now. Distinct conversational style emerges in preschool and doesn't change all that much as kids develop. Unless parents can recognize this fact of life, they uselessly fight to engage kids without respecting something children have little control over: their own way of communicating and "the right" to receive the attuned response our culture now trains kids to expect.

WORDS COUNT—SO DOES TONE

The Language of Listening to Kids

A great deal of twenty-first century work by speech and language specialists, as well as research on what makes

(continued)

certain "healers" great, reveal common patterns of listening that can guide parents. Here are some proven listening techniques to keep the lines of communication open with your kids:

1. Pace yourself to be on a similar wavelength with your child. Specifically, pay attention to his or her breathing, the speed of your questions, and the loudness of your voice. It's been shown that if you mirror another's physiology, he or she more likely will open up rather than shut down.
2. Don't interrupt, don't assume, and don't finish sentences. Kids chronically complain that these are our biggest listening errors.
3. Try not to immediately "fix" as in "you are the best, you are the most beautiful, or it's not so bad." All such efforts to quickly solve the problem make children dig deeper into their negative place and shut you out.
4. Ask concrete questions. For example "What happened then?" is the most powerful question for kids, because they feel like you actually want to hear their story.
5. Help kids tell that story by gently moving them along, and without judgment, bring them towards a beginning, middle, and end of their tale.
6. Stay away from asking, "Why?" Who really knows why, certainly not kids anymore than we adults do? "When, what, and who" are much better word choices.
7. Sometime after a discussion or a story well-told, mention to your children how good it made you feel and how well they expressed themselves. Don't take this for granted—acknowledgment (no hyperbole please) leads to more communication.

ACCEPTING CONVERSATIONAL STYLE LEADS TO CHANGE

Max, a late-elementary school boy, was unhappy about his mother's new husband, Al, and was rejecting him as a step-parent, a family situation I commonly encounter. Nothing was helping—no amount of questioning, soothing conversation, or firm expectations from mom. Al was becoming increasingly frustrated and angry, as well as hurt, and Max's performance in school and even his interest in his usual activities were beginning to suffer.

At that time my knowledge of hard-wired conversational style was just beginning to take shape; I have since used this approach with many families. After inquiring about his talking habits, I discovered that Max generally preferred conversation on the way to school. He rarely spoke in the afternoon, preferring to be left alone and nap, rather than deconstruct the many happenings at school. This was *his* conversational style. Morning was *his* time of day to open up, a fact that was hard-wired, and extremely difficult to change. This style was very different from that of his sister, Carly, who was a "night person" when it came to having discussions.

So instead of attempting to shift this hard-wired fact of life, I asked mom and step-dad to "accept things in order to change things." To do this, I suggested that Al begin walking Max to school in the morning. At first, Max was so dismissive and angry that he speed-walked a good half-block in front, ignoring Al entirely. Al and Max's mother were about to give up, but I reminded them that Max's conversational style was far more ingrained than his anger toward this new man in the house.

For another week they kept walking together. By now, Max had slowed down, keeping pace with his step-dad, but of course he said absolutely nothing to him. Sometime during the third week, however, Max spontaneously mentioned the names of a few boys in his class who "annoyed" him and then said nothing more. A few days later, on his way to school, his hard-wiring finally kicked in and Max began opening up about several of the boys who had been viciously ostracizing him for months. In fact, the bullying had more to do with his bad mood than his new step-dad. What no one noticed was the morning ritual of talking together that Max had shared for years with his mom and that his biological father had fallen by the wayside when Al joined the family.

Both step-dad and step-son's more empathic, best-selves now emerged. Al was so relieved about and responsive to Max's openness that they began to trade stories of how to handle bullies in school, with which Al had his own experiences. Somewhere along the way, Max tried out one or two of his step-dad's suggestions and was thrilled that they made a difference.

A few months later, when I checked in with this family, the morning ritual of walking to school had become a high point in Max's and his step-father's day, a comfortable re-establishment of a ritual this boy truly loved—one that was a natural because it completely suited his conversational style.

Another child whose parents were having communication trouble faced a completely different issue, a dinnertime pattern I've since seen in many families. Julie's conversational style was one in which she could not tolerate questions, especially fast-paced ones that did not allow her time to think. She was extremely sensitive to these queries and experienced them like others do the sound of chalk being scraped on a blackboard. The family came to me not understanding why dinnertime often exploded in fights and x-rated profanities. Being late boomer parents, they weren't particularly upset by the language, but the lack of communication and this descent into hellish bickering was deeply upsetting. Both parents had grown up in sixties and seventies families in which absolutely anything and everything was up for heated debate. "We want to discuss current events, what's happening in the world, and get the kids to think about different ideas," said Julie's well-meaning dad, who lamented that their other daughter, Julie's older sister, had never acted that way at dinner.

After I reviewed Julie's conversational style, which showed a pattern of communication that did not allow for fast-paced, Socratic argument, I encouraged both dad and mom to slow down a bit at the dinner table, and to lessen their well-intentioned, but barbed questions. For awhile, all I heard were complaints about how uninteresting mealtimes had become.

But then, all of a sudden, in the midst of what mom described as the most boring mealtime she could possibly imagine, when Julie's older sister was practically jumping out of her skin and dad was questioning the necessity of returning home in time for dinner, Julie took advantage of the slower pace to start talking about her *own* life, the not-very-compelling subject of middle school fashion.

Given their conversational styles, it was hard for mom and dad not to pounce with questions, not to ask thought-provoking questions about superficial "values," but they held back. This respite allowed Julie to continue airing her thoughts at her own pace. Within a number of weeks, the family had reached a kind of compromise during which part of dinner was spent in heated debate, and another part was reserved for the slower, gentler pacing that Julie required. It was no accident that Julie's slightly less whiny, more self-possessed side emerged during this time.

Different from Julie's easy sensibilities, the conversational style of the daughter in another family I counseled was *arguing*. Take a position and Collette took the opposite one. This is how she felt comfortable communicating, even though it could drive her parents crazy. As I described in *Breaking Through to Teens*, our sessions took the form of constant debates. Here, in part, is one:

Collette: Every adult I know is unhappy, my parents, all their friends. Probably even you.
Ron: Why are we—they unhappy?
Collette: They hate their work. They hate the institution of marriage. They hate everything.

Ron: How can you be so sure of what they feel? You're saying you don't know one adult who's anything but unhappy?

Collette: Well, just about no adults. No, I would say definitely not one. Anyway, what's your definition of unhappy?

Ron: You brought it up, what's your definition?

Collette: Well, an unhappy marriage.

Ron: How are you defining an unhappy marriage?

Collette: Not being happy all the time.

Ron: So, you're telling me being happy means being happy all the time—every single moment. Then I would have to say that, yes, you're right. Absolutely everyone I know, including me, and you for the rest of your life—everyone is unhappy now and is going to remain unhappy forever.

Collette: No, don't be so dense. I don't think everyone is so unhappy every moment of every day.

Ron: But you just said that. You said that everyone is unhappy all the time.

Collette: Well, my parents are mostly unhappy.

Ron: Okay, mostly is different. I know they fight a lot, but that doesn't mean that everybody else, every adult you know, which you can't help becoming one day, is unhappy.

Collette: Oh, I can help it all right. I can help becoming an adult. I just don't have to go with adult values, like working in school, or like, taking it seriously or getting involved with anything extra—it's futile.

Ron: So you're saying everything is futile, everyone is unhappy . . .

Collette: I'm not saying everyone is unhappy!

Ron: Well, let's say mostly everyone is unhappy most of the time, it's all futile—then its no wonder you just lose yourself in reading fantasy fiction and don't get involved in school.

Collette: How do you define reading?

Then we were off to the races again, lost in yet another argument. Just about every meeting proceeded in this manner. I would either tear my hair out in frustration, or sometimes manage to enjoy the sport of it. *But these discussions seemed to be touching something real in Collette.* One day, just "by accident," Collette dropped by the debating club at school. The head of the team told her, "Look, you can't really try out for this unless you get better grades." Collette came away grumbling, and she and I argued about this "senseless" requirement. But she started to go to a few more classes, and got just enough C's and B's to be part of the team.

Needless to say, Collette was a terrific debater; this was her natural conversational style as well as her passion. Over two years, the debate club introduced her to a new world of like-minded iconoclastic kids. Collette made the public school travel debate team. She started to go to matches in different countries and took hundreds of pictures for her journal, which led into another interest, photography. Collette's ability at debate was only second to her sardonic humor, appreciated by her peers, so she was elected president of the debate team. Two years later a boyfriend followed—someone she really loved.

Over the years I've learned that Collette's path is not unusual. The emergence of hidden passion happens more frequently than not when valued adults recognize a child's genuine manner of expression and interests.

COMMUNICATING NEEDS RITUALS—BORING IS BEST

My mother cleaned and vacuumed our house every Tuesday at an appointed time, every single Tuesday afternoon. This was not unlike the unswerving dinner menu: lamb chops on Monday, hamburger on Tuesday, spaghetti and meatballs on Wednesday, etc. (A meal wasn't considered a real meal unless it included a slab of artery-clogging meat—I loved it!) Anyway, on this one particular Tuesday afternoon, I parked myself in the living room as my mom did her weekly search-and-destroy mission for dirt, grime, and lint, all of which could somehow (not without reason) be traced back to me.

But this day was different. I was sitting quietly crying because my girl-friend had broken up with me. My mother stopped her chore, came over, and asked what was wrong. I actually decided to tell her. She took my hand for just a moment, and said, "Don't worry, Ronnie, there are many fish in the sea." Not exactly a high-tech conversation or sophisticated parenting advice, but it stuck. I felt just a little bit better, and here I am writing about it decades later.

Many post-boomer parents, raised in chaotic times much like the free-est generation underestimate the importance of *ritual* and do not see its connection to open communication. Too many of our culture's rituals were left by the wayside when they grew up. During their form-ative years, organized religion, involvement with the PTA, neighbor-hood, and civic lodges were on the decline, and because of this (though as I will show in Chapter Seven, things have just begun to change a bit), most parents today still do not grasp that their kids will open up during the *ordinary,* even the most old-fashioned, rituals of life. It is stunning to see how much more engaged parents feel when they establish and protect what I call "talking rituals" with their children.

Once you've figured out the conversational style of your child, espe-cially the time of day each of your children prefers to open up, it is part of your job as a parent to protect these moments.

The importance of ritual has been suggested by numerous ex-perts, some of the data sensational enough to garner significant public-ity. For example, you've probably heard that family dinners are related to less teen and preteen drinking and sexual acting-out. When I first began to mention this in presentations around the country, I thought it was purely the result of creating family time together. I no-ticed that as soon as I said "the more family dinners you have together, the less active your child may be sexually," every parent in the audience began feverishly taking notes and asking each other: "What did he just say?" They then frantically raised hands to ask whether there were any "special dishes" that were associated with preventing kid drinking and sexual behavior. It all seemed promising and magical at the same time, a ritual that could delay every parent's worst fears.

Years later, as I learned more about life behind the wall of silence, the magical became very ordinary. The prophylactic power of mealtimes was related to a very concrete fact of life I hadn't at first appreciated: most first-time, high-risk behaviors happen, not as one would think, late at night, but between the hours of three and seven in the afternoon. Those kids in a well-to-do suburban high school I once visited, who actually hired strippers for spring break–type flings, did so in the late afternoon and early evening. A lot of smoking-up and hooking-up goes on in very respectable families with very empty houses, again during afternoon hours when parents must be at work. So, one of the secrets of this magical dinnertime was that it cut into kids' time, requiring them to be at home around the dinner table with mom and/or dad instead of in empty houses with nothing to do.

There are many ways, then, to think about rituals: They are a pause in an over-scheduled world; they make sure kids are around when most vulnerable to high-risk behaviors; they establish order and security in a time of uncertainty. But for my money, and for this section, I will focus on the chance to create *talking rituals* that are built around the ordinary moments, the boring moments, and ones that are tailored to your specific child's conversational style.

Making a commitment to protect those rituals is what matters in creating genuine connection and open communication.

Every workshop I give has an interactive portion during which parents describe the talking rituals they have found to pry open even the shyest children, ornery preteens and walled-off adolescents. The examples are always the same, no matter what part of the country I am in. These predictable moments are worth laying down your life for. Much like the exchange I described with my own mother many years ago, I guarantee that they will happen around the most boring times of the day, and they will end up being appreciated by your children for life.

THE TEN MOST COMMON TALKING RITUALS

How to Use Those Natural Times

For over two decades, I've listened to tens of thousands of parents and kids describe their favorite times to open up. Not all are for your home or children, but we can learn from each other to increase the chance of better communication. Here are some of the most frequent rituals that parents report:

1. Bedtime, of course.
2. Online or on the phone with each other, especially while in different rooms in the same house.
3. Right after school or on the way to school—kids' memories are sharp and little else has crowded into their thoughts.
4. In the car—mostly during short runs, though. Long trips require more entertainment, distraction and sib management. Conversation won't usually break through the interpersonal gridlock of a long drive.
5. While playing a board game or other non-action activity. With little except the game going on, semi-boredom can turn into a "By the way" story straight from your child's heart.
6. Doing chores together—cooking, yard-work, cleaning up "the room"—but only if there's no argument or struggle around getting the job done.

7. Cell phone conversations—during predictable kid-transitions—that happen every day. With adolescents, preteens and even elementary school kids increasingly having cells, these provide ample opportunity to check in and communicate from afar.

8. Immediately after a prayer or saying grace before a meal. These moments can clear minds and soften everyone up enough to open lines of discussion.

9. During commercials on TV, watching a favorite show together or while channel surfing. Screens shared together provide ample topics and time to foster extremely interesting talks.

10. Reading and doing work silently side-by-side. Without any expectation for communication, without a direct gaze, with no pressure to relate, communication can happen—and often does

SECRETS OF "VENUS"— WHY KIDS STILL OPEN UP MORE TO MOTHERS

Even when we do protect ordinary talking rituals, parents have a surprising hurdle to move beyond, a stubborn gender imbalance regarding who actually engages in the boring routines of daily life.

Despite the march of time since my mother engaged in her role as a housekeeper, and despite the significant impact of the women's and men's liberation movements, the reality is that post-boomer mothers still do most of the boring tasks of child rearing.

Forget what the glossy magazine covers announce, forget for a moment how much more fathers are doing around the house. The reality is that mothers are still in charge of what I refer to as "the endless list of child-rearing" in my book *When Parents Disagree and What You Can Do About It*. This impacts communication more than anything else—including the advent of the technological revolution. It's not that mothers are necessarily far more skilled in the listening department than fathers. It is because mothers are still the ones most often around for those boring, detail-oriented, and often comforting moments with children that we take for granted. Despite what most of us would like to think, kids do not open up during the "Mr. Excitement" times. No child confides much during the wave at the ballpark or while roughhousing right before bedtime, but rather in the more routine moments.

Whenever I talk about this to audiences, increasingly comprised of a few late boomers and a predominance of post-boomer parents, mothers nod knowingly and fathers take on a somewhat sad expression. The truth is hard to hear, even though most of us are quite aware that the "mom's-in-charge-dad-helps-out" paradigm and "endless list" phenomenon from previous generations is still to some degree true. Old habits and archetypical roles are hard to change. In his and Carl Reiner's classic comedy bit *The Two Thousand Year Old Man*, Mel Brooks said, when asked whether he could still remember the theme song of his cave back from the beginning of time: "Of course, you don't forget a national anthem in a minute!"

Check out the endless-list quiz in the box to find out who feels responsible for and takes care of the "boring stuff" around your house. You will begin to appreciate why kids of all ages still open up more to their mothers.

Talking rituals matter to kids and are worth changing the schedule of your life around (if that is financially possible). But they are also essential to creating at least a slight chance of hearing what is going on in your child's inner world and everyday life. If you don't protect talking rituals, your kids will more than likely open up about true-self matters only during those mindless moments online or in school.

THE ENDLESS-LIST QUIZ

Communication Is in the Details

Kids still talk more to mothers than to fathers, regardless of what the pop culture tells us. As I described back in 1994, in *Why Parents Disagree*, this imbalance is no mystery. Mothers are still in charge of "the endless-list" of parenting. Fathers may do far more than we once did, but mothers are still on the front lines feeling responsible for the small, endless details of life in kid-universe. And, this is when children and teens tend to open up. The devil is in the details—where does the boring detail work fall in your house, because that's where and when your children will choose to open up? Ask yourself a few of these questions:

1. Who first notices the signs that one of your kids is getting sick, then informs the school that your child won't be coming in?
2. Who attended the last parenting workshop in your school church or community center? If both of you attended, who tried the techniques discussed?
3. Who bought the last small "thinking of you" present when your child seemed to be blue?
4. Who thought to call the parents of a friend with whom your child had a bad rift? Who actually made the call? Who spoke to your child about it?
5. Who usually tries to talk to your child when she's feeling sad?
6. Who plans and organizes birthday parties and other special events for the kids?

(continued)

7. Who first notices that shoes are too tight, pants are too short, and sweaters are too frayed?

8. Whose date book contains the dates of the school concert, little-league sign-up, and other kids' birthday parties?

9. Who remembers to bring juice, wipes, and other essentials to the playground, on a day trip, or on vacation?

DOWN TIME COUNTS—QUALITY TIME . . . NOT SO MUCH!

In order to change communication around a twenty-first century house, mothers and fathers must accept that soothing, routine down time is what kids most love with parents.

This is often a surprise for post-boomer parents raised on *Star Wars* special effects, immersed in a brave new world of computerized graphics, just like their own children. In addition, just like our children, contemporary mothers and fathers were brought up on a diet that emphasized "quality time." There's only one problem with this quality-time stance: we're just beginning to discover that what the pressurized free-est generation truly loves is predictable, *down time.*

I remember in the late eighties an articulate young adolescent letting me in on this "secret." When I asked her where she would rather eat, instead of naming one of the local stand-out restaurants, she responded by saying, "I'd rather eat at McDonald's." I said, "Why?" She then went on to say, "Boring is good, but the same is better. I don't like different." Who, but kids, can think like this?

Unfortunately, her words flew in the face of decades-old child-rearing advice. "The Myth of Quality Time," which I first wrote about in my book *Parenting by Heart*, is still very much part of the vernacular. Busy parents incorrectly believe that they must set apart quality time, doing special things in order to connect with their children.

In old-think terms, the definition of "quality" often means that it is expensive, it is a teachable moment, it is enriched and it usually requires waiting on line. My thinking gradually evolved from those early days when experts encouraged quality time to emphasizing "ordinary," comforting moments and finally realizing that what this pressurized generation truly needs is predictable, soothing *down time.*

Damn the stressed-out special effects and all the logistics and the teaching that needs to be done—down time happens in the midst of those moments organized around the ebbs of daily living. They are regular, cost nothing, and are a part of the ordinary fabric of everyday life; they are exactly the moments no one in their right mind would ever stand in line for: setting the table, bath time, commercial breaks on TV, reading side-by-side—time that is soothing, rather than exciting.

When I ask parents to really think about their growing up years, I cannot tell you how many, especially fathers, have begun crying as they remembered when they and one of their parents had an exchange that really mattered. Almost without exception they were in the midst of the most mundane moments of their lives.

The reality that when it comes to communication, "boring is best" continues even after kids have left the house. As Violet, the mother of a university freshman, reported with a mixture of frustration and gratitude, her daughter would call on the cell phone almost every day at the exact same time: those moments walking across campus between classes. For parents of teens facing an "empty nest," there is a glimmer of hope in knowing that once away, kids will still cling to using down time opportunities and call home much more than one could possibly ever have imagined.

And with this generation it doesn't end. Recently we were having dinner with old friends when all of a sudden one of their married children, a twenty-something man, called from San Francisco while in their hotel room to touch base with mom or dad and talk about how the day went—this from a vacation three thousand miles away. We all laughed, didn't think twice about it, and went back to our dinnertime conversation.

TURNING DOWN TIME INTO TALKING TIME

Once today's parents begin to take "boring" seriously, it is amazing how much the free-est generation will open up. Remember, these kids want to stay in relationship with their parents and will talk their real-self hearts out to get some of the advice they need to make it in this complicated world.

They will readily begin to take advantage of such moments and sometimes even give you what the kids call TMI (too much information). As one mom of a mid-adolescent girl told me after acting on these suggestions, "I'm glad your ideas about quiet times worked. But do I really need to hear about this one's penis versus another one's and girls going 'bi' and all the constant drama around love triangles? Actually I do—I'd rather know than not!" Spoken like a true parent in a post-boomer world.

It's not always so x-rated. For example, Zeke a small-town boy between the preteen and adolescent years, was obsessed with snowboarding, inline skating, and alternative-culture music. Forever online, continuously listening to his i-Pod, Zeke practically lived on the mountain in the free-for-all world of snowboarding and its ongoing friction with preppie skiers. Zeke was not doing well in school. Because of his procrastination around schoolwork and generally "slacker" lifestyle, Zeke got into constant arguments with his parents.

To break this destructive dance I encouraged his mom, Melanie, to take advantage of the quiet, comforting moments around the house. In this case, these moments occurred when Melanie read, as she liked to do in the early evenings. Zeke had taken up snowboard magazines. Because Melanie's reading time jived with the boy's schedule and his hard-wired conversational style—casual, slow communication without pointed questions—Zeke would spontaneously sit by mom and the two would read together. Not much was said, but these moments gradually became a soothing part of their routine. With my encouragement, mom kept this time free from schoolwork reminders and logistical machinations. All of a sudden, pretty much out of nowhere, Zeke began to open up about how much he hated the private suburban preppie school he travelled to every day.

With some coaching from the sidelines for mom to hold back from pouncing on the information he was sharing, Zeke's hidden-self emerged. He began explaining to her the heretofore secret rules of snowboarding's anarchistic world, and even (not to my surprise) initiated discussions about a girlfriend, sex, and drinking. Melanie gradually took Zeke's complaints about school seriously and started considering different settings with more students who might share her son's dislike of a monied kid life. This talking ritual ended up changing their experience around the house, creating a predictable time to be together, as well as leading to enrollment in the local public school that did not feel so alienating, a real match for this boy's better, more modest true-self.

Sometimes change does not come so easily—kids may be more ensconced in the second family behind that wall of silence. Molly had been acting out in school, becoming one of the "popular, mean girls" by fifth grade. Even at this early age, she had become addicted to the computer, talking online and joining chat-rooms using various identities. No one in this virtual world realized (or cared) that they were flirting with an eleven-year-old, because of her sophisticated and sexualized banter. At the time, of course, neither her parents nor I knew about her life online, because so much attention was being paid to Molly's "mean" behavior at the top of the grade's pecking order.

When I went over the family's workday and weekend schedule with her mom and dad, it became clear to all of us that she had replaced them with her cybernetic world, and this disconnection was serious enough that one of them needed to be home regularly in the late afternoon. On the surface it seemed as if Molly didn't care all that much whether "the parental units" were around, she was so absorbed in the second family. She loved her freedom, she loved talking online, and she loved being the "queen bee," all because she knew no other way.

At some point, mom was finally able to work out a different schedule at her job, coming in earlier and arranging to be home a couple of hours earlier, two days a week. During these afternoons, she and Molly began to build up an unpressurized, down-time routine that included cooking and watching a couple of TV shows together.

As if on cue, communication began between them, first haltingly and about neutral subjects (teachers Molly did or didn't like); moved into much more touchy areas such as the pressures of being popular, how much Molly felt herself to be in a vice-like grip of social expectations; and finally, one day turned to frank discussion about her online activity—which had actually scared her several times. Molly never did show them transcripts of chat-room conversations, but her mom and dad had now been warned enough to take action and limit her unfettered access to these sites. While this protected her safety somewhat, it was almost an afterthought because the most enduring result was that instead of distance continuing to grow between them, Molly started to yearn for just a little more easy time with mom, rather than only with her friends and followers in school and online. Molly's more empathic and considerate side found expression in these down time moments with her mother.

This was a talking ritual that may have saved a life. It forestalled dangerous acting-out in a preteen, just in time before hard-core adolescence set in. But mother's ability to work out a different schedule with her supervisor was essential for change to happen. Thankfully, greater recognition of a parent's need to balance work and home is beginning around the country, as described in the box.

MAKING WORK, WORK

Staying Available Despite the Job

Ellen Galinsky, President
The Families and Work Institute

Employers and employees are creating new ways to, as Ellen Galinsky puts it, "make work, work." This is not a fantasy, but a growing reality as the research at *The Families and Work Institute* is showing. The fit between work and home is a critical one in creating a community in which the adults are not torn apart by pressures from home and from the job. Ellen is a virtual encyclopedia of cutting-edge initiatives, among them:

- Creating fewer commuting hours for employees by establishing staggered times when workers can arrive in the morning and leave in the afternoon. Less traffic congestion leads to less tension and more time with kids (as well as lower fuel costs and a greener environment).
- Various ways to increase connections at home, one example, seven days on—seven days off for future leave; another example, get paid 80 percent but work 100 percent, which eventually leads to the accumulation of larger blocks of paid time off.
- Part-year work where extra work during the year is balanced by more time off during the summertime, to be with kids when school is out.
- More attention and activities at work that include children and that bring families together during holidays: religious, national and seasonal.

(continued)

- Changes in attitudes towards flexibility where flex-time is seen as a business tool not a perk. Almost 40 percent of workers still believe taking advantage of flexible time and/or leave time carries a stigma and some jeopardy at the job.
- More talks, presentations, events in which home-life is discussed with supervisors present, so that management is mindful of how work demands affect family, and how family life affects workers' productivity.
- Ask yourself: "Do I protect the boundaries at home, or do I jump whenever I am called, contacted or e-mailed from work?" The more my kids see us create boundaries that protect our family, the more they will come to expect that from themselves in the future.

PRAYING AND TALKING—HOW RELIGIOUS AFFILIATION CAN LEAD TO GREATER OPENNESS

From my work with so many families and parents across the country, I've understood the recent nationwide rise in religious affiliation to be partly a result of ritual hunger, especially the kind that celebrates boring moments, creating unexpected conversation between parent and child.

Putting the specific form of spirituality aside for a moment (your choice, of course), those who affiliate tend to share a major part, or even an entire day each week together. Because of how much of the time is structured around slow-moving moments, each child's conversational style can be understood and taken into account.

For example, an observant family I know with three children found that every Sunday, one of the kids preferred to open up in the morning and talked on the way to church. The other opened up in the afternoon following services, during lunch at a local diner. And the oldest spoke intimately to mom while dad napped late. Finally, at dinner, which included family and friends who belonged to the same congregation, everyone was yapping at each other about absolutely everything under the sun—including details of life in the second family that were usually off-limits, but slipped out in the casual Sunday evening melees.

There are many other ways that enlightened twenty-first century faith communities are learning to encourage communication, not only within families but between them. This is an important topic for the free-est generation and its post-boomer parents, one I will focus on in Chapter Seven.

UNPLUG YOUR FAMILY— WELL FOR A FEW MOMENTS, ANYWAY

Two decades ago I used to recommend that talking rituals be encouraged by turning off the phone in the evening, as well as the answering machine and all other electronic devices that had begun transforming families into twenty-four-hour shopping malls, rather than places of intimate relationship.

Looking back now, I realize just how out-dated this notion was quickly becoming. Very soon afterward, technology exploded so quickly and pervasively that the idea of turning everything electronic off now seems impossible, like fighting the ocean tide.

So, trying above all else to be realistic, I no longer recommend disconnecting these devices for evenings or mornings at a time, but for moments, to protect talking rituals.

Again, respect that children have different "open" times of day and then make a commitment to protect those times from interruptions. This is very hard for everyone to do—ignoring that ring-tone or IM or text message is a real challenge—but it is essential to practice this skill in order to foster communication in a post-boomer world.

Our own children, Leah and Sam, used to open up during bathtime, not in the morning, not after school or at dinnertime. So much so that my wife, Stacey, and I ended up getting one of those plastic beach chairs to place by the side of the tub—*and we made a commitment not to be disturbed by anything of a non-emergency nature.* As our kids got older and appropriately modest, they took individual showers with curtains drawn, but they still loved talking at this time and still expected a few minutes with one of us sitting on that beach chair next to the shower. From behind this curtain, "confessions" of the day were screamed out—the best conversations about real life would invariably follow. One day I told our then-nine-year-old son Sam that I had bought a new chair. I meant for my office, of course, but his response? "You mean, so you can sit next to the shower, right?"

Seeing how much this meant, we were able to commit to moments without electronic interruption during dinnertime. It sometimes rips us up not to reach for the phone, and we practically have to tie ourselves to the kitchen chairs, but slowly we are getting used to dinners that are not totaled by jarring interruptions.

LISTENING TO THE TRIVIAL— TURNING NOTHING INTO SOMETHING

There is a classic scene in the legendary TV sit-com, Seinfeld. Jerry and George are sitting at their usual spots in the coffee shop trying to figure out what the pilot show that NBC has just asked them to write ought to be about. Of course, not being able to focus for too long, they inadvertently veer off into a discussion "about nothing," one that thoroughly dissects the difficulty distinguishing "salsa" from "seltzer." George then says: "See, now this is what the show should be about: nothing!"

Boomer, as well as millions of post-boomer parents, and certainly child professionals, have been trained to value "depth," to search for "meaning" and to "relate," in order to get at what is truly important. Decades ago, however, I learned from one of my colleagues, an intern at the Albert Einstein Medical Center, that to get to the important you often have to start with something that seems like nothing.

Whenever he'd meet a new child or adolescent on the ward, he'd begin with something like, "So, do you like baseball?" Or "Who do you like in your school?" or "What are you interested in?" Our supervisors would make mincemeat out of this intern's approach, calling it completely unprofessional, beside the point, and way too trivial to be wasting anyone's time with. The only problem with their smug analysis was that his clients seemed to like him and open up, and in due time talked with him about the things that really mattered.

This unorthodox but commonsense approach made a big impression on me. Years later I was working with a boy named Hank who had been labeled as mute, retarded, and/or oppositional (compulsively obstinate). What this really meant is that one child professional after another had unsuccessfully tried to get Hank to open up by taking the usual route, from the top down. We had wanted him to talk about what *we* thought was important, hoping to get him to move into areas of feelings, motivation, and insight. When Hank resisted, he was hamstrung with these labels and then proceeded to live them out, from therapist to therapist.

One day, after I been working with Hank with little success for several weeks, out of frustration and faced with the same unyielding blank expression, I mentioned something about having trouble with my car that morning. All of a sudden, "retarded" Hank started asking me questions about my lemon of an automobile and embarked on a lengthy discourse about the difficulties with this make, model, and carburetor. Unexpectedly, I discovered that Hank had an entire subterranean life, unbeknownst to previous child professionals he'd seen, and even his parents. The "superficial" details of cars contained the promise and pathos of his life. Talking about them moved us very quickly into discussing his friends, mentors, and what his future hopes and dreams really were. He wanted to work in a garage.

Now, decades later after having many experiences like the one I had with Hank, and after listening to veteran parents describe how often trivial details seem to take unexpected U-turns into meaningful matters, I have become deeply committed to the trivial in order to bring out the hidden, best-self parts of our children. Freud said that "dreams are the royal road to the unconscious." Well, in today's world, the royal road to the unconscious of the free-est generation is the seemingly inane detail of pop culture and second family life.

Unfortunately, most kids believe (often correctly) that we adults and parents, in the half-crazed rush of the day, do not show enough genuine curiosity about the details of their lives.

Creating genuine engagement requires paying attention to exactly the kind of mindlessness we've been taught to think of as "trash."

GET SMART

The Top Dozen "Stupid" Kid-Details
Adults Need to Notice

The best-informed parents are those who understand that the most important information you should look for in kids' communication centers on the "tiny details" of life. In a high-definition world, twenty-first century kids are tuned into seeing, observing and wanting to share the most specific details of their day. Ignore these at your own risk. Pay attention and you will be rewarded:

1. What kids were wearing, whose hair looked different today, what outfit stood out.
2. Who said hello to whom in school—how could you tell?
3. Who was nasty or bullied someone else—what did they do?

4. Who was unexpectedly kind to someone else—what did they do?
5. Who did the teacher call on the most?
6. Who played with whom, or who sat next to whom in class?
7. What specific cell phone, ipod, or video platform does a friend have—what games?
8. What does your child think he/she looked like that day? The tiniest flaws and imperfections matter, as do the tiniest points of pride.
9. Who held open a door, who sat next to whom at lunch, who spent time with each other during "frees"?
10. Who texted whom today, who was left out of the communication loop, and who ignored online or text messaging?
11. What new announcement went up on someone's wall on Facebook—breakups, new couples, etc.
12. What was at served at lunch—who brought in "what" to eat.

First, the talking rituals I've described above most of the time will set the table. Then if you don't get too focused on what is considered important in *your* mind, sticking with the most trivial of details in your kids' lives might just lead somewhere unexpected—and real.

Iris was on the phone with her daughter, Jeanie, who called on her cell about some coins she had just dropped behind a school's vending machine. Instead of getting into how she felt about this or what she was going to do with no money for lunch, Iris began asking about the coins: were they the new state quarters; how did she try to recover them; and who was around watching as she wriggled under the machine? *Staying true to the trivial* suddenly took a sharp turn into something that mattered: no friend was around to help; Jeanie was feeling ditched by some of her closest pals, because she had now become involved in a romantic triangle with a high school classmate. Even more surprising, given where the discussion had begun, mom and daughter that night began talking about how far to go with this boy sexually, and her concerns that he was drinking more than was good for him.

From dropped coins to this? With kids, "nothing" turns into "something" far more often than you would expect, and may provide a look into their true-self concerns.

In another family, one I refer to often, a single mom, Helen, set aside Sunday morning with her son, Rob (who was a morning talker), to chat about the predominant thing that really mattered to him and the one thing she had absolutely no interest in: baseball statistics. For a number of weeks, Helen came back to me, pulling her hair out with frustration at how bored she was with these "trivial" discussions, until she began to notice a pattern. Rob's favorite players always seemed to be underperforming or injured or not living up to their potential. Finally, taking this as a sign of something meaningful, she asked him whether he thought he felt injured in any way. For the first time ever, Rob began talking about how challenged he'd been by reading, and that he was falling further behind by the week. One thing led to another, and after a lot of nothing, something followed: a simple evaluation uncovered her son's subtle reading disability. This small change began to affect Rob's entire outlook and confidence in school.

The trivial had truly turned into a life-altering signal and path toward building this boy's best-self. I knew him for years and watched as he morphed into a more confident kid who matured into a capable student.

TURNING MINDLESS 'POP' INTO MEANINGFUL TALK

As I described earlier, once I opened my therapy doors to kid magazines, teen gossip rags, e-mails, video game manuals, and favorite websites, the kids I worked with began opening up to me.

Marianne brought magazines from my waiting room into the treatment room. Instead of asking her to put them down, to really "talk," I just picked up on where she had left off, giving Marianne room to elaborate on which celebrity she thought was beautiful, which guys she thought were hot. From these openings (which would have had my early supervisors calling me out on the carpet), Marianne finally reached beneath her façade and discussed the cutthroat competition between the girls of her eighth-grade class. They would stop at nothing: piercing, oral sex on the school bus, thongs as outerwear, to outdo each other in attracting both girls and boys in her grade.

At home, and with my encouragement, Wendy and Peter watched reality TV shows like *The Real World* with both their son and daughter. Whether *The Real World* gang was in Vegas or Austin or Paris, its characters constantly got involved with the dramatic details of relationships, friendships, competition, and coming-out. Mom and dad, by committing themselves to these mind-numbing superficialities, ended up having the most graphic conversations with both their son and daughter about who was gay in their group in school, who might be coming out in the future, who was hooking-up with whom, who was technically saving themselves by doing everything sexually without having intercourse. From hidden-selves to slightly more observable real-selves, these kids emerged through engagement in the compelling world of pop.

Even in our house, where my wife, who is also a child therapist, and I were trained to go for depth, the trivial has informed us more than any psychological technique we learned along the way. As you can imagine from this section's opening dialogue between Jerry and George, *Seinfeld* is a topic of conversation around our house. One day,

Sam and I were sitting around trying to think of every "Seinfeldian" phrase that had become part of the vernacular: "high-talker, close-talker, low-talker, re-gifting, level-jumping, not that there's anything wrong with that, yada-yada, sponge-worthy," and so on.

Suddenly, when it came to "sponge-worthy," I found us involved in a frank discussion about safe sex. Our then-fourteen-year-old and I were able to discuss in graphic detail whether Elaine (the *Seinfeld* character) was in danger of contracting an STD because she was only using a sponge. Contraception had been endlessly brought up in Sam's life issues classes at school, but he was under the impression, since this was on *Seinfeld* (the real world), that a sponge must be able to protect from spreading disease or contracting any STDs. What had begun as another of our almost maniacally superficial discussions ended up a platform for the exchange of real information, maybe even something that might one day protect his or somebody else's life.

Stick with the trivial. I know that many times it will not lead anywhere worthwhile. But often, this is the way into a buried concern, what's really on a child's mind, just as it was with Amanda, a fifteen-year-old whose obsession with all things pop was driving her post-boomer, "values-oriented" mom crazy—creating terrible fights around their house.

Here's a compelling case dialogue adapted from *Breaking Through Teens* that mirrors the unexpected that parents often report when they remain "committed to the superficial." It took every bit of my faith in the trivial to stick with the following interaction:

Amanda told me, "I just hung out this weekend. Maggie snuck out in this really cool black tank top. Her parents haven't seen it. And Alice wore these new pants, like around her hips, with a big belt." Restraining myself from moving toward "significant" issues I said, "What about you? What did you wear?"

"I had on these new shoes. I have them on today. You wanna see them?"

I fought my impatience with this dead-end as Amanda displayed her new shoes and pointed out their various features: color, the height of the heel, the special laces.

Far from being the neutral observer, I reacted to each aspect she pointed out, ending with the shallowest observation I could muster, "It sounds like you guys wanted to look pretty good."

"Yeah, there's this new girl," Amanda responded. "Kelly. She's a real bitch. All the guys like her."

Instead of asking, "How do you feel about this new girl, Kelly?" I remained just as deeply grounded in the superficial, replying, "Oh. Who else was there?"

Amanda mentioned a few of the boys.

Reining myself in from the inevitable query about feelings, I channeled a veteran mother I knew and stooped to: "So what was everybody else wearing?"

To my surprise, Amanda perked up even more and said, "Well, just about everybody had on stuff that showed off their tattoos and piercings, because that's what Kelly's into. She's got a few that her parents don't even have a clue about. Her mom knows about her belly-button ring, but Kelly's also got her nipple pierced."

Now I was in a real dilemma: I could barely resist the temptation to explore mother-daughter relationships, secrets, etc. But I held firm and stuck to the trivial, asking, "So where did you guys go?"

We continued on this road to nowhere, discussing the mall, its new stores, and which tattoos Amanda thought were the best. Then, spurred on by my unflagging interest in the details most adults shut off, Amanda unexpectedly opened up about a serious decision: "Well, there's one tattoo I was thinking of. I'd get it on my hip. It's really small and my mom would never see it, because, even if I was wearing a thong, it couldn't really be seen."

I still held off from inquiring about thoughts or feelings and instead asked Amanda to describe the tattoo.

All of a sudden the discussion took a turn. Amanda said, "But just when I was about to do it, I got in a fight with Maggie. She said I was being a poseur, and I was getting a tattoo just because Kelly is now the queen and I'm trying to be like her. The big thing," Amanda added, "is she had her tongue pierced."

Finally, my first traditional "adult" response: "Do you think that's a good idea, this tongue piercing?"

Amanda was then ready to talk. "Well, she can do it, but I'm scared. For her, it's all about hooking-up. The boys really like it. But I'm just not ready for that, I don't think, so I'm just going to go for the tattoo instead."

We were now engaged at a very different level. I asked, "Are you going for the tattoo to look better, so you can find someone to hook up with, or to pose? Maybe Maggie was right. What's the tattoo for?"

"I don't know," Amanda sadly replied. "I have to think about what Maggie said. I don't know if I'm just doing it so Kelly will let me in. She's got everybody else . . . it feels like I don't have the friends I used to."

"You're right," I responded, genuinely moved. "Who's gone?"

The talk had moved from the trivial—malls, clothes, and shoes—to tattoos, hooking-up, and connections with other kids, all the way to abandonment and betrayal and the friends she'd lost. Over the next two weeks, the core of our interactions became everyone who'd moved into a tight circle around Kelly, leaving Amanda behind. Our discussions then began to center on her losses in general, and the decisions she needed to make about how to stay true to herself.

All the while I was helping her mom engage with Amanda by encouraging her to stay truly superficial—and she was reaping the benefits of more depth at home. These discussions with me were soon replaced by far more important discussions about the real world that mother and daughter needed to have.

Although I now teach this in just about every presentation, it took me nearly a decade to realize that by being fascinated with the seemingly trivial aspects of a child's life—who was there, what they were wearing, how did they look, what did they say then—at least occasionally, those trivialities lead to true-self experience and life dilemmas that absolutely need to be shared with an adult.

LISTENING DURING TRANSITIONS— USING THE IN-BETWEEN

A critical reality of listening that leads to authentic engagement in twenty-first century life is that the free-est generation talks during transitions. Post-boomer parents, so used to thinking of transitions—drop-offs, ferrying between extracurricular activities, the witching hour before dinner time—as nothing more than a logistical challenge, a necessary means to an end, often don't make use of the "in-between" to engage kids. Just as with the boring space between bedtime and sleep, kids are surprisingly open during the "Hello I must be going" transitional moments. Here is where "the pressured child," to use Michael Thompson's term, can become *the open child*. After all, we are so scheduled-in it's not as if these moments are rare.

Transitions are not an in-between anymore in which nothing happens. Transitions are so pervasive in the course of everyday living that they have become "way" real—and represent the potential for authentic engagement.

That figure and ground have reversed, and that transitions are soil for connection, is an observation I have repeatedly heard from parents and teachers, with both groups stunned at how the texture of life has changed. If the modern, nuclear family has become "a fortress," this is not your mother's or father's or grandparent's fortress, a castle surrounded by a moat of privacy and propriety. It is not the rigid family battleground of the sixties. It is not the boundary-changing/divorce-remarriage-divorce/family reconfigurations of the seventies. And today's fortress is not the increasingly permeable, leaky family of the late eighties, a frontier of interruption by just-invented electronic devices.

No, the new concept of family as fortress is about *transition*, and totally different from a Newtonian, static image that we continue to hold dear from generations past. The family fortress has taken a quantum leap through a wormhole into a swirling mass of continuous motion, equally familiar to frazzled post-boomers and their free-est generation children.

Like molecules bouncing around, the twenty-first century family is all movement and energy, where there is little chance to break away from swirling and parallel living. However, once we begin to accept that transitions are a usable part of life, we can begin to challenge the disconnection that goes on because we squander these moments. Learning to take advantage of them creates a whole new real-estate of potential engagement.

Viewed in this way, transitions become an invaluable opportunity to create authentic engagement. But first you need to actually recognize how much of your life falls into the realm of "transitions."

TRANSITIONS ARE "THE NEW REAL"

How to Use Them Well

There are so many transitions in the life of a post-boomer child and family one takes many of them for granted. Especially since they can be used to further communication, it is important to become more aware. Following are the most fertile ones as reported by parents and kids—transitions that often lead to connection.

1. Quiet moments during the morning rush—thirty seconds of these do happen, even in the chaos.

2. Before drop-offs and after pick-ups from: school, sports, after-school activities, birthday parties, and play dates.
3. Chilling out after school, or between screen time and homework, preferably with a snack.
4. Getting prepared for dinner or cleaning up together afterwards—as long as these chores are not points of contention.
5. Waiting for the computer to open up or waiting together while downloading files, YouTube videos or links.
6. Sitting together in the doctor's waiting room during those routine physical exams—when not sick-sick or expecting a shot.
7. Talking by cell phone on the way home from work—checking into what everyone's up to at home.
8. Whenever anyone is on the move using mass transit—lately there are almost always hours of waiting-time to check in.
9. Right after the winner of a reality TV show has been named. The choice usually stirs up reactions, opens up heated discussion.
10. Bedtime, of course.

Frank could not establish any meaningful dialogue with his daughter, fourth-grader Gwen. And the distance between them became greater the closer she got to real adolescence. Frank kept attempting to create conversation on *his* schedule, leading with probing questions destined to make his daughter, who preferred indirect conversation, very awkward. (Feeling "awkward" is absolutely toxic to comfort-minded contemporary kids.) After trying different techniques, I asked dad to think about the endless transitions that the family experienced during the course of an evening or weekend, and view one natural "in-between" as a place to start.

After going over this for a while, Frank chose to rise a little earlier to get in his morning run and then drive Gwen to school. He had previously just thought of this as an in-between, not worth much effort, and certainly not a potential time for connection, and at first it wasn't. Gwen actually resisted his involvement, wanting mom to come with her instead. But I encouraged Frank and his wife, Andrea, to stand firm.

I cannot report quick results here. It took several months for anything to actually change, but in small steps it did. First, Gwen, who'd been pretty nonengaged, unexpectedly asked dad for a hug one day before parting. The next week she invited him into the school to meet the staff in the downstairs office. And then, without warning, Gwen began talking about some of the teachers during their morning time. As Frank got used to listening in on Gwen's conversational channel, this once in-between transition became their "real."

As the year progressed Gwen increasingly opened up about what she was expecting in school on that particular day. Frank, now a very different listener, was allowed to offer advice about her feeling excluded gradewide and the popularity wars—issues that as a postboomer he had some personal experience with. It was extremely touching when Frank had to go on a business trip, to see how much his absence now affected this once dismissive daughter.

KIDS TALK AT THE WORST TIMES

There is no way around it. We can pay attention to and respect conversational style, we can turn "nothing into something," we can protect those talking rituals with everything we have, and we can make terrific use of the in-betweens instead of squandering them.

But an inescapable reality of twenty-first century life is that kids seem to open up at the absolute worst times—when we are least available for reasonable discussion.

I've often said that even teens don't really stop talking to their parents; just like younger children, they choose to open up at the most chaotic, gut-wrenching and tension-filled moments. This seems to have increased in recent years with post-boomer parents and their free-est generation kids, because kids are generally so scattered that they become focused and "emotionally literate" (a term coined by school consultant Michael Nerney) mostly when they are deeply upset about a specific issue.

Anger, need, and fear tend to organize kids' scattered minds. This paradox—the more upset a child, the more he or she is able to talk about what really matters—is a manifestation of twenty-first century, culturally induced attention deficit disorder.

Here is a hope as well as a challenge. These times (much like transitional in-betweens) of angst, rage, disappointment, or relentless negotiation provide everyone with a possibility for authentic engagement. As millennium parents we should be prepared, even though the reality of constructive communication during such tension-filled moments is often impossible to imagine.

"AN INCONVENIENT TRUTH"

Kid-communication Often Happens During the "Hottest" Moments

With life so chaotic, it's important to recognize that most kids don't really stop talking, they just seem to open up when you least expect it, which often means the most inconvenient and intense times. Be prepared, and you'll be better at making use of this twenty-first century fact of life. Kids talk:

(continued)

1. When they want something and are deep into relentless negotiating. When there's something at stake it is amazing how much it loosens kids' tongues.
2. When they are mad, scared, sad or upset—these experiences organize their often disorganized minds. The most heartfelt exchanges happen during the worst of times.
3. After you've managed to stand by a reasonable limit, despite their objections kids will often come back sometime later displaying a surprising degree of warmth and openness.
4. Just when they're leaving the house in the morning or before meeting their friends, kids pile on requests, demands, or ask permission—all with no time to think. This is not a moment to speak extensively; instead say, "Next time if you want to go, you need to give me more notice—then we'll have time to talk."
5. When you've been deeply disappointed, hurt, let down, kids will talk—if you show your distressed feelings they will more likely respond with greater openness.
6. Right after an event, being present at that exact moment—which is often logistically difficult. Unfortunately this seems to be necessary if you want to hear what happened before it fades into a distant memory or is lost in their scattered, everyday lives.

TAKE THE CENTER STAGE—WATCH YOUR KIDS OPEN UP

"It's very rare that this happens," says Lynette, mother of children of several different ages, "since we're always focusing on how the kids' day went, but as soon as I start talking at the dinner table about my day, one of them interrupts and takes the stage. If my husband, Stan, and I even dare to start a

discussion between us, then forget it. They cut in like Stan and I should be off-limits to each other. It's amazing, but it almost never fails."

Over the years this phenomenon, which just about every parent can relate to, has gotten even more predictable: take the spotlight from YouTube kids and the orneriest, most recessive child might actually start chiming in with detailed descriptions of his or her day. There are several reasons for this. The most obvious is that the free-est genera-tion is used to center stage. Between YouTube, MySpace, blogs, and endlessly multiplying venues for self-expression, kids are not only comfortable but feel that they are entitled to some kind of celebrity.

Given our contempory context, for kids to open up more, we parents need to demand some of the spotlight that is usually reserved just for our children.

This is not going to be easy. Let's face it. If parents and adults are viewed as two-dimensional, if parents' and adults' history are not even known let alone revered, if what adults do for a living is not cele-brated or met with gratitude, if empathy is considered mostly what kids need rather than a mutual expectation between parents and chil-dren, it is no wonder that talking about yourself is far, far easier said than done.

ARE YOU READY FOR YOUR CLOSE-UP, MOM AND DAD?

Don't Be Afraid to "Hog" the Spotlight (Once in a While)

Post-boomer parents move so easily to the background, they shape themselves so seamlessly around their kids, and are so focused on ceding center stage to children—it almost feels unnatural to think of oneself as a "star." But today's kids listen to parents who can move towards the spotlight of attention. To check out how much of the sup-

(continued)

porting character you've become, ask yourself the following questions:

1. When was the last time you played *your* music in the car?
2. When was the last time you took up a significant chunk of dinner time with a story from your day?
3. When was the last time going to bed included telling your story or a piece of your history?
4. Do your kids know anything about what's going on with you—with your friends, at work, or in your extended family?
5. When was the last time you told your child a dream of yours?
6. When was the last time you and your partner shared a complete story with the kids around?
7. When was the last time you interrupted your child to tell a story of your own?
8. How big a deal do you make of your birthdays, anniversaries, etc.?
9. When you are under the weather, do you expect kids to be considerate or caretaking of you?
10. When you sing along, do you stop singing when your embarrassed kids tell you to?

Parents are so attention deprived, so rarely on stage themselves that their hunger for the spotlight lurks in the shadows. For decades, post-boomers have known what it feels like to be seen and heard, up until the moment they have their own children. The required stifling of this normal need for recognition is a little discussed reason for the vicarious living that today's mothers and fathers do through their kids. This unexpressed hunger can be seen throughout our culture: from the hip, pot-smoking, "friend-mom" portrayed in the movie *Mean Girls* to "heli-copter" mothers and fathers to *Queen Bee Moms & Kingpin Dads* (Ros-alind Wiseman and Elizabeth Rapoport) vying for status and control. Not so secretly, just about every post-boomer also wants to "dance with the stars." As one outspoken mom put it, "If I can't be on stage, I'll just live through my kids being up there."

The child-centered nature of dialogue must change. If parents can be convinced that kids will open up as a result, authentic engagement through mutual communication has a chance.

The good news is that today's kids are completely used to instant exchange in all forums. Given kids' comfort with interaction and con-temporary parents' familiarity with the spotlight, having also grown up in a child-centered universe, there is a lot of room for mutual com-munication, if we can turn some old-think concepts upside down.

Share Your Experiences

Every day, try to remember something about what happened for you. At a moment that's comfortable, such as dinnertime, don't be afraid to sub-stitute *your* memories for all those questions about how your kids' day went. If you want specifics from your children, watch what happens when you take up air-time and get into specifics of your own.

Alicia always made it her business to ask her kids around the din-ner table how school was that day. For her efforts she heard the usual "Fine, Okay . . . not much." After these (typical) sparse answers and false starts, dinnertime would usually devolve into sibling spats, or *South Park* banter about farting, burping, and every other gross-out el-ementary school and preteen topic. Very quickly, the kids would finish dinner, run back to TVs, computers, homework, or all three at once.

With my encouragement, Alicia began to include an event from *her* day in the dinner menu. Let's say, an argument she might have had with a friend, or a difficulty she might have had with her boss. Much to Alicia's surprise, her stories immediately led to tails of fights between classmates: "Yeah, Julie went ballistic because her best friend ditched her." Or, "My teacher, Mr. Smith, was so mean to me; he didn't call on me once during the class."

Alicia was stunned at this change, but it is one I have repeatedly seen. Talk about your day, and it will jog your child's by-then ancient memory of what happened for them that day. Moving the spotlight to focus on you will lead to more evenly distributed attention, and some moments to help parents and kids' true-selves stay more connected.

State Your Opinions

Just about every free-est generation child has opinions galore. And so do you. Kids today expect a constant exchange of beliefs and attitude, and actually find it rather odd that parents hold theirs in check and focus so exclusively on the kids.

If you want to keep the lines of communication open in a "Hardball," "Crossfire," "The View" world, express yourself and see what happens.

In one family I know, a single mom, Brett, who had attended one of my lectures decided she would "for once" include her opinions of the day, while hanging out after dinner with the kids. This was a big change from her almost obsessional preoccupation with what the kids' views were on everything. Whatever her opinion of the day was, about stem cell research, the economic picture, or ordinary issues like the fact that no one got up on the bus for her even though she was loaded down with packages, Brett made it her business to *not* keep her opinions to herself.

All of a sudden everybody in the family, even her youngest elementary school child, jumped into the fray to express their own views. I was not surprised, having told Brett's PTA how kids were so used to instant polls, interactive TV, and the free-wheeling cyber-community that they'd leap at the chance to mix it up with their own parents as well. Even so, Brett was taken aback at her kids' uncensored arguments that began on-topic, i.e., mom's bus experience, then veered off as children do into talking about kid-rudeness and what actually happened to them during the day, what was really on their minds.

Brett's viewpoints, expressed with "attitude" and minus the hesitation, triggered her children as they might yours into becoming less hidden under that façade, and more personal during the rush of twenty-first century life. This is exactly the antidote our children need to the upside-down disconnection that child-centeredness breeds.

Give Your Relationship a Turn

As I've heard many, many hundreds of times, contemporary parents can't seem to get a word with each other in edgewise. My audiences, clients, and friends (as well as Stacey and I) complain endlessly at the way kids butt into any conversation we adults start with each other. This is such a common theme I (almost) believe researchers will discover that when parents do talk, a chemical gets released in children compelling them to interrupt. I really don't know why kids intrude, but it happens with such predictability and at all ages, that you can use it to further open communication.

If you want to get your kids to talk or listen more, then just begin a conversation with your spouse, partner, or a friend on the phone.

In many families, I encourage parents to make a point of talking to each other in full view of the children—not to wait until after the kids are in bed. The free-est generation goes to bed so late adults rarely catch a moment to talk with each other anyway. If mothers, fathers and partners just forge ahead with their discussion, kids will hardly be able to contain themselves; you will quickly find yourself in the unusual position of saying, "Wait your turn!"

I could practically offer an infomercial, money-back guarantee of this outcome, it has been successful with so many families. One family that I knew and wrote about a decade and a half ago, adopted the strategy during dinner, and their three kids became so inspired to join in, mom and dad had to develop a "red napkin" rule. While a family member held the coveted red napkin, only that person could talk, and everybody else had to listen. The same not-wanting-to-be-left-out response helps communication if you'd like to get something through to your child. Instead of talking louder and directly at your kids, talk in a low voice to your spouse, partner, or a friend on the phone. Once again, I almost guarantee that whatever your child is doing, regardless of age, he or she will stop and somehow try to eavesdrop.

Our daughter, Leah, admitted that when she was our young "pupster," every time Stacey and I would begin talking with each other in the kitchen, she'd pretend to be staring at a wall in the hallway, as if inspecting a small spot or irregularity, just so she could listen in on what we were saying. Of course, as Leah has since told us, this was because she was convinced we could only be talking about her. For whatever reason, though, our talking to each other immediately raised Leah's level of interest, as it will with your children at home.

Not only will you feel better about the one type of communication that post-boomer parents most ignore—talking with our partners at home—but you will spark the interest of kids whose attention is so frayed that they often need a less direct approach to trigger more focused engagement.

BEDTIME IS THE BEST TIME

There is probably no more universal experience parents share, especially in a post-boomer world, than the struggle of getting kids to bed at night. It's no wonder: in my interviews with kids and teens, when I ask when they most like to talk to their parents, over 80 percent say with absolutely no hesitation and across all age groups: bedtime!

It is a fact of twenty-first century life that the swirl of transitions, over-scheduling, and chaotic multitasking loads the deck against our ever making it out of that room at night. As kids tell me, "Bedtime is the one time I get my mom or dad's undivided attention."

Even though I've described this earlier and I know it is hard to hear, free-est generation kids understand just how scattered we are; they love bedtime precisely because of how different it is from the rest of the day. The lights are dim; there are usually no pressured attempts at communication; few if any reminders or logistics remain to be managed; and there is time to cuddle no matter how exhausted we are.

If we are open to it, bedtime communicating can take on that authentic tone children and parents desperately need, the kind that heals the dividedness of the day—and brings out the best, most heartfelt parts of ourselves and our kids.

Boomer and post-boomer parents are far less rigid about either a fixed bedtime, a la the advice of Dr. Benjamin Spock, *or* no bedtime at all, as advocated during the counter-culture family bed fad. Even Richard Ferber himself, the greatest bedtime icon of the past few decades, now inhabits a less formulaic middle ground between letting kids cry and staying around. These changes are no accident.

Contemporary mothers and fathers want to finally call an end to the day, but at the very same time we are in no hurry to get out of that room at night. And free-est generation kids, contrary to what we may think about the anxiety of twenty-first century living, don't necessarily want us in the room because of fears—but because they too recognize the chance for real engagement.

This is the last chance of the day to provide an antidote to our parallel living. This is the last chance of the day for a parent to tell his or her story, to create a three-dimensionality. This is the last chance of the day to clear up the unintentional, rushed friction that leads to such dividedness in families; this is the last chance of the day to talk to each other when there is so much noise the rest of the time.

It is no accident that today's parents share with me, often tearfully, how bedtime is *the* time they hear their child's most private thoughts—and it is the time when they tell kids the most poignant memories of their own childhood. So it is an opportunity for kind, true-selves to emerge and to hear each other, if you keep the following suggestions in mind.

Listening in the Dark

Kids open up best when the focus is off of them. They are far more prone to talk when we are in parallel position with them and don't make such a big deal about "relating." With its dim lights, with mom or dad worn down by fatigue or comfortably lying next to or sitting by their kids' side, bedtime is just such a parallel time.

Don't ruin this time with unnecessary expectations. Let it flow by following the no-pressure guidelines in the box below:

TAKING THE TENSION OUT OF BEDTIME

A Dozen Ways to Make Bedtime a Better Time

With life so rushed and chaotic, these days bedtime is not always an easy time. Schedules, several kids, endless technology and wired-up families make this a moment many parents both look forward to and dread. With attention to certain twenty-first century details, it can be turned into a time that adds a positive mood to the remains of the day:

1. Remember, bedtime actually begins about an hour before the kids hit the sheets—start turning off stimulating screen-time, record or TIVO special effects movies and so on, quite a bit earlier than saying "Kids, it's time to get ready for bed!"
2. After weekend or vacation, move slowly back to regular bedtime schedule—to allow child's biological

clock to readjust. Biology will almost always trump your rules.

3. Figure out which foods rev up or slow down your kids as the evening progresses.

4. If at all possible, try to stagger and plan who comes home just before bedtime—or things heat up again.

5. Don't try to relate—don't stare—no probing questions at bedtime.

6. And, please, no reminders, no negotiating, and no logistics to go over, either.

7. Nothing should be mentioned now about future plans—that might create anxiety or too much excitement.

8. If child can't stop—you've tried many other ways—and there are no peer crises in their lives, remove cell phones and laptops from the bedroom. Your child may need some help not being tempted.

9. Use bedtime as a moment to review the best part of the day for both of you.

10. Guided positive imagery is great at bedtime—books such as Maureen Garth's *Moonbeam* provide effective positive meditations before sleep.

11. Play "Lite" music both your and your child like.

12. This is the moment for sentimental and soothing personal memories from your life.

Reading is Good—Telling Your Own Story is Better

Two evenings ago, essentially the very moment I'm writing these words, as our son, Sam, went to bed, he asked me what it was like when it used to snow a lot. I told him how on snow days the whole neighborhood would spend the morning building snow forts in the park. Then we'd go home for lunch, soup and a sandwich, and return to the park, spending the rest of the

afternoon knocking down each others' forts and sleigh riding in between.
He was transfixed—so much snow in a world gone warm. The next day,
Sam approached me after school and said, "You know, in creative writing,
I wrote a story that was started from telling me what your neighborhood
was like when it snowed."

This experience is not unusual. Rather than exclusively reading, which is of course a wonderful part of bedtime, tell stories of your own history. This matters just as much to these pop-saturated, free-est generation kids as the adventures of others. Tell them about your life. Let them hear what it was like for you growing up; help them fill in the lines and connect the dots of *you*. Post-boomer parents need to create for children a narrative of who they are, and bedtime is the perfect time. Your story, making you an understandable person, matters more than you realize.

A father in our circle created a kind of verbal history with his daughter about his life growing up. Night after night, the stories of generations past helped to balance out the girl's daytime preoccupation with all matters pop culture. His daughter, not surprisingly, took up diary writing, a place for her true-self to be privately chronicled as she got older.

A mother I know lamented that the biggest teen change came when her daughter got a loft bed and it became impossible to sit by her side and tell the stories she had loved to share. Almost every night, mom would describe her own life and her family's journeys before coming to this country. A smart woman, keyed in to the pop culture world, she'd alternate by reading comics when her daughter was younger, then books that were mostly tie-ins to current movies. Then she'd go back to her own personal history. But when the loft bed arrived, these moments disappeared. Only after her daughter went off to college and they gradually began using those "anytime" minutes to say goodnight at the end of the day, did this close feeling return. All of a sudden they were again sharing the remains of the day.

There is no end to the kind of sharing that can go on about the world your family once lived in. The quiet, the hush of the evening makes this all possible, and sometimes, as happened with our Sam, it is internalized and used in the twenty-first century world our kids face the next day.

The Gates Are Closing—Creating a Sacred Moment

No matter where I go in the country parents share with each other how they say a prayer or have a special ritual at bedtime. The content doesn't matter. What does matter is that given the hurried, harried, anxiety-filled lives we live, an enlightened, positive prayer and ritual can make a huge difference as kids go off to sleep—and connect with their more compassionate and hopeful sides.

It is not old-fashioned to stress the importance of a bedtime ritual. In this area the old-fashioned is becoming necessary again for post-boomers and their free-est generation kids. Precisely because of the difficulty families have during the day—the "dividedness" that we live with—positive images or prayer at bedtime make a difference. They help deal with the boredom that kids often don't know how to deal with when the day's constant stimulation is over. They soothe the vulnerable, hidden selves of kids on the run and under the gun.

Choose your prayer, one that reflects your values and makes this a sacred ritual, sacred precisely because it brings out the best in all of us.

In our house at bedtime, after talking back and forth, after the stories and reading and sharing of history, a recounting of whatever might have come up during the day—for two decades our children have heard the same exact words. Without them, I don't think we all could really say goodnight:

"Good night. Sleep tight. See you in the morning light . . . I love you."

What will this be in your home? Make it matter, for both you and your children need the engagement of a compassionate word, need the moment of our best-selves saying goodnight, as the gates of the day are closing.

7

ENGAGEMENT THROUGH COMMUNITY

Rebuilding the Village— Twenty-First-Century Style

NEIGHBORHOOD UNBOUND— MR. ROGERS WORKS AT WAL-MART

Years ago, I was working with Alice, a divorced mother of Peter, an early-adolescent boy, who had run away. After Alice and I had been on the phone a number of times for the better part of the evening, I finally said, "You shouldn't be going through this alone, Alice. Why don't you make some calls to his friends' parents? I'm sure they will be sympathetic to what you're feeling."

"But I really don't know anyone well enough to impose on them like that," Alice told me sadly.

As it turned out, Peter was hanging out with a group of kids, having a great time while Alice sat home alone worrying about him. Peter was more connected to his peers than mom was to hers, and that meant that he called the shots. The hierarchy of the family (who was really in charge) had been turned upside down.

This situation, one I encountered a decade and a half ago was a harbinger of things to come. By the late eighties I could see that "the village" had disappeared. For better or worse, the cozy town or neighborhood we remember from movies or documentaries, with its informal adult presence, evaporated a long time ago. And I believe it will never return. Even the mall is losing its unique cachet with kids. In the face of warp-speed changes, malls have resorted to offering extra entertainment such as fishing in stocked ponds, ferris wheels, and interactive games in the hope of creatively luring in youngsters who would otherwise shop online.

After all, while malls are still a weekend attraction, for millions today the internet has become *the* place to be and *the* place to be seen. The free-est generation knows this and recognizes how the Web, suburban sprawl, and urban anonymity create a kid-universe behind that wall of silence. *They "get" that the eyes and ears of town are no longer there to monitor them. They are truly kids who know no bounds, a reality quite familiar to their mothers and fathers.* Post-boomer parents were themselves raised during a time of vast suburban and exurban development. They are not used to the benefits (and confines) of the village either. They no longer expect to know what kids are up to at all times. They try desperately to track kids' every move, but do so with far less success than they would like.

Reacting to the twenty-first century facts of community life, a mother and father recently explained to me their reasons for moving from a comfortable suburban area back to the small-town roots they grew up in: "We want a place where we and our four kids can have lives that *overlap* with people from other families—school, church, stores, community organizations, a neighborhood feeling. The way it works here, while everyone is extremely nice, it's like living in parallel worlds, and that's not what we want!"

This couple is right. When you get down to it, we modern families are too often parenting without the benefit of a safety net, expected to provide a container without having one around us ourselves. We are asked to nurture without being nurtured in return. This insecurity does not bring out our best-selves any more than our children's.

FROM CRUCIBLE TO COMMUNITY

When do many post-boomer parents finally get help for themselves and find the community that they've needed all along? Ironically, we find community support if our children get into serious trouble. Then we go from the crucible of tragedy to a community of peers. When there's a problem, like substance abuse or an eating disorder, failing at school, fighting with peers or a child runs away, that's when parents feel "held" by the community they have needed all along.

By the eighties and early nineties, as I wrote in *Parenting by Heart*, support groups, based on a twelve-step model and focusing on problem behavior, had become the neighborhoods of America. They were the modern answer to what was missing: extended families, organized spiritual affiliations, and close-knit communities of prior generations. Support groups, much like networks of previous times, offer concrete rituals of comfort and guidance, a regular place to meet, religious/ethical/spiritual values, and a common language. In short, these groups provide almost everything that previous generations could take for granted in dealing with the rigors of daily life. They are not to be dismissed. Issue-focused "sharing-caring" groups save countless lives each year and are a bridge between the disappearance of traditional neighborhood and a new type of engaged community.

My major concern is that these groups are sickness-oriented and usually are not joined before difficulties arise. They are not part of normal everyday living.

But I have hope, because over the past decade I've watched the entire nation moving quietly, with stealthlike determination, toward a belief that kids cannot be raised without engaged community.

Almost all of the things we worry about as adults responsible for the kids in our lives—the wild acting-out, the endless ability to go anywhere and be with just about anyone, the increase in high-risk behaviors, the voracious consumerism, the earlier and earlier social cruelty—won't be ameliorated without some change of engagement at the community level.

This chapter is about ways I have personally participated in community-building or have seen communities create engagement as a normal part of life in a post-boomer world, before crises happen.

CREATING A MODERN COMMUNITY— IT'S ABOUT CHANGING ADULT ATTITUDES FIRST

In writing this chapter on a distinctive post-boomer breed of community, I drew from my direct experience with many kinds of organizations—schools, faith centers, social agencies, not-for-profits, and corporations—as well as from my own community of peers: I spoke with numbers of colleagues to find out what they had seen in their travels and whether their views resembled the solutions I recommend in these pages. I needed a kind of reality check, because I believe that our definition of community is undergoing a fundamental change.

The prevalent theme of my discussions with leading experts, along with thousands of families and professionals, is that engaged community starts with a different adult attitude. Despite the way it often feels at home, grown-ups still control the structures of neighborhood: school, church, community organizations. Therefore adult attitudes must change in order to foster the community-building that's needed to guide our free-est generation children.

THE CIRCLES OF COMMUNITY

To see why change in attitude is so important, I'd like you to think about community by using the following image: picture your child as a point at the center of a blank page. Around your child is a circle of the adults most immediately involved in his or her life, you and your family. This closest circle exists in order to hold your son or daughter in what I've called an empathic envelope. As I described earlier, the empathic envelope is made up of *your* beliefs, *your* unique ways of communicating, *your* practices at setting limits, and *your* rituals for spending time together. Unfortunately, this first circle of adult presence and protection is especially permeable in the hyperkinetic, cyber-saturated, post-boomer era. Really, does your home ever feel off-limits to the incursions and unwanted values of the outside world?

The second circle of community is school. The presence of ramped-up school pressure, socially and academically, has such force that in many ways school is *the* driver of kid-life, involving thousands of hours every year and endless interpersonal exchanges every day. It is the instrument for future aspirations and current consumer tastes, with exponentially increased extra-curricular activities. School is the place where kids and parents, logistically, expend more energy than on just about any other part of their lives. Therefore, school is the second circle around our children.

In ways I will describe below, too often there is a chasm or an adversarial tone between the school and family circles. In terms of bringing out the best-self in kids and parents, the first two circles of home and school do not work in ways that create an engaged community around children, a reality that is just beginning to be addressed nationwide.

Now picture another circle around our kids, homes, and schools: the increasing number of faith communities that support children and parents. Throughout the country faith communities strive to find innovative ways to create engagement for families in everyday life crises, with rituals that celebrate the cycles of the year; "social action" to make the world a better place; and ways to search for a communal, spiritually-anchored life. For many families, houses of worship occupy both a place alongside the day-to-day life of school and family and at the same time a presence within the home and soul of the individual.

It is impossible from my perspective to describe twenty-first century community in a post-boomer world without including the impact of faith in the lives of families everywhere.

Next, picture a circle representing the world of work. Kids, families, schools, and church are all affected by the work we do, especially the balance between workplace and home life. Too often we think of "the job" as disconnected, a parallel world of responsibility and stress. But this is changing in wildly creative ways, as I will show below. Initiatives are springing up everywhere to lessen work stress and strengthen community engagement.

Next we find the circle of community agencies: hospitals, day care providers, not-for-profit organizations, wellness centers that provide the emergency services just about all community members need at some point in their lives. Unbeknownst to many, community agencies are also experimenting with innovative ways—prevention, education, easy access—to be helpful in a world in which the landscape has so dramatically changed.

This circle of service agencies is essential in providing a safety net, another container for families too often living at the far edges of connection, both before and after life-crises.

Finally, picture one more circle that is both outside all of us, yet increasingly part of the fabric of our daily lives: the internet. Through everyday points of entry the Web haphazardly connects us, weaving a vast social fabric. As I will show, while parents fear the Web (often for good reasons), innovative cyber networks are having a profound, constructive influence on the ways parents and kids commune with each other, creating an almost invisible scaffolding of connection.

This newest part of community is also the widest ranging, and messiest aspect of post-boomer life. One cannot think about circles of community without considering the internet as an essential part of the new community that has so much potential to protect the free-est generation and its parents.

The image of concentric circles is a way to picture the layered, but parallel life of post-boomer neighborhoods. By being involved with schools, houses of worship, corporations, and service agencies throughout the country, I've learned that expecting community engagement is precisely the attitude change required, the missing ingredient in modern living.

Authentic engagement between these circles of community is the goal of every forward-thinking group I've encountered in every circle of community.

As I describe cutting-edge attempts to re-engage adults with each other, you will notice that certain themes emerge, whether I am talking about school and parents, faith groups, workplace initiatives, or the internet. At its core, the story of community now is one of creating engagement that brings these circles together, sometimes in simple but innovative ways. As a first example, check out the box below.

ADULT CONVERSATION AND COMMUNITY CHANGE

Jim Mason
Beech Acres Parenting Center
Cincinnati, Ohio

Over the last number of years, social agencies around the country have become much more involved in creating communities and partnerships among adults. Among many such social service organizations, Jim Mason's Beech Acres Parenting Center stands out for its innovative approaches and its long-standing community presence. Some of the core ideas are summarized here:

• Beech Acres Parenting Center has moved from primarily delivering services to creating partnerships with

parents in all neighborhoods, especially at-risk neighborhoods.

- The vehicle for change has been simple: Initiating and
  facilitating conversation between the adults in these
  neighborhoods. These conversations focus on expressions of hope, such as "what is your vision for your children, what is your interest in becoming involved, what
  are your strengths as parents or as an adult who works
  with children?"
- Match up parents from neighborhoods with individual
  schools. Pay these parents to become involved. Teach
  parents to participate in schools by offering methods
  that focus on advocacy techniques and individual
  strengths. Hire and train parents to mentor others from
  their communities who are experiencing challenges.
- Connect parents to each other through churches, synagogues and other neighborhood networks that we
  tend to take for granted.
- Peer-to-peer mentoring in which one person's strength
  can help another person who has difficulties.

By focusing on conversation and the inherent
strengths that exist indigenously within neighborhoods,
rather than imposing expert opinion onto neighborhoods,
telling someone what is best to do for themselves—this
community-building approach encourages adults to, as
Mason says, "become the change we want to see."

In this chapter, I will describe more fully the circles of community
that have the most powerful *everyday* effects on our children and families. First I will focus on the two most immediate concentric circles:

school and families and how they need to work hand in hand in order to hold our children and protect them.

THE FIRST CIRCLE OF COMMUNITY:
"IT TAKES A SCHOOL . . ."

"Do you know why," I ask teachers, "you feel over-burdened? It's because your job description has changed and you don't know exactly how. It is because school is the new town center and you are the ones running it."

Teachers and school personnel are stunned to hear this "naming" of their everyday fatigue. A few months ago, a principal came to me looking very relieved, saying, "I think it may be time for us to embrace this, instead of pretending like it's not happening."

Unfortunately, it is difficult to embrace such fundamental change in a part of community we all take for granted. While houses of worship are an equally powerful center of life, school still represents the prime organizer of most children's *daily* schedule. No matter how much our lives have changed, school is where children and teens spend a majority of time when they are not with family.

This is an extremely troubling reality when one considers that the two major adult circles of community, parents and school personnel, are divided by a major schism. The distance between parents and schools is like a divorce in the neighborhood, one of the most daunting challenges in a post-boomer culture.

What is the divide about? To paraphrase the major complaint of school personnel: "We teachers feel like parents are asking us to raise their kids, who are running wild. They are handing them off to us to build character, not just teach curriculum." Parents for their part often feel that schools do not inform them soon enough or well enough: "By the time the teachers said anything to us about our child's problem, it was almost too late. They kept telling us we were just too worried; schools really don't encourage parents to be involved in school."

While blame will not get us where we need to go, I understand how school personnel and parents often feel at odds or disconnected from each other. Teachers and administrators have been gradually transformed into the eyes and ears of our towns. They are on the front line of kid gossip, legally are mandated to be first responders, to recognize the signs and symptoms of various psychological and medical disorders, and to report child abuse. They are involved in endless conflict-resolution between kids, and they are increasingly cast as teachers of ethics and values.

In other words, schools have become the monitors, counselors, judges, and clergy all in one.

Given these spiraling expectations, at every talk I give, teachers blame parents for being lax at home and expecting school to fill the moral vacuum. I cannot tell you how angry teachers are at parents for what they perceive to be an inability to "just say no" to kids who have become so free, so entitled that every request must be accompanied by a lengthy explanation. Just recently a highly gifted director of student plays told me she'd had enough of kids thinking they were really in charge; she was now requiring that they "sign a set of rules and guidelines once they'd gone through the audition process." "Where are their parents?" she asked in an incredulous tone.

Educators feel like they have to clean up after too many parents, the same mothers and fathers who come to school and tell them how to do their jobs. What's worse, teachers feel they're undervalued, unappreciated, and underpaid—even while society wants them to take on more. Is it really part of a teacher's job, they ask me at presentations, to spot emotional problems earlier, to solve social cruelty, or to deal with kids' inability to regulate anger or frustration? Making matters worse, if educators name kids' problems, parents may get defensive and go on the attack. And if a teacher focuses on one child and misses serious issues with another, or takes a firm stand (like wanting to create serious sanctions against a child for bullying behavior), in our increasingly litigious culture he or she—and the entire school—may be open to a lawsuit.

Often exacerbating the divide is a class conflict; educators and parents may be at opposite ends of the economic spectrum. Particularly in urban and suburban schools with large numbers of middle-class and well-to-do parents, teachers feel that mothers and fathers talk down to them, treating them like hired help or babysitters. I've heard the same complaint of parental disrespect from teachers in less affluent school districts. They feel that too many mothers and fathers don't discuss issues, attacking instead by blaming the school's personnel for their children's social difficulties and academic failures.

Interestingly, while No Child Left Behind grabs headlines, the most frequent questions teachers ask me are about parent-conference days, which many dread. They complain that parents rebuff feedback or, on the other end of the spectrum, take constructive suggestions about improvement and then pressure their children relentlessly.

All of this may be true, but there's a parents' side of the story too. Even the most vociferous mothers and fathers report they feel intimidated and shut-out by many educators. From nursery through high school, parents describe their fear of teachers, who hold the key to children's future in this highly competitive world. Parents' fear of school is palpable. Many teachers *do* quickly circle their wagons and create an impenetrable boundary between the classroom and parents, who feel pushed away by pejorative labels such as "over-involved" or are literally kept out of the hallways and classrooms by school policies. Mothers and fathers resent that they can't discuss with teachers what they observe in their children at home more regularly than twice a year. School consultant Michael Nerny offers this pungent observation: "Schools often seem to go out of their way to make parents feel unwanted, yet when something goes wrong, *then* they're called in."

Just today I spent considerable time trying to convince well-meaning parents that they should be open with the school about wanting to seek out counseling for their eight-year-old son. The depth of their distrust, the concern that he might have this as a permanent blot on his record, the worry that private information might become public within the school, and that he could be damaged by bad reports when he moves on to middle school—all of this speaks of the deep schism between home and school.

Talk about disengagement! By the time children get to seventh grade, when classes are departmentalized, parents feel that twice-a-year conferences are a joke. Other than grades, which tell only a small part of the story, they have no idea what their kids are doing for the bulk of the day. In parents' view Nerny is on target: historically teachers have gotten in touch for the most part only when something serious or dramatic happens—cheating, blatant and repetitive truancy, the failure to hand in several months' worth of assignments, or instances of selling drugs. Recently, yet another parent I know received a notice that her child had been late getting to school. Nothing, mom first thought, to really worry about. Then she carefully read the notice which documented over *fifty* late days. "When in the world did they think I should learn about this—after he'd missed an entire year?" she incredulously shrieked.

Sadly, both sides are correct. Meanwhile, kids may go unattended because of this home/school schism, and too often tragedy provides a horrific pause for reflection. In a school in the Northwest, the captain of the fencing team, an A+ student and in many ways a model citizen, hanged herself. Looking back, the teachers realized that they had observed a subtle change in the tenth grader's mood, but either they had not thought to call home or were afraid that their interference might make the situation worse. Parents of other kids also had noticed that the girl seemed a little off, but they were afraid of sounding critical of another parent's child. The adults simply never got it together, never compared observations, or shared concerns. Would that have changed anything? No one can know for sure, but in all likelihood it wouldn't have hurt.

ENGAGEMENT THROUGH PARENT-SCHOOL PARTNERSHIPS

In order to deal with this chronic and sometimes fatal disconnection, schools and parents need to develop "partnerships."

Having been involved with schools over the past two decades, I've seen significant movement toward creating bridge-building partnerships. Ten years ago when I wrote about them in *The Second Family*, I was pretty sure the few alliances I'd learned about signaled the beginning of a paradigm shift. Now, with so many more schools and parents on board, I am convinced that the shift has occurred.

However, as I have learned through my experiences, creating a parent-school partnership is not an easy process, nor is it simply bringing in a faddish set of techniques. I've witnessed countless schools purchase communication-oriented packages to get the process going—for example, social-emotional modules, programs to deal with conflict resolution and anger management, or an emphasis on ethics—but they may fall short. What schools and parents forget is that the real goal is not a specific skills package—it is the idea of a partnership embracing the entire community of children, school personnel, and parents.

This creation of a twenty-first century village, with the school as a town center that reaches out to both children and adults, is part of the radical shift I have seen spreading around the country. Nothing less than this systemic change in attitude—the expectation of bringing together the circles of parents and school—will help post-boomers live in an engaged community.

THE CHOREOGRAPHY OF CHANGE

By the mid-nineties I had begun to help a number of schools create partnerships that would ultimately change not only the way adults conducted themselves, but the way they regarded one another. As these efforts have borne fruit (or not), one thing has become abundantly clear—forget the kids, they are not enough.

All the meetings and general scaffolding of partnerships are inconsequential unless the adults are willing to address beliefs that created the parent-teacher divide in the first place.

This kind of new venture takes time; up to four years is often necessary to effect movement toward real parent-school connection and to create programs that actually work. It is essential to include all parties: parents, administrators, teachers, and eventually, the kids. If one or two important constituencies won't participate, the effort will likely fail. The key is to involve major constituents and to be purposeful, to move with what faith communities call "intentionality."

Creating a partnership is about what I think of as "the choreography of change." If one ignores the community's different moving parts, resistance will certainly emerge. In several schools, for example, the PTAs were put off when the new partnership between parents and school did not include them from the beginning. They opted-out of supporting attendance at major partnership events. Additionally, teachers in almost every school (as their workloads expand), become extremely resentful if they are not compensated for the extra time required to develop programs—in effect creating more, rather than less resentment toward parents and administration. In other schools kids are brought into meetings way too early, and they rebel against becoming involved with anything so closely intertwined with adults.

These examples illustrate more than just inclusiveness or professional sensitivity or turf-battles or underlying resentments over time and compensation. They represent how carefully we must proceed when trying to change a system. Attitudes are ingrained and must be respected. One extremely astute and irate sixth grader put his finger on the real issue of this paradigm shift a decade and a half ago: "What are you parents doing getting together—who do you think you are; only kids are supposed to talk to each other!"

Be forewarned. In the face of these challenges, before you advocate for a parent-school partnership in your own backyard, learn from others. Use the guidelines suggested below to get alliances off the ground.

Partnership Step 1: Define Membership

As in the formation of any group, the first issue is to define its membership. This is also the trickiest. Not everyone will want to be involved, but just about everyone will be insulted if not asked.

FORMING THE TEAM

As I wrote in *The Second Family*, the first and most important step is to choose wisely from the school's different constituencies. While varying from school to school, successful partnerships usually include:

- Two or three highly proactive parent leaders, especially those already involved with the PTA of the school.
- Representatives from the administration—in particular, the principal of the school and a couple of deans, if your school has them.
- Teacher representatives and guidance counselors—but only those who are committed to the project and who can hopefully be remunerated for their efforts.
- Student representatives—a balance of "cool" and less "popular" kids from different grades.
- Representatives from health or wellness centers connected to the school.
- Law-enforcement personnel, if any are involved with the school.

Partnership Step 2: Articulate the Mission

The second task is to conceptualize the mission of the partnership. For example, Geoffrey Jones, head of The Potomac School in Virginia, points to the partnership's mission statement as central to changing the entire culture of the adults in the community.

As Jones summarized, "Articulating what we stood for allowed us to make powerful connections despite and because of our diversity. In working on this together we understood that the school's mission is to make connections throughout the community; we wanted to build on the idea of seeing oneself in the context of people who are different from each other, but at the same time want to make a difference in the world."

Potomac's mission statement was the work of many representatives of the community. During a consultation I was deeply impressed to see parents, teachers, administrators, and student representatives around me. Their words described the over-arching umbrella under which the alliance was protected, as well as the inner compass that helped create a coherent partnership for the entire school. Whatever your community's values are, articulating the mission of a parent-school alliance creates clarity and what I call "readiness for change."

The moment that the mission statement includes the idea of changing the adults, rather than just the children, is the moment when a partnership begins—all for the benefit of figuring out how to bring out the best-selves of our kids.

Essential to the mission at Potomac was an emphasis on "old-fashioned" values: courage, honesty, commitment to others, and compassion. Sometimes ordinary moments demonstrate that stated goals can have a profound transformative impact on taken-for-granted attitudes of the community.

Jones told me the following story: "One of our best football players, a senior who had been recruited to go to play college ball, suddenly leaves the bench in the middle of a game. Where is he going? This 'guy's-guy,' this major 'jock' in the community walks over to his father who is about to head off on a business trip. In front of all of his football buddies, his coach and parents in the stands, this teenage all-American boy hugged his dad, gave him a kiss goodbye, and reminded him to call when he arrived safely at his destination."

"What was so special to you?" I asked. Jones replied, "I don't believe this scene would have been remotely possible even a few years ago, without our stressing the courage to show compassion openly." Potomac's mission was a more compassionate, balanced culture—humanistic as well as academic. Through many different forums—classes, assemblies, curriculum, parent meetings, and guest speakers—this value was repeated to everyone in the community over a period of years. But articulating it as a goal was the beginning of change.

Partnership Step 3: Modest Expectations—Ask for Feedback—Develop Trust

Parents and school must develop not only a specific mission, but a patient time line so the initiative doesn't tax everyone too heavily or lead to disappointment. The goals that "rally troops" (in other words, are urgent enough to involve over-extended post-boomer families) vary from everyday issues such as lowering stress to handling social cruelty to developing a code of ethics to dealing more effectively with high-risk behaviors. You might want to focus on just one such key goal at first.

For example, in one school "stress" turned out to be the issue that motivated people toward a parent-school initiative. In the high-pressure atmosphere of this community it seemed to touch kids, school personnel, and parents. As one of the initiative's proponents told me, "We need to pick something that affects the most people, stick with it, and have realistic expectations of slow progress."

In another setting, New York City's 92nd St. "Y," an organization with a renowned toddler parenting center, nursery and pre-K, fostering "imaginative" play became the overarching mission. Why imaginative play? The staff had become extremely concerned that the nonstop interactive atmosphere of the free-est generation was robbing even younger kids of their ability to play. The initiative, called Wonderplay, focused on imaginative skills in the early years to help children deal with interpersonal problem solving, handle boredom and transitions, and increase verbal as well as written expression.

Even such a non-controversial mission as this required modest expectations. Besides helping to articulate their mission, I also worked on a several-year time frame for realistic change. After about a year of professional training on the topic, some interested parents were invited in. Fretta Reitzes, the executive director of the program, and co-author with Beth Teitelman of *Wonderplay, Too,* understood the need for slow, steady progress rather than splashy events. Even with this extremely patient time frame, the ordinary tensions of enthusiastic but typically harried staff and overly pressured parents needed to be attended to in order to keep the momentum of change going. Steadiness shows: the program has been extremely successful at increasing the number of staff involved in training possibilities, and slowly creating a common language to further dialogue with parents about their children.

Part of creating a steady, well-choreographed process is to stop along the way and get feedback. Most schools regularly ask parents to evaluate presentations, and some send out brief surveys requesting the critical issues on parents' minds. (I cannot overemphasize how even a decade ago, many school administrators were afraid to allow parents to express views for fear of starting "gripe" sessions and community "revolution.") Times have changed. The same administrators now regularly seek out parents' and teachers' thoughts before and after presentations to get a reading of the community's pulse.

Feedback is crucial to creating twenty-first century partnership and community. We do not live in the more authoritarian world of the greatest generation, where much will be taken on faith. Interactive feedback is now an essential part of trust-building and program continuity.

The issue of trust, which has been brought up over and over to me, is the subtext of creating any successful partnership among the adults in a community. Post-boomers raised on nonstop interaction need to feel that their opinions will be valued, that more work won't be added on to their already half-crazed days and nights, and that this project won't become another bureaucratic infrastructure to weigh them down.

Trust-building also has its utilitarian side: the attempt to lessen the divide between the circle of school and home costs money! So it is especially important for parents and potential funders to trust the process in order to fund these initiatives from the ground up.

SHOW THEM THE MONEY

Ways To Fund Partnerships

I have been involved for decades with not-for-profit initiatives. Paradoxically, charitable experience makes one sophisticated about finances, especially the importance of effective fundraising techniques. Building a neighborhood partnership is expensive, including as it does teacher remuneration, monies for special events, promotion costs, and overtime fees to keep communal spaces open for after-hours adult involvement.

Following are some ways that schools at all points on the economic spectrum have found the money, even when they thought they couldn't:

- Silent sponsors from the parent body, especially those who are emotionally connected to specific issues
- Alliances with neighborhood businesses
- Consortiums of schools that partner for events

- Grants from local and state governmental agencies for specific aspects of the partnerships—for example, a community health day
- Discretionary funds from local elected officials
- Fundraising events co-promoted by the school and PTA, such as potluck dinners, auctions, flea markets, and 50/50 raffles

Partnership Step 4: Creating "A Community of Learners"

One of the most important "attitude" changes I have seen in bringing the circles of adults together is an emphasis on redefining parents and teachers as "a community of learners"—grownups who continue learning not just for ourselves, but to better understand who our kids are.

Despite such a commitment, narrowing the divide is hard. And one of the main reasons is very simple, indeed. Until recently parents and teachers have learned in different corners of a child's world, turning to very different sources about the same kids they are involved with each day.

Several examples come to mind. In one, an early-adolescent girl, Crystal, keeps to herself and doesn't participate in class often, though when she does she has extremely intelligent things to say. More worrisome, she doesn't mix with the other children and is often seen alone, even eating by herself during lunch.

Crystal comes from a broken home, her mother having left the family when she was an infant. In addition Crystal has lived with several relatives over much of her life. The teachers believe that because of this troubled history, Crystal's social issues and lack of passion about learning are essentially emotional. Having just been through a number of professional trainings on the benefits of systems-oriented treatment (meaning family therapy), the teachers and guidance counselor strongly recommend a therapeutic approach for Crystal.

Crystal's parental guardians have been doing their homework as well. And using different source material, they have come to a very different conclusion. They are concerned that Crystal may have attention deficit disorder (ADD) and other learning issues that prevent her from becoming interested in anything that requires sustained focus and dedicated passion. In their view, therapy is the *last* thing she needs, after academic remediation and a possible pharmacological intervention.

Meanwhile, months pass without anything being done, until a crisis develops when Crystal suddenly refuses to go to school.

As I listen to these two estranged adult camps, it is clear that they are in such different places not because of bad intentions, but for a good reason: they have been doing their homework about childhood disorders and child development in totally different contexts. It is no wonder they cannot come together on what to *do.*

Until recently, few parents and schools recognized that if they began to learn together about what to look for, they might end up on the same page a lot sooner. This is central to the development of an effective partnership between home and school

Another situation illustrates the damage done when these two circles of community use basically different learning resources. Precocious Adam is considered so advanced by his teachers in his high-powered suburban community school that they strongly recommend he be moved ahead one grade. Rarely have they seen such verbal abilities in a second grader. With a lot of coaxing, his single mom and grandmother finally agree against their judgement to move Adam up a year.

Almost immediately, trouble begins. Once the leader of his class, Adam immediately becomes a follower and the least developed kid in the social pecking order. In his own words many years later, Adam poignantly told me, "If I were a baseball player, you'd have pictured me going up until third grade, and from then on I'd be going nowhere but down to the minors." What makes this tragic is that if parents and school had been learning together from what are now accepted tenets of child development—don't rush kids along, especially boys—they might well have come to a different decision. By high school, the results of this division are painfully clear: Adam's self-esteem is in the pits, and the adults are at war blaming each other for the trouble he's in.

Another situation was even more heartbreaking, even for a seasoned professional like me. Amy was so severely taunted by classmates in her elementary school that by junior high she had begun secretly purging herself and engaging in early sexual experimentation. Neither the school nor Amy's parents could ever get together on who she really was: the obstinate and ornery stand-out who created her own destructive fate, or a victim of unnecessary peer abuse who desperately needed to be contained by the adult community.

Neither home nor school had learned how to understand the victim/perpetrator dynamic in its most current perspective. In short bullying is increasingly viewed as a destructive power-play purposely meant to hurt another who cannot easily respond because of his or her lower social status in the peer group. Bullying is not usually an event "created by the victim," who ought to handle it alone in a kids-will-be-kids world. Indeed, many bullies are empathically gifted and use that gift to their advantage, rather than suffering from some emotional-intelligence deficit. Because of this lack of understanding of the bullying dynamic, neither the home nor the school could approach Amy in a coordinated way. Until the adults began to develop some humility and accept that they needed to learn together, poor Amy didn't stand a chance. Once they did, however, I was able to convince both parties to listen to the same enlightened voice regarding peer abuse—and the taunting and Amy's purging finally began to ebb.

What is the solution to this ordinary but tragic quandary? Parents and teachers must become a community of learners. They need to learn the same language from similar sources, so they can complement each other.

Partnership Step 5: Learning Together—New Basics We Can Count On

It is a revolutionary notion that we now know enough about child development and parenting—information that is not going to change with next week's science news—that we adults can be on the same page to guide the free-est generation.

The myth that everything about parenting is relative, a matter of individual belief, and that there are very few "facts" parents can count on, stifles an effective adult voice in post-boomer communities. This myth also inhibits adult collaboration. Contrast this contemporary lack of confidence to the certitude of the greatest generation or their rebellious boomer kids.

It is astonishing how the schism begins to narrow when parent-school partnerships cull the latest literature on tough twenty-first century parenting issues. In fact, information gathering and synthesizing is one of my most important tasks when adults get serious about becoming a community of learners. To give you an idea what I mean check this box for a brief outline of some new basics you can count on:

THE REAL WORLD

Post-Boomer High-Risk Behaviors Adults Need to Know

Sticking one's head in the sand or entirely letting kids live off in their own parallel world, does not help parents or kids deal with the realities of twenty-first century life. Adults need to keep up with the ordinary high-risk decisions that are part of everyday living.

1. Kids are not usually peer-pressured into being bad—in fact, today's children of all ages pride themselves on not pressing their values onto others.

---

2. Kid networks are almost seamless—for example, word about an unsupervised house makes the rounds in minutes—astonishing, but true.

3. Peer-bonding—wanting to be connected—is a greater reality than peer-pressure; today's kids do things to feel connected, not because someone "made" them do it.

4. There are few ways to completely protect your child's exposure to sexual, violent, or graphic material—the best protection is your knowledge of their interests and willingness to talk about them.

5. Issues with body-image and food begin in elementary school, and are no longer just part of "girl-world." Boys have begun buying into the alpha-beauty message. Know your child, watch their eating and exercise habits.

6. Life issues classes are often a couple of years ahead of today's kid-concerns. Check the school's curriculum to make sure they talk about what's happening right now—friendship, triangles, parties, exclusion, lunch-room politics—not sexy, but real.

7. Money is on kids' minds a lot—keep track of yours, have a sense of where it is going, quickly notice when figures don't add up.

8. Pop-culture is not just for kids—learn it, or at least some of it, so you can "learn" your child. Do you know the videogame, magazine, computer sites that count?

9. Don't entirely despair or freak out—studies repeatedly find that kids are more cautious on-line, about sexual behavior and friendships than we give them credit for. Our guidance matters far more than we know, but children and teens also think about what matters more than we realize.

Busting the myth that every bit of new information about parenting and child development contradicts the last is central to becoming a community of learners. So I will include here a few key areas of "must-have" information, focusing specifically on several tough twenty-first century concerns that are central to the creation of engagement between parents and school. Recognizing *what we now know* allows parents and schools to more readily agree on remedies.

ADULT-ED: THE FREE-EST GENERATION AND SUBSTANCES

Despite their own pretty wild experience growing up, today's parents and teachers know far too little about changes in post-boomer drug and substance life, certainly not enough to be able to have much impact on their young charges. Today's realities about alcohol, marijuana, and other hallucinogens, as well as harder drugs such as cocaine and meth, are not always common knowledge to either the parent body or school personnel. Similarly, few parents and teachers know the seamless way that kids keep in touch with each other regarding upcoming parties. Nor do they grasp the realities about raves, loft parties, and leaving a house empty without adult supervision, as well as the changing laws on parental supervisory responsibilities. To test yourself on how much you know about the current view on kids and substances, check out the box below.

YOU CAN MAKE A DIFFERENCE

Facts from One of the Country's Foremost Experts on Kids and Substances

Joe Califano

Joe Califano, one of the country's leading experts on substance use and abuse, as well as a former U.S. Secretary

---

of Health, Education, and Welfare runs The National Center for Alcohol and Substance Abuse (CASA) at Columbia University. Joe is one expert who knows both the research and parenting realities in this area. He and the professionals at CASA are working on a book, *Parent Power*, to help parents raise drug-free kids. Here are some select observations and guidelines for mothers and fathers:

1. Why is talking to kids or having clear expectations important? Sixteen years of CASA research has found that a child who gets to age twenty-one without smoking, using illegal drugs, or abusing alcohol is almost certain to never do so. In other words, delay . . . delay . . . delay.
2. Seventy-five percent of kids who use alcohol or other drugs in college were using them in high school. So parents raising teens have a great influence on whether their kid will binge drink in college.
3. Parents should be honest (using one's own personal standards of privacy as a compass) about their own histories with their kids and use their own experience to guide children to make clear choices about alcohol and drug use.
4. Tell your kids that marijuana has a significant impact on memory, motor skills, and the brain, itself; in fact, more kids are in treatment for marijuana dependence than for alcohol and all other drugs combined. Be sure to use the Internet and show them the brain images of individuals addicted to marijuana (or other drugs) compared to those who do not use.
5. Emphasize to your children that alcohol and drug

(continued)

abuse is the one major activity (besides unsafe sex) that can affect their lives for the worse, sometimes with tragic consequences—affecting their futures more than their grades or the college they get into.

6. For kids who do not abuse alcohol or substances, parental disappointment is the most important factor, so set clear rules for your children and show them when you are let down.

7. Teen perceptions of immorality, parental disapproval, and harm to health are far more powerful deterrents to teen smoking, drinking, and drug use than illegality of substances. As kids become college juniors and seniors, stressing illegality has more of an impact— probably because jobs and graduate school are around the corner.

8. The more often children have dinner with their parents, the less likely they are to smoke, drink, or use drugs. The relationship between substance use and family meals is so strong, on a chart it would show that as dinners per week go up, the likelihood of teen substance use goes down.

ADULT-ED: KIDS AND SOCIAL CRUELTY

Similarly, I have been startled by how much learning needs to go on in the area of social cruelty—how helpless twenty-first century parents still feel in the face of kid meanness. It is striking to hear the seasoned heads of today's schools admit to me that they just don't know how to handle the kind of sophisticated peer abuse that has become an everyday occurrence: a boy who is chronically tormented about his social awkwardness or a girl who last year was the enemy of the entire grade for being too outspoken. It is startling to hear the academic dean of a high school admit that he has no idea how to help students who have been typecast and tormented as appearing "gay." And it saddens me to listen to a dean of student life admit that he had no more tools left in his bag of tricks to help a child, now a loner, who did the courageous thing and reported another kid stealing students' property from cars in the school's parking lot.

Clearly these well-meaning adults need to have consistent information about twenty-first century social cruelty, and it's there to be had.

STOP BULLYING NOW

Stan Davis and Barbara Coloroso

Stan Davis and Barbara Coloroso are two of the leading experts in the country on serious childhood bullying. They have spent decades dealing with the most practical ways we can lessen taunting, threats, and ostracism among kids of all ages. Both emphasize the following steps in mind-set and behaviors adults need to take to protect our children:

- *Bullying is not a necessary rite of childhood.* It is not an expression of normal aggression between kids; rather it is an ethical/moral issue, one that requires adults to decide where they stand.
- *Bullying is not primarily about aggression between equals.* It is most often a power play in which one child with a greater power position and/or social status seeks to increase his or her dominance, regardless of its effect on the other.

(continued)

- *Adults need to understand when to intervene, which levels of social cruelty merit adult attention.* Adults do not always understand when it is essential to step in vs. when it is best to stay out and let the kids handle it. Stan Davis defines three levels.
  1. Green represents kids simply choosing not to be friends with other kids; this is a normal part of childhood and requires no intervention by adults.
  2. Yellow represents taunting and bullying that is likely to get in the way of the schools' core mission: a child's ability to learn. When this happens, school faculty must stop the behavior and demand greater restraint.
  3. Red indicates that a child's psychological or physical safety is likely to be threatened. In these cases firm, clear consequences, such as suspension and even expulsion, may follow.
- *Encourage greater ethical/moral thinking in kids.* Barbara Coloroso's work has focused more recently on this area. In order to lay a foundation of empathy, rather than social cruelty or bullying, kids need to develop the ability for critical thinking about the ethical dilemmas involved in schoolyard politics—at the earliest grades. "Do I go along with this? Should I step forward? What is my role as a bystander, and my responsibility towards a fellow classmate?" Barbara's work on bullying has led her to believe that unchecked power imbalances are indeed dangerous. In her view, it is a surprisingly short distance from cruel taunting to hate crimes and even to genocide.
- *Both Barbara and Stan believe we need to focus on youth who bully and bystanders to change their behav-*

> *iors, not primarily on victims to change themselves.* Leaders' skills need to be acknowledged and channeled into more constructive behavior. Bystanders must be protected by the adults to step forward, so they can do the right thing without fear of retribution.

ADULT ED: SHARING INFORMATION WITHOUT HURTING YOUR CHILD OR LOSING THEIR TRUST

Unfortunately, learning more about difficult contemporary issues such as high-risk behavior and bullying isn't enough. Adults must also learn how to share information about these issues with each other. This is a skill that parents and teachers should practice from the earliest years of school—not wait until adolescence hits.

Neither parents nor school personnel feel comfortable stepping forward if they hear about troublesome or potentially dangerous behavior. Most free-est generation kids threaten never to open up again if mom or dad mentions a word to anyone, even though the "top-secret" info might be on someone's wall in Facebook for every kid to see anyway. An example of this involved someone I know who called up absolutely paralyzed about what to do with information her son had shared. It seems that several girls he knew had been posting graphically sexual pictures online and drinking secretly before going to parties. None of the other parents appeared to have a clue. Their son was worried, to be sure, but he was dead serious about maintaining confidentiality, as he'd witnessed others kids being ostracized for years when they broke the code of silence. This normally proactive mom had no idea how to share information without entirely endangering her son or breaking their trust.

When a friend's daughter was in seventh grade, a pal of hers talked to his closest buddies for several weeks about feeling down. Though all his friends were worried, true to second family code, none of them told their parents or teachers. Finally, suspecting the boy might be suicidal, one of his classmates confided in her mother that she was worried about him. In the absence of concrete guidelines for dealing with such problems, her mom had misgivings, and no idea what to do. Finally she asked my advice. What would happen if they called the school? What was their responsibility? What about the boy's parents? Would the girl be ostracized for breaking the code of silence?

Teachers have the same set of questions, even though they may be based on different concerns. For example, school personnel often don't get involved because they're afraid of making a situation worse. A teacher at a workshop told of calling a student's home because she was worried about the boy's depression. During the phone conversation she could hear mother and son screaming at each other. The boy did not show up at school for several days afterwards, plaguing the teacher about whether she had done the right thing. Like the parents I mentioned above, teachers question what their responsibility is, when and how to call a parent, and whether they will be violating the trust of their students.

Different schools have different policies regarding teacher disclosure, but most parents are stuck. So, here are suggestions to consider when you learn about something worrisome. It definitely may be time to call a licensed counselor or therapist if these don't work for you.

"MOM, DAD, YOU CAN'T TELL ANYONE WHAT I TOLD YOU!"

How to step forward without hurting your child or your relationship

With the wall of silence so daunting, many parents and kids face tremendous difficulty stepping forward when they know something troublesome about another child.

Here are some ways to do so. They are not a guarantee your child will receive no kid blow-back, but they will lessen that probability and allow you to do what your conscience dictates.

1. Recognize that in areas of life and death safety, as a parent you do have responsibility to share information. To help, ask yourself, what if something does happen—afterwards the first question is always why the adults who knew did nothing.
2. Unless danger is imminent, discuss first with your child before taking action. This is not about permission, rather to prepare the best way to step forward.
3. Say clearly you've got to do something—set a time limit that fits the urgency of the situation—and try out different options by role-playing with your child.
4. Identify one adult—another parent or school personnel— who can be absolutely trusted with confidentiality and protecting your child's identity. Sometimes this is not always possible, but the other adult also has the responsibility to support your child and you.
5. Lobby the school for safe "connections of concern," such as anonymous answering machines, e-mails, etc., as well as school personnel who are designated as "vaults," who will hold and act on sensitive information. Some schools point out several of these vaults to kids from the first day.
6. Take the blame yourself for needing to share information—this helps a child to say "My mom or dad did this on their own."

(continued)

7. Lobby the school to officially write guidelines for stepping forward: outlining parents, and kids' legal and ethical responsibilities, so everyone will feel more concretely supported. Concrete guidelines help parents to be courageous.

8. Pressure the school to gradually change its culture, so that showing concern is labeled as being "heroic," rather than being a "tattler." This is beginning to happen around the country.

A COMMUNITY OF LEARNERS— "PUTTING ASSES IN THE SEATS"

It is inspiring to know that by paying attention to details, the decision to learn together can grow into something much longer-lasting than a "one night stand" about a specific topic. It can grow into a community of connected adults.

In large numbers of schools I've worked with, one-night "special" presentations have led to seminars with other child professionals on subjects identified from the initial workshop. This has been followed by more workshops based on questions parents and teachers came up with from previous presentations. A hunger for learning had been created.

In several suburban communities, much larger events were created by the schools' personnel and proactive parents, including workshops by experts, teachers, *and* students. Topics examined many areas of twenty-first century living, such as daily health issues like STD's, the ethics of stepping forward, academic pressures, and the real-world of ordinary high-risk decisions.

Poignantly, the leader of one parent-teacher-student association said to me, "When parents and teachers were able to sit side by side and learn together, they began to use the same language." Two differ-

COME ON PEOPLE

Tips for Community-Building

Alvin F. Poussaint, M.D., Professor of psychiatry,
Harvard Medical School

Dr. Alvin Poussaint, co-author with Bill Cosby of *Come on People,* has spent much of his lifetime focusing on creating effective communities in some of our country's most economically hard-pressed neighborhoods. Dr. Poussaint believes that these suggestions are important guidelines in neighborhoods at all socio-economic levels. They are meant to increase parents' comfort with school and faculty's involvement with, and understanding of family life, as well as institutions around the school. In this way he hopes to increase shared information about child-rearing, the challenges that parents face, find out what mothers and fathers think and what they think they need—not to assume that just the professionals know.

- To reach parents, we need to go where parents already are, not necessarily bring people into the school, but go out to churches, synagogues and community centers.
- Church and school leaders must connect with each other so that they can ultimately connect to parents. Religious leaders in neighborhoods can easily encourage outreach at school.
- Many parents are intimidated by institutions and school systems, and need to become familiar with advocacy for their children that does not antagonize faculty, to

(continued)

make the kind of demands that do not seem aggressive and entitled. Even the skill of "chit-chat" with those adults that are authorities over children is helpful.

- Adult learning centers at local colleges can help create a community of learners—by helping parents not only learn subjects, but understanding again what it feels like to sit in the classroom.
- Encourage non-threatening adult activities: non-PTA meetings, non-curricular meetings, encouraging the kind of get-togethers that are easy-going and allow for human dialogue—the more comfort, the more ability to work together for the kids.
- Open the school's doors to parents in all the ways that are possible: field-trips, "good-deed-doing projects," involvement in lunchrooms, and as aides in the classroom.

ent vocabularies had once served as a wedge between the circles of adults; now their mutual experience in a community of learners was helping to join them in spirit and in action.

INCENTIVES THAT WORK

*Ways to Acknowledge
Teacher and Parent Efforts*

Despite the best of intentions to create a community of learners it is a challenge to increase both parent and teacher participation. I have been involved with countless organizations that struggle with different ways to fill those seats. The key concept is that because so much is already demanded of parents and school personnel, one must think beyond information alone as an incentive and accept that these harried grownups have a right to ask "what's in it for me?" Here are just a few ideas that have worked in other communities. See what feels right for your own:

- Teachers/professionals should not only be financially compensated, but awarded continuing ed credits.
- Parents can receive "certificates" of participation for being involved with educational events; many are motivated by being recognized as developing expertise in the community.
- Teachers who become involved should be labeled as "heroes." States have begun to raise the level of public perception with such programs.
- Time is our most precious commodity—successful programs always keep an eye on how to inform in the most efficient way—some schedule educational evenings on the same night as school elections or regular PTA meetings, others have symposiums that are coordinated with major child events, so only one trip is necessary.

Partnership Step 6: Community Engagement Means That
Adults Listen Respectfully to Each Other

After a presentation I gave to several hundred parents and teachers in a suburban school system, one of my colleagues (Anthony Wolfe, author of Get Out of My Life, but First Could You Drive Me & Cheryl to the Mall?*), who had presented earlier in the evening, came over to me and said, "Ron,*

I've never seen anyone get parents to talk to each other in such a large group like this."

My training with one of the great pioneers in family therapy, Dr. Salvador Minuchin, had unintended consequences. He gave me the skill to shape interpersonal choreography among anxious and angry parents. That is the art of family therapy, and as a result, my workshops are highly interactive without getting out of control. I always ask that audiences, whether parents or professionals, talk to each other—not just to me—focusing on what matters to them. These public discussions have given me a wonderful perspective about what is on parents' minds; this is really my "secret" for finding out about parenting and educational trends across the country before an issue hits the radar of news headlines or becomes an area of research.

For better or worse, then, I see the attitudes parents have when addressing each other, not just the content of their concerns. From my vantage point in front of a group, I witness the far-from-subtle signs of disrespect and competition between the adults in a child's life.

The reality is that the first circles of adults, those responsible for children's everyday welfare, have a terribly difficult time listening to each other respectfully. How in the world do we expect kids to treat each other with greater respect when the grown-ups around them treat each other with disrespect as well?

A mother haughtily says to a neighbor in front of hundreds of others "My kids tell me everything that goes on in their lives—what's your problem!" A dad in another workshop brags about how his children never skip a chore in *his* house and belittles another family's complaint about how hard it is to pry their kids away from the computer. And, this right in front of many other parents his kids go to school with! I can't begin to describe the derisive comments made to me privately after an event or repeated as gossip at home. As *Reviving Ophelia's* Mary Pipher told me, reflecting the combat-style discourse she too has witnessed in school auditoriums around the country, "Words are being used these days more as weapons of destruction than a means to communication."

I became aware of adult-to-adult disrespect in the late eighties. As an antidote I suggested the creation of "peer groups for parents"—mothers and fathers learning to talk together in a constructive and safe manner—by forming support networks (similar to their kids' group of friends) *before* something tragic happened in a community. Peer groups for parents as described in my book *Parenting by Heart* struck a chord among countless isolated families, as it had in my talks around the country.

Yet despite this positive feedback (much more than I have space to detail here), I also became aware that a weakness of the adult-partnership approach was how poorly parents, teachers, and school personnel were able to respectfully listen and talk to each other. As I'd seen in countless workshops, the adults had to learn the basics about genuine, respectful communication before they could begin to guide their own children.

Through a series of starts and false starts over many years, I began to understand what contributed to this tension and disrespect among the adults. Not only were the issues themselves tough to resolve, adults were unclear about the ground rules of talking to each other. Both parents and administrators were used to stewing in their discontent. They had concentrated so much on conflict resolution and social-emotional programs for the kids that they themselves were not aware of how to talk together without a tone of blame and disrespect.

It is interesting that whenever I bring up the topic of more respectful dialogue between parents and teachers, almost every professional says to me, "This is our most difficult challenge."

CREATING "RESPECT" BETWEEN ADULTS
TO HELP OUR CHILDREN

The view of the Churchill School Center's former head, Kristine Baxter, is emblematic of this revolutionary change. "I always emphasize to both parents and teachers that we each see a different child, the one that is in school and the one that lives at home—and that each of us has some knowledge the other needs to know, and we should talk."

It is no longer enough to get parents into peer groups for support, or for the school to score better on standardized testing, or to develop a good "college" list. Regardless of whom I talk to, no matter where I've traveled, I see that the days of disconnection between parents and teachers are coming to an end. If only as a survival mechanism to protect our kids, parents are realizing that for children to treat each other more compassionately, adults must accept that "the apple doesn't fall far from the tree."

In response to this reality, Rosalind Wiseman, author of the influential book *Queen Bees and Wannabes*, has moved from working primarily with kids in order to lessen social cruelty, to focusing on parents and their attitudes toward each other. In her follow-up book *Queen Bee Moms & Kingpin Dads*, Wiseman underscores the reality that if we want our kids to change, parents must engage each other more respectfully. Rosalind and I experience the same derisive adult-to-adult tone in countless school auditoriums. She is working hard to help bring change about.

Regardless of Wiseman's wise words, at this point, most of the programs aimed at fostering more respectful and caring communication *still* focus on our children. Listen to the following example of a child-centered program and ask yourself, as I have, shouldn't adults be using the same guidelines about communication with each other?

The Responsive Classroom movement has been initiated in several hundred schools throughout America. In this program, students and teachers are taught the basics for empathic and respectful com-

WISE WORDS ABOUT MEANNESS FROM THE KIND "QUEEN" OF QUEEN BEES

Rosalind Wiseman

In her work with social cruelty, Rosalind Wiseman has shifted her focus to creating communities of enlightened adults, willing to look at themselves in order to change the kids they love. Rosalind counsels adults to work together to lessen kids' social cruelty. Among her suggestions are:

- Adults need to have the *courage* to do what we ask our kids to do when it comes to greater emphasis on and expression of kindness.
- The first act of courage is to recognize that social cruelty is not everybody else's problem, it is our own, and we have the possibility to change it.
- Adults, parents and faculty need to set examples and watch out for subtle ridicule, mockery and humiliation towards each other, behavior kids pick up from us.
- At the same time, administrators in schools must be convinced to join the community in changing the culture, understanding this is not just an acceptable problem of childhood, or an issue that exists in other schools.
- Schools can help by respecting teachers more—when teachers are disrespected they lose morale, spirit and a sense of hope for change.
- By involving the adults to become aware of social cruelty, taking responsibility for their own behavior, and initiating programs to make a change, we create hope that this age-old problem can be lessened.

munication, such as making eye contact with whoever is speaking, showing with a nod of the head or some response that one has heard, not interrupting each other, and tolerating differences of opinion. One teacher told me that this approach made such a difference in the tone of her class she was inspired to begin greeting each child at her door with a morning handshake and a "How are you, today?"

Principals have raved to me about the positive results in the younger grades, pointing to its impact not only on lessening exclusion but also on improving kids' problem-solving skills. As one headmaster put it, "By slowing down the pace of interaction, we can see that even the youngest kids take a beat to think about how it may feel to another child to not let them join during a recess game or to gang up on them in public."

In some communities parents react negatively to the idea of a responsive classroom, feeling that it is far too "authoritarian" or that it will cut down on their children's spontaneity. In fact, when the approach was adopted in a suburb of one major city, I was called by the local newspaper to comment on parents' complaints that their kids creative spirits were in danger of being squelched.

I do not agree. I have been around too many of the free-est generation and their post-boomer parents to be worried: A little skill building in the area of respectful listening is not going to make the slightest dent in our children's sense of entitlement and freedom to speak their minds almost everywhere and to almost everyone. Instead, respectful listening is a constructive method of nurturing more empathy and tolerance. But again, as welcome as this movement is—and though its effectiveness has not yet been refined as kids move into the rough and tumble middle school years—without including responsive classroom guidelines for adults, it is simply not enough.

Similar ideas have a way of popping up in many languages and cultures across the globe. For example, The Reggio Emelia program is an educational experiment in the Tuscany region of Italy, and it is a powerful example of this emerging trend. "Reciprocal listening," a

Reggio cornerstone, is the goal of helping adults, not just kids, learn to listen respectfully to each other, with genuine curiosity, a tolerance for differences, and an emphasis on understanding another's experience. The theme of mutual respect and collaboration is clear.

But, Reggio goes further than most other programs. If reciprocal listening is to be increased, guidelines and rules are not enough: *increasing the amount of everyday communication about the thing that matters most to both parents and teachers—kids' welfare—seems to be necessary for creating respectful dialogue. Distance and lack of shared information increase suspicion instead.*

What are some avenues to encourage opportunities for communication?

Reggio's "open book" is a way for parents and teachers to informally "talk." A book is left out in an accessible school area for teachers to write notes and observations about a child's daily experiences: the way a child approached material, a new kind of interaction with another child, how kids are doing in a class project. Teachers spend this time documenting the experiences of each child in order to communicate with parents in "pick up" areas so that parents and teachers have the same understanding of what's going on with a child. Obviously this means that schools must keep their doors open, at least during specific moments, rather than subtly discouraging involvement with labels such as "helicopter" moms and dads. The sharing of photographs from school and videos of kids in action is another way for parents and teachers to be sure they are talking about the same child. Computer photographs take seconds to send back and forth, and our children absolutely love to be the focus of the spotlight, so they usually don't object.

Without too many formal rules, ongoing communication creates its own respectful guidelines, bringing the circles of adults together. This approach has gained such traction that a "Reggio" conference in New York City in 2007 attracted almost a thousand participants from around the country. We cannot wait for those twice-a-year conferences to make adult connections about who our kids are and what they are doing; this is a twentieth-century paradigm that seems outrageously inadequate in our fast-moving twenty-first century world.

Other communities use a multipronged approach to nudge the circles of adults together. For example, Geoffrey Jones of The Potomac School talks about establishing dialogue from day one. Jones describes "regular 'town meetings," meetings with each division of the school, and ongoing "curriculum coffees." Parent forums are run by parent facilitators—almost always with teachers and administrators present. Events are scheduled at different times of the day and on different days to increase the number of parents and faculty who can attend. Parent activities are sponsored, and guest teachers come to lecture, to both parents and teachers, on the same day or even in the same auditorium.

Initiatives like these give me hope that we can make progress changing the mindset of the disconnected adults in our communities. So keep some guidelines in mind: you should expect parents and school personnel to create a formal partnership, with ongoing education for both parents and school, and with an emphasis on mutual respect and concrete collaboration during the school year around tasks that matter. You should no longer be satisfied with infrequent conferences and report cards. I've seen e-mail dialogue, online hours for specific questions, and access between teachers and families become part of normal life (not just when a child gets into social or academic trouble), even in suburban and urban schools with upwards of several thousand kids. These changes take time.

But without partnerships, changing adult attitudes comes hard. In one such situation, mom and dad hesitated for months, telling the classroom teacher that they were not only on the edge of a divorce, but that the mother had a life-threatening illness. Would their son be singled-out? Would the teachers treat him differently from the other boys, making him feel less a part of the group?

And, just recently, it took me several months to convince the parents of nine-year-old Rayna that their child's teachers needed to know that her lack of focus was partly the result of newly diagnosed attentional difficulties. Mom and dad were wary about letting the school in on such information, especially the fact that medication had been prescribed.

With some guidelines I provided on how to speak to school personnel, mom's meeting with Rayna's teachers not only went well but suddenly led to her teacher opening up about her own daughter who was showing signs of the exact same difficulty focusing. The dialogue unexpectedly began a mutual exchange of ideas, information, and referrals that kept the lines of communication open for the entire year.

You need to decide how to share info with your child's school. But one thing is clear: given the many examples I've described, the days of adult to adult disrespect, mutual wariness, and the rigid boundary between school and home must be put behind us.

GO ONLINE TO CONNECT TO OTHER PARENTS

Of course, in a twenty-first century post-boomer world, there is always the Web. If you have difficulty imagining a partnership in your school, take advantage of online possibilities.

One of the central educational cyber-sites in the country for closing the circle between school and home is GreatSchools.net. This is a nonprofit Web site whose mission is to help parents choose schools, support their children's education and improve schools in their communities. Parents can subscribe to free e-mail newsletters. The "My School Stats" feature helps parents understand school data. Grade-by-grade newsletters (*My First-Grader*, for example) help parents understand what to expect in the classroom, and Parent Advisor guides parents through the school year with timely topics. The site also features a library of more than 1,000 articles on education-related topics, such as how parents should talk to teachers. A vibrant community section allows parents to be able to create their own pages and network directly with each other.

Greater collaboration in those first circles around our kids, the parents who love them and the teachers who are with them every day, is a must. This free-est generation will continue to challenge us adults toward more collaboration, rather than distance and blame. What's more, in some intuitive way, kids are telling us it's time to get our act together.

HOW TO TALK TO A TEACHER: CONVERSATION, NOT CONFRONTATION

adapted from Mary Beth Castell
GreatSchools.net *September, 2004*

First of all, follow your "gut." If you have a feeling something's not right with your child, that means something's *not* right . . . there is this unwritten rule that you can't go in and express what you see to a teacher because you're not a teacher. As a parent, you know your child better than anyone, so give yourself credit.

Go to the teacher and say, "This is what I've noticed." Observe your child and tell the teacher specifically what you see. The more specific you are the better.

Then, ask the teacher, what do you think? You might not get an answer right away. Teachers rarely say, I don't know. Many teachers are even told not to say they don't know because it opens them up to legal liabilities. A good teacher will offer to find out for you.

When you have your first discussion with the teacher, whether it's a phone call or face-to-face, you want to document it in writing. It's easiest if you just keep a running log or journal. It doesn't have to be formal or fancy, but you need to note: What it is that you and the teacher are each going to do, and when?

If you suddenly realize that for the last four months everything anyone did for your child was wrong, you need to step back and say, maybe I've been the one with the issues. You may want to say to the teacher: "I feel like we got off to a bad start, and that I've made things worse. I want you to know that I still want some changes for my daughter, but I realize I've kind of lost sight of the long-term process here."

Most teachers are good, compassionate people. They want to know that a parent is going to be approachable, is going to listen, and is going to be fair. They want to know that you're going to give them a fair shot; not make assumptions about them based on your earlier experiences. That's sometimes hard for parents because they do have past negative experiences with teachers.

Let the teacher know that you want to take the time to communicate with them and that they matter. Treat them as a fellow human being. Find out something about them. Do they have children? Is this their first time teaching this grade? Do they have a child or family member or friend who struggles with learning? What are their hobbies? Are they on the planning committee in the school building? As with any communication between two people, the more you know about them, the more you can make connections.

The last thing is, when a teacher is doing something you like, notice it and take the time to tell them. There are many fabulous teachers that go the whole year without one compliment from parents.

If we want authentic engagement with children of all ages, we must create community with each other first. In this effort, not only school, but religious organizations and faith centers can be of great help.

SPIRITUAL COMMUNITY—WHY THE FREE-EST GENERATION LOVES ENLIGHTENED RELIGION

Paraphrasing what I hear from so many clergy and lay leaders, Zeke Pipher, Lead Pastor at Heartland Evangelical Free Church in Central City, Nebraska, told me, "We now regularly meet with many people who feel defeated or confused or ashamed as parents. It's hard for a person to have joy and a clean conscience if he or she doesn't feel like a good father or mother. We try to help adults to be part of a community that will strengthen them to be the parents they and their kids deserve."

I've also heard from many kids, increasing numbers of whom are becoming more involved with spiritual life, that the friends they make through religious groups are different from their friends from school. They'll say, "We want to keep them forever." "Why?" I ask. "They seem to care about what happens in the world," they'll answer. "They want to make a difference, and they're not afraid to show it."

While this doesn't make headlines, many children today gravitate toward faith centers as safe havens from the endless dissing and social competitiveness at school and online. Instead of responding to the code of "cool," they welcome a code of compassion and the kindness that comes with the turf of enlightened religious communities.

I'm a "progressive" psychologist so it may be surprising to hear, but for decades I've felt strongly that faith communities have become the other center of town. This realization developed as the list of my speaking engagements came to include churches and synagogues of all denominations throughout the country. Enlightened religious institutions understand how the village has become deserted, and they are working hard to fill the void. So much so, I believe that one of the secrets behind the success of positive, inclusive mega-churches, synagogues, and religious community centers is that they create a place for the free-est generation and its post-boomer parents to affiliate.

I know how much parents and kids love the engagement and the coherent set of values offered. In my discussions across the country it is clear to me that the politicization and divisiveness regarding faith that has entered the national discourse is a tragedy.

Together with school-parent partnerships, an essential part of creating twenty-first century community engagement is the need for parents and children together to believe in something more important than the individual—to experience themselves as part of a spiritual community built on belief, mutual support, and contribution to the world.

Over many years I have worked with leaders of enlightened church and synagogue organizations, consulting to programs in schools, neighborhood-outreach organizations, and summer camps working to foster the teaching of values, a service mentality, and intergenerational bonding—all in a fun and a natural way that recognizes the importance of genuinely engaging today's kids and families.

To the extent that faith centers deliver on these goals, they become another town center, connecting otherwise parallel circles of community while providing greatly needed security around our kids and schools.

WHERE PASSION CAN BE COOL

It is striking to see cyber-driven kids of all ages, whose graphic repartee rings in the schoolyard and even at home, welcome the expectation of kindness that comes with the turf of many faith communities. As the child I quoted above described (and as our own children have told Stacey and me), kids of all ages recognize the difference between schoolyard values and those informed by nonpunitive spirituality. Children, no matter how comfortable with everything "pop," experience social compassion as an antidote to everyday life. Why *wouldn't* kids love to be guided from a set of compassionate ground rules, even if for a few moments each week—when the rest of the time just about any-thing goes?

Susan, a late elementary school girl, said to her mom, "Every day I worry about the way I look, every minute. It makes a huge difference on Sunday when I don't have to be thinking about it for just a little while."

It is also striking to see how less self-conscious kids are about ex-pressing *passion* in an enlightened community. Discussing an upcom-ing program to go overseas and build houses in a Third World country, it was inspiring for me to witness seamlessly hip teens go all out with praise of the program, calling it one of the coolest things they'd ever done. "This trip changed my entire life," said one kid after the other, pointing out that no TV show or internet site could prepare them for the cultural differences they experienced and the goodwill they created. These are not sentiments one normally associates with oh-so-jaded twenty-first century adolescents.

Likewise, it was impossible not to be touched by the passionate singing at a camp I heard in the backwoods of a Georgia religious re-treat for kids. The outpouring of unself-conscious enthusiasm was such a striking difference from the ironic detachment I see every day in schools around the country that it would be impossible for most parents not to be affected. The content of the compassionate message was not the only thing that mattered to the kids; it was also the chance to let go about something meaningful in a way usually reserved only for "raves" in secular life.

Unself-conscious passion is a gift that needs to be endorsed and protected by grownups—and enlightened faith communities provide one of the few such outlets for today's kids.

CREATING RELAXED CONNECTION
WITH MENTORING ADULTS

Almost every church or synagogue leader I've interviewed has stressed the importance of mentoring kids. Our children's lives have become so heavily stacked in favor of peer-to-peer engagement that there is a dearth of adult mentoring. Kids cannot live engaged only with other kids or technology, without feeling adrift in the world. Across all socioeconomic strata, faith communities provide a chance to engage with adults in noncompetitive situations, a counter-balance to so many adult-run academic and sports activities. And these programs are staffed with grown-ups who tend to stick around for more than a season, or the time-limited course of an extracurricular module.

MAKING SPIRITUAL SERVICE PAY OFF FOR THE FUTURE

Faith communities are also beginning to grasp that in order to involve kids of all ages, especially as they enter adolescence, experiences should have some relevance and use in kids' secular lives. In response, spiritual initiatives are quickly developing partnerships with service programs such as Christian Relief Fund, Habitat for Humanity, and American Jewish World Service, among literally thousands of others. Kids who participate earn service points that go toward building a more robust college resume.

Though they may be lured in primarily for that reason, kids come back from these programs having replaced a free-est generation glib and often sarcastic view of kindness, utterly stunned at how much they were affected. The first time whets kids' appetites for more. This is exactly what Deborah Spaide found, for example, in the wildly successful growth of Kids Care Clubs I described earlier. Beneath the veneer of free-est generation cool lies a yearning to be inspired, feel compassion, and make a difference.

The scope of programs kids are connected to through faith communities is a phenomenon. Many are nominally priced or subsidized, targeting kids from all backgrounds, and partnering with organizations that work in every corner of the world. If your faith center does not have programs for your children, check out the Charity Navigator at www.charitynavigator.org/ to find one that fits your beliefs. The astonishing choice is a metaphor for how much this generation and its boomer parents want to contribute to the larger good.

BEYOND ISOLATION, DIVISION, AND MATERIALISM

When you read the sections below, please keep in mind that if I focus on a particular set of communities it is without any intention of leaving out the thousands of others that offer equally creative and perhaps even better programming. I also would like to make clear that in citing these particular institutions, in no way do I feel their spiritual message is more important than the message of any other group or denomination.

In considering the value of such programs, it is critical to recognize three themes of engagement I have repeatedly found that connect almost every positive faith community, regardless of geography, religion, or denomination. They are:

First, engagement between families who would otherwise feel more isolated in the community; second, engagement through intergenerational activity; third, engagement through compassion and good-deed-doing. All three authentically connect both children and adults with their best-selves and with each other.

HELPING FAMILIES TO BE ENGAGED

I tell the following to every group I present to: "Yes, I came here to teach something new about the way I see child rearing. But another reason is to help you begin to speak to each other. I want you to find wisdom and comfort from each other before trouble finds your kids."

Around the country faith communities are engaged in exactly this same mission—helping families become engaged before tragedy strikes. Probably the most repeated sentiment from religious leaders I've spoken to is the idea expressed by Deb Hardman of Christ Episcopal Church in Ponte Verde Beach, a community near Jacksonville, Florida: "Our community has a spiritual aspect, of course, but it is just as much about lessening isolation between families for everyday problems."

Faith communities employ many avenues beyond weekly services to create this kind of engagement. For example, prayer chains are a familiar and extremely popular way to make sure that congregants are available to help one another in concrete ways. Zeke Pipher describes how a prayer chain meets the concerns of his approximately 400 regular congregants: "If someone has a particular need, no matter how ordinary, a call is made and it is addressed anywhere from within fifteen minutes to two hours." For example, Mary finds herself without childcare because her four-year-old daughter suddenly develops a fever. A call to the prayer chain is made, and within a very short time a grandparent or an out-of-work mother or a neighbor in the congregation fills in. The speed of this response rivals communication among today's kids, which is exactly the point. It *is* an antidote to contemporary living—we are living upside down if our children take care of each other more quickly and more efficiently than we adults do.

Both small and large churches do a great deal of community service. Christ Episcopal Church in Jacksonville, Florida, has over 6,500 congregants and is situated in a fast-growing Sun Belt area. Obviously it has a more developed infrastructure than Zeke Pipher's smaller church, but the goal is exactly the same: in a spiritual setting, to provide ordinary help for ordinary problems so that isolation and disengagement can be lessened, even in a sprawling suburban and urban environment. So, if a congregant has an unmet need, such as emergency transportation or a trip to the hospital for chemotherapy, a con-

HOW COMMUNITIES CAN HELP EACH OTHER— THE WAY THAT KIDS DO

I've heard of so many examples of adults helping each other in ordinary and extraordinary ways that I include here only a small fraction of them. What is extraordinary is how simple these examples are:

- For everyday needs, families within congregation are on "speed-dial" for immediate contact
- In one family of five boys, twins were born prematurely and remained in the hospital for several weeks; the church watched their other children, while providing meals for the family.
- For a child with Engelmann's Syndrome, congregants planned Sunday morning care for him from 9 A.M. to noon.
- When a couple adopted a child from Oklahoma, congregants took in their other children to offer valuable time, set up a crib, and gave the family a Walmart gift card, as well as food and clothing.
- If church volunteers need childcare, teenage girls come in at 7:30 AM for two weeks at a time.
- Teen boys ride the bus to help out with younger kids.
- Families regularly make large, home-cooked meals to freeze at church for unexpected life emergencies.

gregant, referred to as a "shepherd," is called by the appropriate ministry. In order to deal with the burgeoning needs of a large community, as many as twenty ministries deal with such everyday issues as flowers for births and deaths, food preparation and delivery during an emergency, help with a newborn child, and so on.

At Congregation B'nai Jeshurun, a mega-synagogue with over 3,500 members in the urban canyons of New York City, the congregation has an informal community constellation called *Havurah*. These are comprised of congregants who join small groups that study and discuss mutual interests, such as the challenges of specific phases of the life cycle, spiritual learning, or social justice. Such small groups help narrow the distance between isolated members in a megasize city.

Even if one is not directly connected to a faith community, these days a thriving cyber-community is just a click away. Wendy Schuman was the managing editor when I wrote for *Parents* magazine. Now she is projects editor at Beliefnet. The activities and services provided on this site are truly astounding. Check out the box below, keeping in mind that this is just one of the many sites available.

CYBER-FAITH COMMUNITY—A MOMENT AWAY

One Site, Millions of Connections

If you are more comfortable using the Web to make spiritual connections or to find those that fit your needs in your area, this is a site that offers a great deal. Check out some of their highlights to see if a cyber-community fits your family's spiritual path. Here is a brief description:

Beliefnet (www.beliefnet.com), the largest spiritual website on the internet, is the multi-faith hub for community connection and spiritual resources on the web. Every faith has a place on Beliefnet, and the site's mission is to help people meet their spiritual needs, whether it's deepening their faith, learning about other traditions, helping their children grow spiritually, or seeking more inspiration

(continued)

and meaning in life. Beliefnet attracts three million unique visitors each month and has 11 million subscribers to its inspirational and faith-oriented newsletters.

Highlights:

1. Beliefnet Community offers thousands of discussions, support groups, and prayer circles, including areas where parents can connect with each other about family and child-raising issues.
2. Popular member groups include: Parenting the Facebook Generation, Raising Kids with Learning Disabilities, Family Traditions that Draw Families Together, Favorite Spiritual Books for Kids, and many others.
3. Beliefnet Video gives access to the best spiritual teachers, clergy, and authors in the world.
4. Beliefnet's Family channel features articles, quizzes, family movie reviews, expert interviews, and resources to help parents raise children with faith and values.
5. Beliefnet's Tools help users find prayers for every need and occasion, search sacred texts, learn about religious holidays and life-cycle rituals, and much more.
6. Beliefnet blogs give commentary on faith, culture, and values from a variety of viewpoints.

Wendy Schuman, Projects Editor, wschuman@belief netstaff.com.

FOOD THAT'S GOOD FOR THE SOUL

Almost every faith community I've spoken with devotes a dinner during the week or an after-service luncheon bringing community members together.

Wednesday evenings seem to be a favorite. These events follow a similar pattern across different congregations. A potluck buffet dinner is served for the first hour, after which the larger group breaks down into smaller groups, usually study-based for the adults, and activities for the kids that include hanging out, "chilling time," or bible study, depending on age.

The connections formed through these regular dinners can spread out into the wider community. Irene, who is in an observant Jewish woman, has two children who have launched into adulthood and left home. Suddenly her husband of thirty-five years died of a heart attack. As Irene told me two-and-a-half years later, she did not spend one single Friday evening without being invited for Sabbath dinner by congregants from her family's synagogue. "I can't imagine what my life would have been like without this. It gave new meaning to those thousands of dinners Stan, me and the kids had shared with other families all those years before."

The creation of community is now purposeful—an intentional antidote to twenty-first century disconnection, rather than only an historically based religious ritual.

Years ago, when I wrote *Parenting By Heart*, I referred to a family going to a local diner every week after church and treasuring this time together. But such wonderful moments were spent alone. Now, I hear many more stories of families regularly getting together with each other, valuing not just the ritual, but using these occasions to be part of a larger community. Communal experiences, first initiated by a church- or synagogue-sponsored event, and then spreading among families within a neighborhood, are a powerful development bringing the kind of horizontal connection between families that for recent decades has been associated exclusively with kid peer groups.

FAMILIES HELPING EACH OTHER THROUGH TOUGH TIMES

It is not only the ordinary that requires community, of course. Tough life events surely need the engaged hand of others to see families through.

In Jacksonville, therapist Deb Hardman has led many parent-to-parent groups, as she calls them. This is based on the notion that mothers and fathers have a great deal of information to share with each other about raising kids in a twenty-first century world—a concept I've been proposing since 1982, which I call "peer groups for parents." Back then this seemed a luxury. The idea was for mothers and fathers to make time to discuss ordinary matters: what their kids were getting for allowance, who was being invited to which party, where a sleepover was being held on the weekend.

As the years progressed and families felt ever more pressured, the need for alliances became obvious—and for some, these were best anchored in spirituality, outside the hothouse of school and academic life. Suddenly, many more faith communities began offering parent groups for tough times and theme-focused groups for people who needed to heal from specific life events.

At Christ Church under the umbrella of *Christ Church Cares* healing and educational groups deal with topics that may vary from sudden death to divorce to chronic illness to job loss or any other traumatic family event. This is not therapy. This is about community—a distinction made very clear by practically all clergy and lay leaders I've spoken to.

Some faith communities go so far as to provide an ongoing support-person to be a companion as individuals recover. In Jacksonville, the Stephen Ministry is such an effort, in which a volunteer is available twenty-four hours a day and is willing to meet weekly with the "journeying" individual, for up to a year. Again, this is not about therapy, though Stephen ministers do get intense training and ongoing supervision. It is really about adults engaging each other so that individuals and their children can feel *held* by the circles of community.

THE JOY OF INTERGENERATIONAL ENGAGEMENT

Zeke Pipher and Deb Hardman say it well, in almost the same way that I have phrased it to audiences for two decades: "It is essential for kids to be involved and engaged with at least one responsible adult who is not a family member."

It is striking to me that the very work I've done for over twenty years is mirrored by faith communities who recognize the necessity of engaging responsible adults in the lives of the free-est generation. A decade ago, almost all attempts to get children involved with spiritual journeys were organized around the idea that activities needed to be age-stratified and that kids, especially as they approached adolescence, should be segregated from the adults. Without this "space," preteens and adolescents would not become engaged, it was thought.

Times have changed, but adult mentoring is easier said than done. In a world that provides plenty of opportunity for free-est generation kids to endlessly engage with each other, there are relatively few nonacademic or nonsports-related opportunities for adults to be involved in ongoing ways. It takes some thinking to challenge this almost taken-for-granted fact of twenty-first century life. And that is exactly what many faith communities are doing.

For example, Christ Church developed an alternative service for families whose short-attention span kids could not sit through the regular service. Anyone whose children felt more comfortable being able to move around was invited to be in another space in the community hall, engaging in an informal service with contemporary music. Soon, many people began to gravitate toward that space—people of all ages. Grandparents, parents, children, and even teens would congregate, so many, as Deb Hardman told me, "They were standing like sardines, practically shoulder to shoulder."

This other event became so popular it was given a name, All & All. Far from experiencing it as a loss to the main adult service, the clergy felt it was a wonderful way to get people across generations to share the same space. Hanging out together is a way for adults to see the faces and hear the voices of their children's friends—a rare experience, indeed, for today's parents, so used to kids socializing off on their own or in the far reaches of the cyber-community.

Good ideas that speak to a common need have a way of popping up all over. A couple of years ago, at Congregation B'nai Jeshurun, the adult-oriented Saturday morning service became augmented by a Junior Congregation service. In no time, more than a hundred congregants, children between the ages of five and twelve, as well as grandparents and parents, were participating, creating an ear-popping service in their own space with their own brand of enthusiasm. "Forget the music," many parents told me. "More important is that all of a sudden I had a chance to see the faces of my kids' friends in a fun spiritual event."

Most of the faith communities I've been involved with now use the pop culture to bring adults *and* kids in. Much like their post-boomer parents, many churches and synagogues no longer view "pop" as the enemy; rather, they've begun reaching out in ways that cater to twenty-first century sensibilities.

For example, numbers of communities have begun "jam sessions"—time for teens and preteens to get together and show off their skills. In Jacksonville, these tiny gatherings have grown into regular community events that attract upwards of forty kids. *Word spread, and now the seemingly impossible has begun to happen.* Numbers of parents and other adults have joined in on jam sessions, creating an event consistent with the idea that like no generation before, the free-est generation is open to engagement with adults.

The realization that the generations can mix is accompanied by a growing belief that they should mix. Most clergy I've spoken to echo an inter-generational sentiment that has been missing for several decades.

As Zeke Pipher put it: "We believe it's good for the adults to know what's going on in kids' lives, to see them, so that they can feel the freedom to collaboratively raise not only their children, but be knowledgeable and involved in raising their friends' children as well."

Experiences such as these have been increased by adding numbers of intergenerational events outside the walls of churches, chapels, and synagogues. Pipher described with great poignancy his own reaction going on a two-day fishing expedition down Nebraska's Niobrara River with his child and a number of other families from the congregation. The age span, almost impossible to imagine decades ago, was from four to seventy years. "This was inspiring even for me," said Pipher. "I watched my son interact for thirty-six hours with men of all ages. It was very meaningful as a father to see this."

In many communities, local service agencies not directly affiliated with faith communities also focus on inter-generational activities. Their enlightened mission is most often anchored by spiritually-based, humanistic values. The Academy of Healing Arts (AHA!) is a project of the Family Therapy Institute of Santa Barbara, California. The program involves approximately 300 teens who meet up to four or five times a week after school. They engage in a multicultural curriculum that focuses on building character, creative expression, and tolerance toward diverse cultures. Emphasizing the inter-generational aspect, one exercise asks each person to share how rumors or gossip have ever hurt them—adults and teens participating equally. In the same vein, AHA! places great emphasis on mentoring, with a ratio of one adult to every five teens. As Jennifer Freed and Rendy Freedman, co-directors of the program describe, "Each member is a meaningful part of the whole, and each is acknowledged for their strengths, and aided in their weaknesses."

In our post-boomer world, the extraordinary experience of the generations passing time in each other's company, doing good deeds or having fun together, is indeed a sight to behold.

GIVING GONE WILD

The Growing Philanthropy of Today's Kids

While it rarely makes the headlines, today's kids are perhaps the most "giving" on record. The numbers of opportunities and participants boggles the mind. Here are just a handful of examples. None of the following are endorsed by the author; rather they are just a few illustrations of the incredible work that goes on every day around the globe. For specific, concrete recommendations upon which to make decisions, check out other parents' experience, your school and faith center in your area. *Never send your child to a program without speaking to others who have gone.* Adult diligence notwithstanding, the trend towards giving is an essential part of what makes this generation and its parents so special.

1. Kids Care Clubs (Funded by Quaker Oats)
   www.kidscare.org

Kids Care Clubs are groups of young people who work together to help others in their communities and around the world. Clubs are formed in schools, churches, synagogues, Volunteer Centers, and other community-based organizations. Today there are more than 1,400 registered Clubs and 75,000 kids in the United States and countries including Australia, Canada, China, and Nepal. Kids Care Clubs members begin volunteering as early as pre-school, with projects designed for ages five through thirteen years old.

2. Youth Now! (Collaboration with AmeriCorps,
   Volunteer Center of Southern Arizona, United
   Way and six other partner agencies.)
   gocyf.az.gov/CYD/GRT_YNC.asp

Youth Now! strengthens communities by mobilizing people and resources to develop creative solutions to community problems. Its mission is to engage youth in meaningful volunteer opportunities, increase literacy rates for children by utilizing youth and adult volunteers, and expand service learning activities for youth. Their goal is to engage volunteers of all ages, including young people themselves—for youth ages 11 to 18.

3. Bliss Women and Children Project
   www.blisswomenandchildrenproject.org

BWCP is a Christian nonprofit organization ministering to the poor in Kaptembwa, Nakuru, Kenya through relief, education, feeding programs, training, literacy, health and social care programs. These are acts that restore dignity and relieve human suffering. They offer volunteer opportunities for kids under 12 and teens 13–17. If the kids are too young to travel they can help with the website and other domestic programs.

4. Students Travel and Exposure South Africa
   www.staesa.org

A registered Non-Governmental Organization (NGO). STAESA works very closely with groups, individual, schools, colleges, universities, communities and NGOs in capacity building, development and sustainability.

(continued)

STAESA has been in existence since 1995. STAESA programs are not just for students—everyone can participate. (Teens 13–17)

Today STAESA sends over 100 volunteers to more than 60 communities in more than 15 countries in Africa, connecting over 100 foreign NGOs and individuals, schools, colleges, and universities to programs, events, and community projects in Africa.

Mission: To enhance and promote a safe, fair and sustainable future for both local and foreign students, non-students, NGOs, schools, colleges, universities, and communities in Africa. It supports global friendship through culture, work exchange, education, and friendly tourism, the advancement of quality of life of the African communities socially, economically, and spiritually.

5. Best Buddies www.bestbuddies.org

Best Buddies® is a nonprofit organization dedicated to enhancing the lives of people with intellectual disabilities by providing opportunities for one-to-one friendships and integrated employment. **Best Buddies Middle Schools** matches students with intellectual disabilities with other middle school students and creates one-to-one friendships between them. In today's middle schools, students with intellectual disabilities enter the same building and walk the same hallways as their peers, but are very often left out of social activities.

6. Do Something Clubs www.dosomething.org

Do Something Clubs are a fun, free, and easy way for teens to take action in their community and impact the causes that they're passionate about. The Clubs program launched 2 years ago and already has over 150 clubs in 37 states and Canada. All club resources can be found online! Teens start the DS club themselves, requiring only five members to start! Do Something stays in touch with clubs via monthly eblasts, individual calls and emails, social networking sites like Facebook, and biannual physical mailings.

Just about everyone with kids in their lives is beginning to understand that to bring out the best-selves of the free-est generation, we must bring the circles of our communities together, for child rearing alone is an impossibly disconnected way to live. In the manner they seek each other out, our kids who know no bounds are urging us to move beyond the dividedness of post-boomer life. Authentic engagement that fits these times is what children of all ages yearn for, in loving, limiting, listening, and creating community.

*

A long time ago I had a dream that has stayed with me for life, one I've described in various ways in different presentations. It feels particularly fitting at the end of this section on spirituality, and after the long journey we've taken through these pages.

In the dream I find myself in a basement. A figure stands at the top of the stairs and says to me, "Come here." "Why?" I ask. "God is here," is the answer. As I climb the stairs I am increasingly worried. At this point in my life, each step represents to me another concern, familiar to all parents: "Will my kids be safe? "Am I doing right by them?" "Will they be prepared to survive in this world," the questions that are on our minds every day. By the time I reach the top of the stairs, I am trembling. I slowly open the door and the figure says to me, "This is God." I look up and see a warm, softly glowing light. It is filled with life, love and acceptance. For days I carry this feeling around with me until it gradually fades, but is never forgotten.

The worries I had with each step mirror the unnecessary blame and pressure on today's parents and kids I described in the first pages of *Childhood Unbound*—we climb stairs of doubt every day. For the good of our children, this doubt must be replaced by an enlightened child rearing: the glow of shared knowledge, the ease of mutual acceptance, and the comfort of a collective support that families deserve. This is what we need to bring out our kids best-selves. For when the lights finally go out at the end of long, long days, our children and even our teenagers look up, whispering with their eyes. Without saying a word, they are asking us to hold them with our hearts, to never stop trying to guide them.

They are asking us to travel with them through a world of new challenges and into a world of new hope together.

ACKNOWLEDGMENTS

Since this is a seminal work for me, the process is much like what one says of a painting: *Childhood Unbound* took about a year and a half to write, but it has been twenty years in the making. Behind the entire journey, however, is my long time editor-in-chief of *The Psychotherapy Networker*, Rich Simon. Not one of my books could have existed without his offering me a platform for my ideas, no matter how edgy. This has been a once-in-a-lifetime professional relationship, a collaboration that remains special in its durability and creativity to this day. Thank you, Costello.

And, as I wrote in the introduction, I would again like to thank all the contributors to *Childhood Unbound*—who were generous beyond words with their time and expertise. Their specific input has been apparent (and I'm sure appreciated) as you've gone through these pages.

I would like to thank Linda Loewenthal, my agent, whose humanistic values and grit should make her literary agency, David Black, extremely proud. Linda is wonderful at nurturing a balance between the hope of the new and the need for concrete movement. She is an ultimate professional who feels like family to me—the kind of family that helps you to look forward, as well as toward the past.

This brings me to thanking my current publisher Free Press and its editor-in-chief Dominick Anfuso, who immediately saw the promise of these ideas and editorial assistant Danielle Kaniper for helping to make this vision happen. Danielle is a godsend: professional, clear and the embodiment of quick thinking when deadlines loomed. Free Press is lucky to have such a quality person.

And through it all, there's the editor of *Childhood Unbound*, Emily Loose. You met her as you read these pages. Working together, *Childhood Unbound* evolved along the way. As a senior editor, Emily has dealt with some of the "biggest" people in our culture, as my parents used to say of any professional who had a spiffy car in our neighborhood. Despite having developed a following through the years I am not such a person, but Emily and I worked together in a mutually respectful manner, which was unparalleled in its fluidity around ideas and ongoing teamwork. She is a gifted, smart, and compassionate person, exactly what was needed to match the incredibly sharp kids and intense times described here. I've been lucky with all my editors, but even in this good company, Emily's slightly unconventional but thoroughly disciplined heart, intellect, and spirit stand out.

As always, I want to thank my wife, Stacey. Without Stacey nothing happens, with her almost everything can. And, now that they are a bit older (though we're not completely out of the woods yet—still being teenagers and post-adolescents), our children, Leah and Sam, were always there, with *a lot* to say. Together, they are the "incredible lightness of my being" and the "rock of my ages."

Acknowledgments are usually written at the very end of the process, which is my way as well. Finishing such a long, intense project is, paradoxically, a fiercely poignant time—one of feeling exhilarated, relieved, and vulnerable all at once. As I write these words I am touched by of all things, my own mortality. For this I give thanks—to be blessed enough to have been able to write *Childhood Unbound* and to have had these generous people in my life.

NOTES

Chapter 2

19 *"The Second Family"*: Ron Taffel, "The Second Family," *The Family Therapy Networker* (May/June 1996).

23 *"The new anger"*: Ron Taffel, "The New Anger," *The Family Therapy Networker* (Sept/Oct 1999).

23 *Psychotherapy Networker,* "Discovering Our Children" (Sept/Oct 1999).

25 *"Like deer frozen in the headlights:"* ibid.

27 *In a poll of hundreds of teens in heartland America:* Judy Emerson, "Hearing Our Future," *Rockford Register Star* (Dec. 20, 1996)

33 James Gleick "Addicted to Speed" *New York Times Magazine,* Sept. 28, 1997.

33 *We were becoming, as a famous* New York Times *article put it in 1997, "addicted to speed":* James Gleick, "Addicted to Speed," *New York Times* (Sept. 28, 1997).

33 *"We had become managers of our kids":* Taffel, "The Divided Self," *The Psychotherapy Networker* (July/August 2006)

34 *how families actually spent time at home:* "Kids and the Media at the new Millenium," *The Kaiser Family Foundation* (1999).

37 *"wall of silence":* Taffel, "The Wall of Silence," *Psychotherapy Networker* (May/June 2001).

43 *"I just can't take it anymore":* Taffel, "The New Anger."

48 *The Divided Self:* R.D. Laing, *The Divided Self.* Penguin Psychology, New York: 1965.

49 *The Magic Years:* Selma Fraiberg, *The Magic Years.* Charles Scribner's Sons, New York: 1959.

Chapter 3

53   *I suddenly grasped that the second family of peers was as important to get to know as the first family at home:* Taffel, "The Second Family."

59   *the Yankelovich Youth Monitor, one of the most respected public opinion research organizations:* "Zapping the Gap," *Yankelovich Youth Monitor* (2005).

60   *Yankelovich called this very recent phenomenon:* ibid.

60   *many parents are now considered by their children to be their best friends:* Barbara Hofer, "The Fine Art of Letting Go," *Newsweek* (May 14, 2006).

60   *Rick Pearlstein described this new parent-child relationship: New York Times* online, August 5, 2007.

65   *Twenty percent of the population now has at least one parent from another country:* Michael D. Hais, Michael D. Hais, *Millenial Makeover.* Rutgers University Press, New Jersey: 2008.

71   *becoming a common rite of passage in middle and high school:* Julia Baskin, Lindsey Newman, Sophie Pollitt-Cohen, Courtney Toombs, *The Notebook Girls.* Grand Central Publishing, New York: 2006.

72   *By all measures teen pregnancy is down dramatically*, "Youth Risk Behavior Study and Surveys of Teen Sexual Behavior," *Center for Disease Control* (2006–2007).

77   *66 percent use instant messaging:* "Media Multi-Tasking: Changing the Amount and Nature of Young People's Media Use," *Kaiser Family Foundation* (Mar. 9, 2005). www.kff.org/entmedia/entmedia03095nr.cfm. Accessed 8/11/08.

78   *it is projected that by 2010 there will be 10.5 million preteen users:* Lisa Foderaro, "Child Wants Cell Phone," *New York Times* (Mar. 29, 2007).http://www .nytimes.com/2007/03/29/fashion/29cell.html?_r=1&scp=1&sq=Child%20 Wants%20Cell%20Phone&st=cse&oref=slogin. Accessed 8/14/08.

78   *when 69 percent watched broadcast, and 50 percent watched cable:* "Multi-Media Tasking."

78   *the average time spent reading or being read to is 40 minutes:* Yankelovich Youth Monitor 2003; Yankelovich Preschool Study 2005; Kaiser Family Foundation, *The Media Family,* May 2006.

80   *muscles in the brain that kids no longer learn to easily use:* Robin Marantz Henig, "Taking Play Seriously," *New York Times Sunday Magazine* (Feb. 17, 2008).

Chapter 4

86   *With twenty-first century kids of all ages, there's no escaping it: The "edge of relatedness":* Darlene Ehrenberg, *The Intimate Edge.* W.W. Norton and Company, New York: 1992.

89   *These dances discovered by family therapy pioneers decades ago:* Joan DeClare, Daniel Goleman, John Gottman, *Raising an Emotionally Intelligent Child.* Simon and Schuster, New York: 1998.

92   *The idea that kids have different temperaments:* Stella Chess, Alexander Thomas, *Temperament and Behavior Disorders.* New York University Press, New York: 1968.

94   *They had been arguing a great deal about Amy's curfew:* Taffel, *Breaking Through to Teens.* Guildford Press, New York: 2005.

100 *"clear expectations create strong":* "Nurturing Good Children Now," *JAMA,* September 1997.

100 *clear guidance and absolute rules to safeguard them:* "Nurturing Good Children Now," *The Johnson Institute* (1999). p 218.

103 *we can't remold our children's basic temperament:* Jerome Kagan, Nancy Snidman, *The Long Shadow of Temperament.* Belknap Press, New York: 2004; William Carey, *Understanding Your Child's Temperament.* Macmillan, New York, 1997.

Chapter 5

140 *As movie and social critic David Denby wrote:* David Denby, Annals of Popular Culture, "Buried Alive," *New Yorker,* July 15, 1996.

142 *research by those who have studied interpersonal communication:* DeClare, Goleman, and Gottman, *Raising an Emotionally Intelligent Child.*

150 *children as young as two-and-a-half to strengthen their skills at solving interpersonal situations:* Myrna Shure and Theresa Foy, *Raising a Thinking Child,* Pocket Books, New York: 1996.

156 *the actual "hole" in the prefrontal lobe of kids' brains starts to fill in during adolescence:* Emma Young, "It's Not Fair: Brains May Compel Teens to Tantrum," *New Scientist,* February 25, 2008. http://www.newscientist.com/channel/being-human/dn13373-its-not-fair-brains-may-compel-teens-to-tantrum.html. Accessed 8/21/08.

161 *Deci found that the more we praise children, especially when it is inauthentic:* Edward Deci, Richard Flaste, *Why We Do What We Do.* Penguin, New York: 1996.

169 *Nothing illustrates this better than the following exchange I had with Kyle:* Taffel, *Breaking Through to Teens,* Guilford, 2005.

171 *fathers asking their young charges for guidance:* Yankelovich Youth Monitor, "Zapping the Gap."

179 *Numerous programs already exist in which consequences and incentives are combined:* "Examining Conditional Cash Transfer Programs." Benedicte de la Briere and Laura Rawlings, World Bank Institute, June 2006.

Chapter 6

187 *I began to notice this phenomenon fifteen years ago when I wrote about Phillip:* Taffel, *Parenting by Heart.* Da Capo Press, New York: 2002.

197 *Our sessions took the form of constant debates (Collette and Ron):* Taffel, *Breaking Through to Teens.*

Chapter 7

251 *In a school in the Northwest, the captain of the fencing team, an A+ student:* Taffel, "The Second Family."

257 *Fretta Reitzes, the executive director of the program, and co-author Beth Teitelman:* Fretta Reitzes, Beth Teitelman, *Wonderplay, Too.* Running Press, New York: 2007.

INDEX

ABOUT THE AUTHOR

Ron Taffel, Ph.D., is one of the most esteemed and in-demand special-ists nationwide on child rearing, having presented to parents and pro-fessionals across the country for over two decades. He has written a half-dozen books and over a hundred articles on children and fami-lies. Dr. Taffel founded the Family Therapy Division at the Institute for Contemporary Psychotherapy, a not-for-profit organization which provides training in psychotherapy as well as counseling for more than 500 clients a week. He serves as chairman of the board of directors of the Institute, while continuing to run a thriving child and family therapy practice in New York City, where he lives with his wife and two children.